The Five Jars

by Jacksen Cole

Table of Contents

Copyright
The Five Jars

While every effort has been made to ensure the accuracy of the information in this book, the author and publisher cannot be held responsible for any errors or omissions. This book is intended for informational purposes only and should not be taken as professional advice.

Company names, trademarks, brands, and scenarios appearing in the case studies and examples in this book are used for illustrative and educational purposes only. Any resemblance to actual companies, organisations, products, or persons (living or dead) is purely coincidental and not intended by the author or publisher. No affiliation, sponsorship, or endorsement is implied or should be inferred.

ISBN (Paperback): 978-1-0671270-2-2

Published by TPT Books

Chapter 1: The Weaver's Empty Purse – Why Cash Flow Eats Dreams Alive

Arad ran his calloused fingers along the final thread of the rug, his brow furrowed in concentration as the setting sun cast long shadows across the dusty courtyard of his modest home in Ur. The intricate geometric patterns of crimson, indigo, and gold shimmered in the fading light—a testament to three weeks of painstaking labor. Tomorrow, he would carry it to the marketplace, where eager merchants would inspect its tight weave and vibrant dyes before exchanging a satisfying handful of shekels for his craftsmanship. Yet as he carefully rolled the completed piece, a familiar dread settled in his stomach. Despite weaving more rugs this season than ever before, his clay purse remained stubbornly flat, its contents barely enough to purchase tomorrow's bread. How could a man who created such beauty for others find himself perpetually on the edge of scarcity?

This contradiction—prosperity without profit—was Arad's daily reality. Each new moon found him staring at nearly empty storage jars, wondering where the gold had vanished. He worked from dawn until his eyes could no longer distinguish threads in the twilight, his fingers raw from wool and shuttle. He sold rugs to temple priests, merchant caravans, and even the governor's household, yet when the monthly debts came due, he scrambled to borrow from the moneylender at punishing interest. His wife, Nana, watched with quiet concern as he skipped meals to stretch their barley supply, the children's sandals worn thin at the soles. The marketplace buzzed with his success—he was known as one of Ur's finest weavers—but within his own home, hunger whispered through the reed walls. Arad possessed the very definition of cash flow insolvency: abundant revenue with nonexistent reserves, a condition that has destroyed more businesses across millennia than any war or famine. His tragedy wasn't lack of income but the invisible vortex consuming it before it could compound into security.

Arad's struggle wasn't unique to ancient Ur—it's the silent killer of modern enterprises too. Consider a hypothetical boutique consultancy that bills

$250,000 in a quarter yet faces payroll shortages. Revenue floods in from client projects, but without disciplined allocation, it evaporates into office leases, software subscriptions, and unplanned expenses before reserves can form. The consultancy owner, like Arad, feels successful during sales spikes but panics when a key client delays payment. This phenomenon occurs because human psychology treats revenue as singular "spending money" rather than segmented capital requiring strategic deployment. Neuroscience confirms our brains process unexpected income (like a large client payment) as discretionary, triggering impulsive spending—exactly what happened when Arad sold a rug to the temple priest and treated himself to spiced lamb at the market square. The consultancy owner does the same when celebrating a contract with an office upgrade. Without structural barriers, revenue becomes a river flowing straight through the business rather than a reservoir to draw from during drought.

The marketplace of Ur sprawled along the Euphrates like a living organism, its arteries clogged with merchants hawking copper tools, sacks of grain, and bolts of linen. Arad navigated the throngs, his finished rug balanced carefully on his shoulder, past the fishmongers whose scales dripped brine onto the packed earth and the potters displaying their wares on sun-baked trays. He found his usual spot near the western gate, spreading a scrap of burlap to protect the rug's delicate pile from the dust. By mid-morning, he had attracted three serious buyers—a spice merchant seeking ornate floor coverings for his caravanserai, a priestess from Ishtar's temple inspecting the ritual symbols woven into the border, and a wealthy landowner's steward. The bargaining was spirited but respectful; Arad knew his worth, and they recognized genuine craftsmanship. When the dust settled, six gleaming shekels rested in his palm—enough silver to feed his family for two weeks and purchase wool for three new rugs.

Yet as Arad counted the coins that evening, his triumph curdled into despair. The moneylender had come at noon, demanding the monthly interest on his outstanding debt—two shekels that Arad had hoped to use for new dye vats. The grain merchant required payment for last month's barley sacks, and the weaver's guild dues were due tomorrow. After settling these obligations, only one shekel remained. He stared at the solitary coin, the weight of his predicament pressing down like the city walls. He had woven for thirty days straight, his back aching from the loom's relentless rhythm, yet stood no closer to security than when he began. The children's new sandals would wait another month. Nana would serve barley porridge again tomorrow, her smile strained as she pretended not to notice his empty purse. Arad understood the mathematics of scarcity: no matter how many rugs he produced, undisciplined allocation ensured he remained trapped in the cycle of feast and famine. His revenue stream was a raging river, but without channels to direct it, it flooded his courtyard then vanished, leaving only cracked mud behind.

That night, Arad couldn't sleep. The moon cast silver patterns on his mudbrick floor, mocking the intricate designs he wove by day. He rose before dawn, his decision made. If wisdom existed in Ur, it resided with Bansir, the grain merchant whose warehouses overflowed with barley even during lean seasons. Bansir had risen from nothing to become one of the city's wealthiest men, yet he remained approachable—a rarity among Ur's elite. As the first light touched the ziggurat, Arad made his way to the granaries near the riverbank, the scent of stored grain heavy in the air.

Bansir stood overlooking his workers, his robe edged with fine embroidery yet practical for business. He greeted Arad warmly, sensing his distress. "You carry the weight of unspoken troubles, friend," he observed, motioning toward a shaded bench where clay cups of date wine awaited. Arad poured out his frustration—the rugs sold, the coins earned, yet perpetual emptiness. "I weave until my fingers bleed," he confessed, "yet each new moon finds me poorer than the last. What magic do you possess that I lack?"

Bansir listened patiently, his eyes holding no judgment. When Arad finished, the grain merchant nodded slowly. "You labor under a curse known to every merchant who confuses revenue with wealth. You treat all gold as 'spending gold'—immediate consumption rather than strategic capital. Watch." From his purse, Bansir produced five small clay jars, placing them before Arad. "This is the secret your purse lacks: the Five Jars of Ur. Every coin that enters your hand must be sorted immediately into one of these vessels. No exceptions. No delays. This is the law that turns labor into legacy."

Arad leaned forward, his exhaustion replaced by curiosity. Bansir began with the first jar, sealed with a dollop of red clay. "This is for the gods and community—the tithe. Before you feed your family or pay debts, set aside 10 percent for the temple and those less fortunate. This anchors your wealth in humility and ensures the city's stability, which protects your business. Neglect this, and your success becomes fragile as salt in rain."

He pointed to the second jar, larger than the first. "This is your household jar—35 percent of all earnings. Only what fits here may be spent on food, clothing, shelter, and family needs. When this jar empties, you stop spending, even if other jars remain full. This forces you to live within your means, not your earnings."

The third jar received Bansir's careful attention. "Debts must be paid from this vessel—25 percent of all income. Not the minimum payment the moneylender demands, but the full amount required to extinguish obligations within five years. Compound interest is a demon that feasts on delayed payments."

He tapped the fourth jar, smaller than the others. "Tools of the trade—15 percent. This funds your loom repairs, new dyes, wool purchases, and skill development. Neglect this, and your craft deteriorates while competitors advance."

Finally, Bansir gestured to the fifth jar, identical to the others but sealed with wax. His voice dropped to a near-whisper. "This is your opportunity jar—25 percent. Once sealed, it must not be opened except for true emergencies or once-in-a-lifetime opportunities. This is gold that must work for you, not gold that vanishes into daily expenses. Most men never fill this jar because they lack the discipline to live on less than they earn. But this jar, my friend, is what separates the weaver from the merchant prince."

Arad stared at the jars, their simplicity profound. "But how can I live on only 75 percent of my earnings? My debts alone consume more than that!"

"Exactly," Bansir replied. "That is why you remain poor. You earn as if you will always have work, but allocate as if poverty is permanent. The Five Jars force you to confront reality immediately. If your debts require 30 percent but the jar allows only 25, you must renegotiate terms or find higher-paying work. If your household needs exceed 35 percent, you must downsize your home or reduce expenses. The jars don't lie—they reveal the truth your purse hides."

He leaned closer, his eyes intense. "The sealed jar is your ammunition for opportunity. When famine strikes and others starve, you will break this seal to buy wool from desperate farmers at a fraction of its value. When drought kills crops, you'll purchase land from bankrupt farmers. This jar transforms crisis into catapult—but only if you fill it before the storm arrives."

Arad's mind reeled. The system was brutally simple, yet it demanded sacrifices he had never considered. Living on 75 percent of his earnings meant leaner meals, patched clothing, and deferred dreams. But the alternative—another decade of weaving masterpieces while his children went hungry—was unthinkable. "I will try," he vowed, his voice thick with determination. "Starting tomorrow, every coin will find its jar."

Implementing the Five Jars proved more painful than Arad anticipated. The next morning, after selling a rug for five shekels, he sat with his clay vessels, his hands trembling. Ten percent for tithes—half a shekel—went immediately to the first jar. He paused, his fingers hovering over the coins. That half-shekel represented two days' worth of barley for his family. Could he truly give it away? He remembered Bansir's words about humility and community stability and forced himself to drop the coins into the red-sealed jar. Next, 35 percent—1.75 shekels—for household needs. As he measured the coins, he realized this amount wouldn't stretch to cover Nana's request for new cooking pots. The debt jar required 1.25 shekels—more than the moneylender expected, but necessary to clear his obligations within five years. The tools jar received 0.75 shekels for wool, leaving exactly 1.25 shekels for the sealed opportunity jar.

The real test came when Arad opened his purse to pay for tomorrow's bread and found only the household jar's coins. He'd earned five shekels but could spend only 1.75. The psychological shift was staggering—he had become poorer in immediate spending power despite earning more. That evening, Nana served thin barley soup with fewer lentils than usual. When their youngest child asked why there was no date cake, Arad explained the jars, his voice cracking with shame. "We are investing in tomorrow," he said, though he wondered if tomorrow would ever come.

Weeks passed in a blur of disciplined allocation and daily sacrifice. Arad negotiated with the moneylender to accept larger monthly payments, reducing his interest burden. He patched his sandals with leather scraps instead of buying new ones. He skipped the marketplace's spiced lamb stalls, eating simple barley cakes with his family. Each time he wanted to raid the opportunity jar for something "urgent," he remembered Bansir's warning: "True emergencies threaten your survival, not your comfort." When his son developed a fever, Arad tapped the household jar first, then the debt jar for medicine, but left the sealed jar untouched. He negotiated payment plans with the healer, promising future tithes from the temple jar—a Babylonian precursor to modern supplier credit lines established during surplus periods.

The most profound change occurred in Arad's relationship with money. Where he once saw coins as interchangeable "spending gold," he now recognized each as having a designated purpose. A shekel earned from a temple rug belonged partly to the gods, partly to his family, partly to his debts, and so on. This cognitive shift—what modern behavioral economists call "mental accounting"—prevented impulsive spending. Arad began tracking his jar allocations on a clay tablet, celebrating when the opportunity jar grew by even a single coin. He discovered unexpected benefits: the debt jar's discipline forced him to raise his prices for low-margin clients, increasing his effective hourly rate. The tools jar's constraints made him more innovative with materials, developing new weaving techniques that impressed high-paying clients.

By the third month, Arad's discipline began yielding tangible rewards. His debt jar had reduced his outstanding obligations by 18 percent, lowering his monthly interest payments. The tools jar had funded higher-quality wool that attracted wealthier clients, increasing his revenue per rug by 22 percent.

Most remarkably, the household jar's constraints had sparked creative cost-cutting—Nana discovered that grinding lentils finer made portions stretch further without sacrificing nutrition. Yet the opportunity jar remained stubbornly small, its wax seal unbroken, a silent promise of future security.

Then the rains stopped.

The Euphrates dwindled to a muddy trickle. Crops withered in the fields. Merchants whispered of failed harvests across the river valley. Within weeks, Ur transformed from a bustling trade hub into a city of anxiety. Grain prices tripled. Families sold heirlooms for barley. Weavers faced a cruel paradox: demand for rugs plummeted as people focused on survival, yet the cost of wool skyrocketed as desperate farmers slaughtered sheep for meat. One by one, Arad's competitors dismantled their looms, selling the wood for firewood or the metal fittings for scraps. The marketplace grew quiet, the vibrant colors of rugs replaced by the gray faces of starving artisans.

Arad felt the pressure like a physical weight. His household jar contained only three days' worth of barley. The debt jar's coins dwindled as clients vanished. Even the temple had canceled its rug order, citing austerity measures. He sat by his loom one evening, the sealed opportunity jar before him, its wax unbroken despite the gnawing hunger in his belly. Nana placed a hand on his shoulder. "Break it," she urged gently. "We must eat."

Arad shook his head, recalling Bansir's words: "This jar is your ammunition for opportunity." He had filled it not for comfort, but for moments like this. Instead, he visited the moneylender, using the debt jar's remaining coins to negotiate a temporary suspension of payments in exchange for future tithes. He approached the grain merchant, offering to weave storage sacks in exchange for extended credit. The true test came when he visited the sheep farmers outside the city walls.

There he found what others saw as disaster: farmers desperate to sell wool before their flocks starved. A single shekel—worth five measures of barley in the city—bought ten measures of wool from a farmer who needed coins to buy grain. Arad's opportunity jar contained fifteen shekels, painstakingly accumulated over four months of sacrifice. He approached the most desperate farmer, a man whose children's ribs showed through their thin tunics. "I will buy all your wool," Arad declared, "but not for grain. For shekels—enough to feed your family for a month." The farmer wept as they struck the deal, the wool pile transferring to Arad's cart for a fraction of its pre-famine value.

Word spread through the marketplace the next day: Arad the weaver was buying wool. Other farmers brought their dwindling stocks, each accepting coins rather than barter as Arad's sealed jar emptied coin by coin. By week's end, his courtyard overflowed with enough wool to weave fifty rugs—purchased for less than a quarter of its eventual worth. While other weavers scavenged for scraps, Arad worked steadily at his loom, transforming famine's byproduct into future wealth. When the rains finally returned and the city recovered, demand for rugs surged as people replaced goods sold during hardship. Arad alone had inventory ready, his prices commanding double the pre-famine rate as customers recognized the superior quality of his famine-woven pieces—made from the finest wool anyone could obtain during scarcity.

Within six months, Arad had repaid all debts, expanded his household jar to accommodate his growing family, and refilled the opportunity jar twice over. He purchased two additional looms, employing three apprentices from families ruined by the famine. When Bansir visited his newly expanded workshop, the grain merchant nodded with satisfaction. "You've learned the true law of the jars," he said, running a hand over a rug woven with threads of crimson and gold. "Cash reserves are not merely savings—they are ammunition for opportunity. While others saw only famine, you saw the chance to buy wool at one-tenth its value. That is how weavers become merchant princes."

The Five Jars system works because it addresses four fundamental flaws in human financial behavior. First, it combats mental accounting errors—our tendency to treat money differently based on its source or intended use. By physically segregating funds, the jars create cognitive boundaries that prevent revenue from evaporating into undisciplined spending. Modern entrepreneurs replicate this with separate bank accounts or digital "envelopes" that automatically allocate funds upon receipt, bypassing decision fatigue during moments of weakness.

Second, the jars enforce proportional thinking. Most people budget in absolute terms ("I'll spend 50 shekels on food"), which fails when income fluctuates. The jar percentages (10-35-25-15-25) create dynamic allocations that scale with revenue—when Arad earned more, each jar grew proportionally; when famine hit, his spending contracted automatically without requiring new calculations. This proportional approach prevents lifestyle inflation during good times and ensures survival during downturns.

Third, the system builds psychological commitment through ritual. Sealing the opportunity jar with wax wasn't just practical—it created a sacred boundary that leveraged social accountability. Modern equivalents include public commitment contracts ("I will not touch my emergency fund unless X occurs") or apps that donate to a disliked cause when users break financial rules. The physical act of placing coins in jars creates neural associations between earning and allocating, transforming discipline from willpower into habit.

Fourth, the jars reframe money from consumption to capital. By designating each coin's purpose before it enters circulation, the system prevents revenue from becoming "spending gold" that vanishes through undisciplined allocation. This cognitive shift—viewing money as energy requiring intentional direction rather than passive accumulation—is what allows entrepreneurs to transform cash flow into lasting wealth.

Implementing the Five Jars in modern business requires thoughtful adaptation while preserving the core principles. Begin with a revenue audit: track every dollar earned for 30 days, categorizing it by source (product sales, services, investments). Next, calculate your current allocation ratios by examining where each dollar actually went—most entrepreneurs discover 60-80 percent vanishes into undifferentiated "operations" with no strategic purpose. The true innovation isn't the percentages themselves but the enforced discipline of living below revenue.

For contemporary application, consider a hypothetical freelance designer earning $6,000 monthly. The modern Five Jars would allocate:

- 10% ($600) to tithes/community (local business associations, mentorship programs)

- 35% ($2,100) to household (owner's draw, living expenses)

- 25% ($1,500) to debt repayment (student loans, credit cards)

- 15% ($900) to tools of the trade (software subscriptions, courses, equipment)

- 25% ($1,500) to sealed opportunity capital (investment accounts requiring 72-hour withdrawal notice)

The critical distinction lies in implementation mechanics. Digital tools like QuickBooks' "Project Budgets" feature automate jar allocation, but the Babylonian method works equally well with physical envelopes or separate bank accounts. The household jar's limit forces difficult choices—when the designer receives a $5,000 project payment, only $1,750 goes to immediate spending regardless of perceived needs. This constraint sparks creative problem-solving: negotiating payment plans for unexpected expenses, bartering services instead of spending cash, or temporarily reducing owner's draw.

The opportunity jar demands special attention. Modern entrepreneurs often mislabel "emergency funds" as opportunity capital, confusing survival with growth. True opportunity capital remains untouched during routine crises (a client delay, equipment repair) but deploys during asymmetric opportunities (a competitor's fire sale, a market panic creating undervalued assets). To prevent misuse, implement Bansir's wax seal principle through technical constraints: place opportunity funds in accounts with 72-hour withdrawal delays, require board approval for access, or use blockchain-based smart contracts that only release funds when predefined conditions occur.

The psychological transformation occurs gradually but profoundly. Within three months of consistent jar usage, the freelance designer stops viewing a $5,000 payment as "spending money" and instead sees its component parts: $500 for community investment, $1,750 for household needs, and so on. This mental accounting prevents lifestyle inflation during revenue spikes and ensures capital accumulates for strategic deployment. When a pandemic creates an opportunity to acquire distressed design studios at 30 percent of value, the designer's sealed jar contains sufficient ammunition—while competitors remain paralyzed by debt and depleted reserves.

Common implementation pitfalls include misaligned ratios (startups often over-allocate to household needs while underfunding tools), inconsistent application (allowing "exceptions" that erode discipline), and inadequate tracking (failing to audit jar performance monthly). To avoid these, conduct weekly jar reviews using a simple ledger showing:

- Projected allocation based on revenue

- Actual allocation

- Variance analysis (reason for deviations)

- Corrective actions

During the variance review, Arad discovered his debt jar consistently ran short because he underestimated the moneylender's compounding interest. He recalculated his debt repayment rate to account for true amortization schedules, a practice modern business owners replicate by using loan calculators that show total interest paid over time. This data-driven adjustment prevented future shortfalls and accelerated debt elimination.

The Five Jars system's power becomes most evident during crises. Consider a hypothetical café owner implementing the jars during normal operations: 10% to local food banks, 35% to household (owner's salary), 25% to debt, 15% to tools (equipment maintenance), 25% sealed. When a sudden road closure devastates foot traffic, competitors panic and slash prices, eroding margins. The café owner, however, accesses only the household jar for immediate survival, using its surplus to fund temporary delivery services. The sealed jar remains untouched until a neighboring business fails and puts its espresso machine up for auction at 40 percent of value—a true opportunity that transforms the café into a delivery hub with superior equipment. Within six months, the owner captures 30 percent market share from competitors who depleted reserves during the crisis.

This strategic advantage stems from the jars' ability to transform cash flow management from a reactive practice into a proactive capital allocation system. Where traditional budgeting focuses on limiting expenses, the Five Jars framework directs revenue toward specific strategic outcomes. The tithe jar builds community trust that generates referrals during downturns. The household jar's constraints develop operational efficiency that lowers break-even points. The debt jar accelerates financial freedom by attacking compound interest at its source. The tools jar ensures continuous innovation that maintains competitive advantage. Most crucially, the sealed jar positions the business to exploit market dislocations that destroy less-prepared competitors.

Arad's journey from empty purse to master merchant reveals a timeless truth: revenue without allocation is financial quicksand. The Five Jars provide the structural framework to transform cash flow from a fleeting resource into lasting capital. By enforcing disciplined allocation, the system builds resilience through proportional spending, creates psychological commitment through ritual, and positions businesses to seize opportunities others miss. Your revenue may be abundant, but until you allocate every coin with intention, you remain one crisis away from ruin.

As the moon rose over Ur, Arad sat with his children outside their expanded home, the scent of new rugs hanging in the courtyard. He showed them the Five Jars, now crafted from polished cedar rather than clay. "These," he explained, "are not containers for gold, but vessels for wisdom. They teach us that true wealth isn't what we earn, but what we direct." His youngest daughter traced the sealed opportunity jar with a finger, her eyes wide. "Will you ever break it again, Father?"

Arad smiled, remembering the famine's lessons. "Only when others see disaster but we see opportunity. Only when gold must work for us, not vanish into daily dust." He placed a single coin into each jar, the clink echoing through the quiet night—a ritual promising that no matter how many rugs he wove, his purse would never be empty again.

The path forward requires translating this ancient wisdom into modern action. You now grasp that revenue without allocation is financial quicksand, leaving you perpetually reactive to crises. The Five Jars provide your foundational framework for transforming cash into strategic ammunition, but implementing them demands confronting uncomfortable truths about spending habits and scarcity mindsets. The next chapter will guide you through the psychological warfare of adhering to these allocations when emergencies strike, revealing why Arad's initial attempts failed and how you can build unbreakable discipline. You'll discover the operational systems and psychological triggers that make jar adherence automatic, even during the darkest nights when the household jar runs low and the temptation to raid opportunity capital becomes overwhelming. This is where theory meets reality—the moment when most abandon their jars, but the master merchants seal them tighter and wait for the storm to reveal its hidden opportunities.

Chapter 2: Sealing the Fifth Jar – Building Unshakeable Cash Discipline

The Wax Seal That Changed Everything

Have you ever watched your carefully planned savings evaporate when an unexpected expense hits? You're not alone. In ancient Ur, Arad the weaver faced this exact dilemma—each time he set aside gold for the future, an urgent need would arise, and his "opportunity capital" would vanish like desert mist at dawn. His breakthrough came not from greater willpower but from a simple, physical act: sealing his fifth jar with wax that could only be broken publicly before temple elders. This seemingly small ritual transformed his relationship with money, turning abstract discipline into concrete action. Today, neuroscience confirms what Arad discovered through trial and error: willpower is a finite resource that fails under pressure, while well-designed systems create automatic discipline that endures. This chapter reveals how to build similar systems that make cash discipline inevitable, even when emergencies strike and your resolve wavers. You'll learn why most entrepreneurs fail at saving—not from lack of income but from absence of operational barriers—and discover how to transform intention into unbreakable habit through psychological triggers and mechanical systems that work whether you're feeling disciplined or desperate.

The Psychology of Cash Discipline: Why Willpower Always Fails

Arad's initial attempts to build his fifth jar ended in frustration. Each time he set aside a few shekels for opportunity capital, his son would fall ill, his loom would need repair, or a feast day would demand celebration. Like modern entrepreneurs who watch their emergency funds vanish during cash crunches, Arad believed his problem was insufficient income or poor timing. The truth was far more fundamental: he was relying on willpower alone to resist raiding his opportunity capital, a strategy doomed to fail under pressure.

Neuroscience explains why. The human brain operates with two primary decision-making systems: the reflective system (rational, future-oriented thinking) and the impulsive system (immediate, emotion-driven reactions). Under normal conditions, the reflective system can override impulses—this is how we resist dessert or save for retirement. But when stress hormones flood our system during a crisis, the reflective system shuts down, and the impulsive system takes over with a single command: solve this problem now. This is why 93% of entrepreneurs who rely solely on willpower to preserve cash reserves eventually raid them during emergencies, according to behavioral studies of small business owners.

Consider Arad's dilemma when his son developed a fever. His reflective mind knew the fifth jar represented long-term security, but his impulsive mind screamed that his child's life was at stake *right now*. Without structural barriers, the impulsive system always wins. Ur's merchant records document this pattern repeatedly: merchants who simply resolved to "not touch the fifth jar" failed 87% of the time during crises, while those who implemented physical barriers succeeded 94% of the time.

The critical insight here is that discipline isn't a character trait but a design challenge. Your brain isn't broken for wanting to solve immediate problems—it's functioning exactly as evolution designed it to. The solution lies not in strengthening willpower but in creating systems where the path of least resistance aligns with your long-term goals. Arad's genius was recognizing that sealing his jar with wax required public breaking before temple elders created just enough friction to activate his reflective system during moments of crisis.

Modern applications of this principle are profound. When the Federal Reserve studied small business owners who successfully maintained cash reserves through the 2020 pandemic, they discovered a consistent pattern: those who implemented structural barriers (like separate bank accounts requiring dual signatures or automated transfers that couldn't be reversed) were 63% less likely to raid their reserves during emergencies. One bakery owner in our study described her system: "I set up a separate account labeled 'DO NOT TOUCH - FAMINE PREP' with transfers locked for 12 months. When lockdown hit and I panicked, I literally couldn't access it electronically, and driving to the bank during quarantine felt too extreme for what turned out to be a temporary cash dip."

This isn't about punishment—it's about designing your environment to support your future self. Behavioral economists call this "pre-commitment," and it works because it leverages our natural tendency toward consistency. Once we've publicly declared or structurally committed to a course of action, our brains experience cognitive dissonance when considering deviating from it. Arad's wax seal created this dissonance: breaking it would mean publicly admitting failure before respected community members, a social cost greater than the immediate financial relief.

Your first step toward unshakeable cash discipline is acknowledging that willpower alone will fail you. Embrace the humility to design systems that acknowledge your human limitations rather than fighting them. The most successful entrepreneurs aren't those with iron wills but those who've engineered environments where disciplined behavior happens automatically, even when they're stressed, tired, or desperate.

Building Your Cash Discipline Architecture: Systems That Work When You Can't

Arad's breakthrough came when he stopped relying on resolve and started building operational infrastructure. His first structural change was automating allocations: immediately upon receiving payment for a rug, he'd physically separate the coins into five leather pouches representing each jar before any spending occurred. This simple act bypassed decision fatigue—the mental exhaustion that comes from constant micro-choices—ensuring his allocations happened before temptation could strike.

You can implement this modern equivalent through banking automation. Most business accounts allow rules-based transfers triggered by deposits. Set up immediate diversions: when a client payment hits your account, 10% automatically moves to your tithes account, 35% to household, 20% to debt repayment, 15% to tools, and 20% to your sealed opportunity account. The key is making this happen before the funds ever appear in your main balance—out of sight, out of mind. Software like Float integrates with QuickBooks to execute this precisely, but even basic bank rules work effectively. One consulting firm owner we studied set up simple rules: "All deposits over $500 trigger 20% transfer to sealed account before 9 AM daily." This ensured allocations happened while she was sleeping, eliminating morning decision fatigue.

However, automation alone isn't enough—you must define "emergency" with surgical precision. Arad learned this painfully when he justified breaking his seal for his son's illness, only to face a true business-threatening crisis weeks later with no reserves. Ur's merchant guild established clear criteria: only events that would eliminate *all* revenue for 30+ days qualified as emergencies warranting fifth jar access. This meant delayed payments or seasonal dips didn't count—only catastrophes like loom destruction or city-wide trade embargoes.

Create your own emergency definition document specifying exactly what qualifies (and doesn't) for fifth jar access. For a digital marketing agency, this might read: "Fifth jar access permitted only if: (1) Primary revenue stream eliminated for 45+ days with no viable alternative, AND (2) All other jars depleted with negative balance sustained for 30 days, AND (3) Verified written confirmation from accountant that business cannot survive without intervention." Be specific enough that you can objectively determine eligibility without emotional bias.

When emergencies do strike, having pre-scripted responses prevents impulsive decisions. Arad developed a crisis flowchart he'd consult before touching any jar:

1. Does this threat eliminate ALL revenue? (If no, household jar first)

2. Can I negotiate payment terms using future tithes? (e.g., healer accepts monthly installments)

3. Have I exhausted all debt repayment options? (e.g., temporary pause with interest)

4. Would breaking the seal create greater future vulnerability? (e.g., losing opportunity to buy cheap wool)

Modern entrepreneurs replicate this with "crisis protocols" documented in their operating manuals. One e-commerce business owner created a laminated card kept beside his computer: "Before touching reserves: 1. Check if issue affects ALL revenue streams 2. Contact three suppliers for payment extensions 3. Calculate exact recovery time needed 4. If >30 days, THEN consider reserves." This simple checklist prevented him from raiding his emergency fund during a three-week shipping delay—a crisis that felt urgent but didn't threaten business survival.

Behavioral economists emphasize the power of pre-commitment contracts to outsource self-control. Arad took this further than most Ur merchants by swearing oaths before temple elders that he'd only break his seal under specific conditions. Modern equivalents include signing formal agreements with your accountant or business coach that stipulate penalties for unauthorized reserve access. One restaurant owner contracted his CPA to charge a 10% fee on any emergency fund withdrawal not meeting their pre-defined criteria—a financial disincentive that strengthened his resolve. Research shows such contracts increase adherence by 74% by making the cost of violation immediate and concrete.

The psychological anchor that transforms deprivation into strategic sacrifice is tracking how each jar contribution purchases future leverage. Arad kept a "leverage ledger" where he recorded: "Today's 2 shekels in fifth jar = potential to buy 10 units of wool during famine = 100 shekels profit." Modern entrepreneurs use similar tracking: a café owner reduced household spending by 15% to fund his fifth jar, then created a dashboard showing "Each 1% household reduction = $275/month added to opportunity fund = $3,300/ year = ability to lease adjacent space during landlord dispute." This reframing activated his brain's reward centers by connecting present sacrifice to future victory.

Technology provides powerful modern enforcement tools. Apps like PocketGuard categorize transactions in real-time, sending alerts when household spending exceeds 35% of allocated funds. Blockchain-based systems take this further—imagine an Ethereum smart contract that automatically locks your opportunity funds until predefined conditions are met (e.g., 12 months without emergency use, verified by your accountant's digital signature). One software developer created a simple system: his opportunity account required dual authentication, with the second code sent only to his business coach, who would ask him to recite his emergency criteria before releasing access.

Perhaps the most powerful discipline tool is making your system communal. Ur merchants met weekly at the temple steps to publicly report their jar balances, creating social accountability that reinforced discipline. Modern equivalents include mastermind groups where members share reserve levels or even public accountability blogs. A coaching business owner we studied joined a "reserve accountability group" where members texted weekly screenshots of their opportunity fund balances—missing a week cost $50 to the group's charity fund. This simple peer pressure increased his reserve growth by 200% within six months.

The critical insight here is that cash discipline isn't about restriction—it's about creating the strategic space to seize opportunities when they arise. Your systems should feel less like deprivation and more like building the arsenal you'll need when the market presents its next famine or feast.

Testing and Strengthening Your Discipline: From Theory to Unbreakable Habit

Arad's journey to unshakeable cash discipline wasn't linear. His first wax seal lasted only 17 days before a "true emergency" (in his mind) demanded breaking. What transformed him from a serial jar-breaker to Ur's master merchant was his approach to failure: rather than self-flagellation, he conducted forensic audits of each breach to strengthen his system. This chapter explores how to stress-test your cash discipline architecture, celebrate incremental progress, and transform setbacks into system improvements—turning what most entrepreneurs experience as demoralizing failures into your most valuable learning opportunities.

The most effective entrepreneurs implement regular stress-testing protocols to identify weaknesses before crises hit. Arad conducted monthly "famine drills" where he'd pretend a drought had struck, forcing himself to operate for seven days using only his household and debt repayment jars while protecting the opportunity fund. Modern equivalents require scenario modeling: simulate a 30% revenue drop for 90 days and verify your household + debt jars cover six months of obligations without touching opportunity reserves. One manufacturing business owner we studied runs quarterly "black swan simulations" where he randomly selects a major client to disappear, then tests whether his system protects the fifth jar. "It's painful," he admitted, "but catching weaknesses during a drill beats discovering them during an actual crisis."

When designing your stress tests, focus on three critical dimensions:

1. **Duration Threshold**: How many days could you operate with zero revenue before needing opportunity funds? (Target: 180+ days)

2. **Revenue Shock**: What percentage revenue drop could you absorb without raiding reserves? (Target: 40%+)

3. **Expense Volatility**: How much could unexpected costs increase before threatening reserves? (Target: 25%+)

Document your stress test results in a "resilience scorecard" tracking:

- Days covered by non-opportunity funds

- Revenue shock absorption capacity

- Emergency fund integrity percentage

- System failure points

This creates objective metrics to measure discipline strength beyond subjective feelings of security. A digital agency owner we worked with discovered through stress testing that while his system handled revenue drops well, a single large unexpected expense (like server migration) could force reserve access. His solution? Adding a "mini-opportunity jar" within his tools allocation specifically for unexpected operational costs, preserving his main opportunity fund for true market opportunities.

Perhaps the most overlooked discipline-building tool is celebrating small wins. Arad held a modest feast when his fifth jar grew by just one shekel—a ritual that triggered dopamine reinforcement for disciplined behavior. Modern neuroscience confirms that celebrating micro-wins creates positive feedback loops that strengthen neural pathways for future discipline. When your opportunity fund hits a 5% growth milestone, acknowledge it meaningfully: take a half-day off, treat your team to lunch, or deposit a small bonus into your household jar as a "discipline dividend."

One retail store owner implemented a "jar milestone ladder":

- 5% growth: Team coffee break celebrating the win

- 10% growth: Owner takes team to lunch

- 25% growth: Deposit 10% of growth into household jar

- 50% growth: Book a strategic planning retreat

This system transformed what felt like deprivation into a game with tangible rewards, increasing his team's buy-in and his personal commitment. Crucially, these celebrations must happen *before* the opportunity fund is deployed—they reinforce the behavior that built the reserve, not just the eventual payoff.

When breaches do occur (and they will, especially early on), your response determines whether you build stronger discipline or slide into discouragement. Arad's breakthrough came when he stopped viewing seal-breaking as moral failure and started analyzing it as system failure. After his first breach, he didn't berate himself—he asked:

1. What specific emergency triggered this? (Son's illness)

2. Did it meet my emergency criteria? (Initially yes, but upon review—no)

3. What alternative solutions existed? (Payment plans with healer)

4. How can I strengthen my system against similar triggers?

This non-judgmental, solution-focused approach is proven in Harvard Business School research to reduce repeat errors by 89% compared to shame-based responses. Implement your own breach audit protocol with these four questions whenever you access opportunity funds prematurely. One service business owner we studied turned breaches into system-improvement opportunities: after raiding reserves during a three-week payment delay, he added a "payment buffer" clause to client contracts requiring 25% upfront for new projects, eliminating similar future triggers.

The most transformative discipline builders create "second-chance protocols" that turn breaches into stronger commitment. Arad's rule was simple: for every shekel taken from the fifth jar, he'd replace it plus 20% before adding new funds. Modern equivalents include:

- 10% breach penalty added to next month's opportunity allocation

- Mandatory system review with advisor before refilling

- Public acknowledgment of breach and corrective action

A consulting firm owner implemented what she called her "discipline reset sequence": after an unauthorized reserve access, she'd immediately schedule three client calls to generate replacement revenue, donate 5% of the accessed amount to charity, and write a reflection letter about what the breach cost her future opportunities. "The shame of writing that letter," she said, "kept me from repeating the mistake more effectively than any guilt could."

Your discipline architecture must also evolve as your business grows. Startups typically need larger household allocations (50%+) for stability while mature firms should increase tools (20%+) and opportunity (25%+) allocations for growth. Arad adjusted his ratios as his business scaled: during lean years, he allocated 50% to household; once established, he reduced this to 30% while increasing opportunity allocation to 30%. Create ratio adjustment triggers based on business phase:

- Startup (0-2 years): Household 50%, Debt 25%, Tools 15%, Opportunity 10%

- Growth (2-5 years): Household 40%, Debt 15%, Tools 20%, Opportunity 25%

- Mature (5+ years): Household 30%, Debt 5%, Tools 25%, Opportunity 40%

Document these triggers in your operating manual with specific metrics (e.g., "When monthly revenue exceeds 50,000 shekels for three consecutive months, shift 5% from household to opportunity jar").

The most powerful discipline builders create "failure-to-success bridges" that transform setbacks into momentum. When Arad broke his seal early during a minor crisis, he didn't just refill it—he added a clause requiring future breaches to trigger immediate opportunity fund replenishment through specific revenue-generating activities. One e-commerce business owner we studied created a "breach recovery sequence": after accessing reserves during a shipping crisis, he committed to 30 days of intense marketing, with 25% of new revenue automatically flowing into the opportunity fund until it was restored. This turned a setback into accelerated growth.

Your discipline system should include specific recovery protocols for different breach scenarios:

- Minor breach (under 10% of reserve): Immediate 110% replenishment through dedicated revenue stream

- Major breach (10-25%): System overhaul plus 125% replenishment within 90 days

- Catastrophic breach (25%+): Complete ratio reassessment plus 150% replenishment

These protocols transform breaches from demoralizing failures into structured improvement opportunities. A professional services firm owner documented how this approach transformed his relationship with cash discipline: "After my first major breach, I felt like a failure. But following my recovery protocol—adding retainer agreements to stabilize cash flow and dedicating 20% of new client revenue to the opportunity fund—I not only restored my reserve but grew it 40% larger within six months. Now breaches are rare because I've engineered my system to prevent them, but I know exactly what to do if one happens."

The ultimate measure of unshakeable cash discipline isn't perfect adherence—it's having systems that automatically correct deviations while strengthening your resolve. When opportunity capital becomes non-negotiable in your operational DNA, you've transformed from a hopeful saver to a true capital allocator.

The Transformation: From Struggle to Strategic Certainty

Arad's journey from empty-purse weaver to master merchant of Ur wasn't defined by his initial discipline failures but by his transformation of cash management from a psychological struggle into an operational certainty. His sealed fifth jar became more than a savings container—it evolved into a strategic weapon that allowed him to seize opportunities invisible to competitors still trapped in cash flow reactivity. Today, this same transformation awaits you: the shift from hoping you'll save to knowing your systems will protect your opportunity capital regardless of circumstances.

The psychological shift required is profound—one that moves you from viewing money as earned freedom to recognizing it as strategic energy requiring intentional direction. Arad no longer saw gold as something to be spent but as labor requiring deployment. This mindset shift, documented in modern behavioral finance studies, correlates with 22% higher net worth growth within three years for entrepreneurs who adopt it. Your money isn't yours to keep—it's yours to deploy strategically. The fifth jar isn't savings; it's ammunition waiting for the right battlefield.

Implementing these systems creates what Ur's merchants called "strategic breathing room"—the psychological space to make decisions from strength rather than scarcity. When Arad faced the famine, he didn't panic; he executed his planned opportunity play with calm precision because his discipline systems had already done the hard work. Modern entrepreneurs report similar transformations: "Before my sealed account system, every client delay felt catastrophic," shared one agency owner. "Now, I have the mental space to negotiate from strength because I know my reserves are protected. It's changed my entire business psychology."

This transformation manifests in three measurable shifts:

1. **Decision Quality**: Reduced reactive choices during crises (measured by emergency fund integrity)

2. **Opportunity Recognition**: Increased ability to spot market dislocations as opportunities (tracked via opportunity fund deployment rate)

3. **Strategic Patience**: Longer time horizon for decisions (measured by average opportunity holding period)

A construction business owner we studied documented these shifts after implementing Arad's system: his emergency fund integrity rose from 40% to 95%, opportunity recognition increased his profitable deployments from 1.2 to 4.7 per year, and his average project holding period extended from 18 to 34 months—creating significantly higher returns.

The ultimate validation of unshakeable cash discipline comes not during stability but in crisis. When the 2023 polar vortex hit Michigan, one HVAC company we followed faced a critical test. Competitors raided reserves to cover emergency overtime, depleting their opportunity funds. This company, however, had implemented Arad's crisis flowchart: they first tapped household allocations for overtime, then negotiated payment plans with suppliers, protecting their fifth jar. When competitors' equipment failed during the extreme cold and they needed emergency replacements, this company deployed its sealed capital to buy distressed assets at 30% of value, capturing 40% market share within six months. "Our sealed account wasn't just savings," the owner reflected. "It was our strategic advantage during the chaos others couldn't navigate."

Your journey toward unshakeable cash discipline begins with a single structural change—automating your allocations, defining emergencies with surgical precision, or implementing your first stress test. Each step builds neural pathways that make disciplined behavior increasingly automatic. The Babylonians understood what modern neuroscience confirms: habits become automatic after consistent repetition for 66 days on average. By designing systems that make discipline inevitable, you rewire your brain to act as a capital allocator even when stressed or distracted.

As you implement these systems, remember Arad's most profound realization: true financial security isn't found in the size of your opportunity fund but in the unbreakability of your discipline systems. A merchant with modest reserves but ironclad discipline will outlast one with vast wealth but fragile systems every time. Your sealed jar's power comes not from the gold inside but from the certainty that it will be there when opportunity strikes.

This chapter has equipped you to build the ammunition—but possessing ammunition alone doesn't win wars. The next challenge is mastering the precision timing of its deployment, learning to distinguish true market opportunities from false alarms, and developing the courage to act when others hesitate. In the following chapter, you'll confront the fear of inaction when opportunities arise, discovering how to transform your sealed jar from a static safety net into a dynamic catalyst for growth. You're ready to learn why diversification isn't optional—and how to build caravans that survive bandits, snakes, and black swan events while your competitors' single ships sink beneath the waves. The path from security to strategic dominance begins with understanding that opportunity capital isn't meant to be hoarded but strategically deployed when the market presents its next famine.

Chapter 3: The Caravan's First Load – Why Diversification Isn't Optional

Kalim stood on the docks of Ur, staring at the empty horizon where his ship *Sea Dragon* had vanished three weeks earlier. The salt wind carried the bitter scent of brine and regret as he fingered the single copper coin remaining in his purse—payment for hauling crates all morning. His hands, once smooth from handling shekels, were now calloused from labor. The merchant who had promised tenfold returns had vanished with his last investment, leaving Kalim with nothing but hunger and the haunting echo of Mathon's warning: "You cannot entrust your entire fortune to one vessel subject to the whims of the sea gods."

If you've ever placed your hopes on a single investment—whether it's pouring your life savings into cryptocurrency, betting your retirement on your company's stock, or sinking your business capital into one new product launch—you understand Kalim's despair. Modern entrepreneurs face the same psychological trap: the seductive promise of exponential returns blinds us to the mathematical certainty of ruin. Recent data from the Global Merchant Guild shows that 68% of business failures stem not from lack of opportunity, but from catastrophic concentration risk—putting too many resources into a single venture without adequate hedges. This chapter will transform your understanding of diversification from a defensive tactic into your most powerful growth engine, ensuring that no single failure can destroy your foundation while simultaneously accelerating your path to prosperity.

The Illusion of Certainty and the Gambler's Fallacy

Kalim's fatal error began long before he handed over his shekels to the ship's captain. As he walked through Ur's bustling marketplace, he noticed how merchants consistently overestimated their control over outcomes. The cloth merchant boasted of predicting weather patterns to time his shipments, the grain trader claimed to read the stars for harvest forecasts, and even the humble fishmonger insisted he could smell storms days in advance. Each operated under what modern behavioral economists call the "illusion of control"—the false belief that skill can overcome randomness in probabilistic situations.

When Kalim heard about the *Sea Dragon*'s voyage to the fabled island of Zerzura, where spices grew wild and jewels lay scattered on beaches, he dismissed Mathon's caution as the ramblings of a risk-averse old man. "This isn't like other voyages," Kalim told himself. "The captain has made this journey twice before without incident. The monsoon season has passed. The gods favor bold ventures." His mind constructed a narrative of near-certain success, ignoring the fundamental truth that maritime commerce operated on probabilities, not guarantees.

This cognitive distortion remains pervasive in modern business. Entrepreneurs routinely overestimate their ability to predict outcomes when evaluating opportunities. A recent simulation by the Academy of Merchant Scholars demonstrated this vividly: when presented with identical investment opportunities, 74% of participants rated ventures described with confident narratives ("The market is ripe for disruption!") as having 80%+ success probability, while the same opportunities framed neutrally received only 55% probability ratings. Our brains are wired to seek certainty, making us vulnerable to stories that eliminate ambiguity—even when reality is inherently uncertain.

Consider a contemporary parallel: a software entrepreneur evaluating two potential ventures. Venture A promises 5x returns with a 20% success probability (high risk, high reward). Venture B offers 1.5x returns with an 85% success probability (moderate risk, moderate reward). Most entrepreneurs instinctively choose Venture A, captivated by the outsized potential while underestimating the 80% chance of total loss. Yet the expected value calculation tells a different story:

- Venture A: (5.0 x 0.20) + (-1.0 x 0.80) = 1.0 - 0.80 = 0.20

- Venture B: (1.5 x 0.85) + (-1.0 x 0.15) = 1.275 - 0.15 = 1.125

Despite the seemingly "less exciting" returns, Venture B delivers nearly six times the expected value of Venture A. This mathematical reality explains why Mathon's caravan strategy consistently outperformed Kalim's shipwreck approach across generations of Ur's merchants.

The psychological barrier to proper diversification isn't just mathematical illiteracy—it's emotional. When Kalim stood before Mathon's seven camels, each loaded with different goods, he felt contempt for what seemed like timid, unambitious thinking. "Where is the glory in small gains?" he demanded. Mathon's response cut to the heart of the matter: "Glory feeds no family after the ship sinks. Certainty builds empires while hope leaves men hauling crates at the docks."

Mathon's Caravan Strategy: The Mathematics of Resilient Growth

Mathon's caravan wasn't merely a collection of camels carrying goods—it represented a sophisticated risk management system refined over generations of Ur's merchant class. As Kalim reluctantly accepted work as Mathon's camel driver to repay his debt, he began to understand the method behind what had initially seemed like excessive caution.

Each caravan followed a precise allocation formula:

- Two camels carried grain sacks (drought-resistant but vulnerable to rodents)

- Two camels transported wool bales (famine-resistant but susceptible to moisture)

- Two camels bore copper ingots (recession-resistant but targeted by bandits)

- One camel carried temple offerings (war-resistant but low-margin)

This seven-camel structure wasn't arbitrary—it represented the optimal balance between risk reduction and growth potential. Ur's merchant records reveal that caravans with fewer than five routes had catastrophic failure rates exceeding 40% during the Great Drought of 1782 BCE, while caravans with more than ten routes suffered from management dilution that reduced overall returns by 22%. The "magic number" of seven emerged from centuries of trial and error, representing the point where additional diversification yielded diminishing returns.

At the heart of Mathon's strategy was what modern portfolio theory calls the "efficient frontier"—the optimal balance between risk and return. The Ur merchants had discovered through painful experience that spreading capital across uncorrelated assets didn't merely reduce risk; it actually increased long-term growth potential by preventing catastrophic losses that would require starting over.

Consider how Mathon evaluated a single caravan route:

1. **Upside Potential**: Maximum possible return (e.g., 3x for wool during famine)

2. **Probability of Success**: Historical success rate (e.g., 75% for grain routes)

3. **Downside Magnitude**: Maximum possible loss (e.g., 100% if bandits strike)

4. **Correlation to Other Routes**: How this route performed relative to others (e.g., grain and wool routes had negative correlation during droughts)

Using these four factors, Mathon calculated an Expected Value (EV) for each opportunity:

EV = (Upside Potential × Probability of Success) - (Downside Magnitude × Probability of Failure)

For Kalim's doomed ship voyage:

- Upside Potential: 10x

- Probability of Success: 30% (based on historical shipwreck rates)

- Downside Magnitude: 100% (total loss)

- EV = $(10.0 \times 0.30) - (1.0 \times 0.70) = 3.0 - 0.70 = 2.30$

This positive EV might suggest the investment was rational, but Mathon would have added a crucial fifth factor: **Concentration Risk**. When Kalim allocated 100% of his capital to this single venture, he transformed what appeared to be a positive EV opportunity into near-certain ruin. The true calculation should account for the probability of total portfolio failure:

True EV = EV × (1 - Concentration Risk)

For Kalim (100% concentration):

True EV = 2.30 × (1 - 1.0) = 0

For Mathon (14.3% allocation per route):

True EV = 2.30 × (1 - 0.143) = 1.97

This mathematical reality explains why Mathon's approach consistently outperformed. He didn't merely diversify for safety—he engineered his portfolio to maximize long-term growth by eliminating the risk of total failure.

The Ur merchants formalized this understanding through what they called the "20% Rule": no single venture should ever consume more than 20% of total capital. This meant Kalim's mistake wasn't investing in the ship—it was allocating 100% of his resources to it. Had he invested only 20% of his capital in the *Sea Dragon* while diversifying the rest across other opportunities, even the ship's sinking would have left him with sufficient resources to continue trading.

Modern investors have rediscovered this ancient wisdom through quantitative analysis. A comprehensive study by the Academy of Financial Wisdom tracking merchant portfolios over 200 years found that those adhering to the 20% Rule achieved compound annual growth rates of 9.8%, compared to 6.2% for concentrated portfolios and 4.1% for over-diversified portfolios (those with more than 15 holdings). The data revealed a clear mathematical optimum: limiting individual investments to 15-20% of net worth maximized long-term growth while minimizing ruin risk.

Building Your Uncorrelated Opportunity Matrix

Kalim's most profound realization came not from understanding the mathematics of diversification, but from discovering how to identify truly uncorrelated opportunities—those that don't rise and fall together during market shocks. During a sandstorm that stranded the caravan for three days, Mathon explained how Ur's merchants categorized risk exposures:

"Look at these routes," Mathon said, sketching in the sand. "Grain caravans thrive during droughts when fields fail but suffer when rains come too early. Wool caravans flourish during famines when people need warm clothing but decline when harvests are plentiful. Copper routes are steady during recessions but vulnerable to banditry during wars. Temple offerings are slow but certain during conflicts but less profitable in times of peace."

He drew intersecting lines representing how these different routes performed under various conditions, creating what modern investors call a correlation matrix. The key insight was that true diversification requires assets with negative or near-zero correlation—not merely different assets that move in the same direction during crises.

Consider how a modern entrepreneur might apply this principle. Instead of simply investing in multiple businesses (which may all suffer during an economic downturn), they would seek opportunities with fundamentally different risk profiles:

- **Cyclical Business**: Restaurant (thrives in good times, struggles in recessions)

- **Countercyclical Business**: Debt collection service (struggles in good times, thrives in recessions)

- **Defensive Business**: Healthcare services (steady demand regardless of economy)

- **Innovation Business**: Software development (volatile but high growth potential)

The Ur merchants operationalized this understanding through what they called the "Triad Test" for new opportunities:

1. **Captive Demand Test**: Does this solve a problem people will pay for regardless of economic conditions? (e.g., grain during famine)

2. **Infrastructure Reuse Test**: Can I leverage existing resources to enter this space? (e.g., camel routes for multiple goods)

3. **Correlation Test**: How does this opportunity perform when my core business struggles?

When Kalim later established his own trading business, he applied this framework rigorously. His core business remained cloth trading (vulnerable to droughts), but he added:

- A small grain storage operation (thrived during droughts)

- A contract weaving service for temple garments (steady demand regardless of weather)

- An information brokerage service selling shipping forecasts (profited when others suffered from poor planning)

This structure created what Mathon called "opportunity resilience"—the ability to maintain cash flow through any market condition. During the next major drought, while Kalim's cloth business suffered, his grain storage operation doubled in value, his temple contracts remained steady, and his information service saw unprecedented demand as merchants scrambled for reliable forecasts.

Modern entrepreneurs can create their own opportunity matrix through systematic analysis:

1. **Map Your Current Risk Exposures**: List all significant threats to your primary business (e.g., economic downturns, supply chain disruptions, technological changes)

2. **Identify Counterbalancing Opportunities**: For each threat, find businesses that would benefit from that same condition

3. **Assess Implementation Feasibility**: Evaluate how much new infrastructure each opportunity would require

4. **Calculate Correlation Coefficients**: Estimate how each opportunity would perform relative to your core business under stress

For example, a modern bakery owner might create this matrix:

Risk Exposure	Core Business Impact	Counterbalancing Opportunity	Correlation Estimate
Economic Downturn	Sales drop 30%	Discount bulk bread for shelters	+0.2 (low positive)
Flour Shortage	Production halts	Alternative grain sourcing service	-0.7 (strong negative)
Health Regulations	Compliance costs rise	Sanitation consulting service	-0.4 (moderate negative)
Labor Shortage	Operations disrupted	Staffing coordination platform	+0.1 (near zero)

Using this matrix, the bakery owner could strategically invest in the alternative grain sourcing service and sanitation consulting—opportunities with negative correlation to their core business that would actually thrive when their bakery struggled.

The Risk Ledger: Your Diversification Command Center

As Kalim worked with Mathon, he began maintaining what the merchants called a "risk ledger"—a simple clay tablet tracking three critical metrics for every investment:

1. **Capital Deployed**: Percentage of total portfolio allocated

2. **Maximum Acceptable Loss**: The most he could afford to lose before impacting survival

3. **Correlation Score**: How this investment moved relative to others (-1.0 to +1.0)

Mathon insisted that Kalim update this ledger weekly, forcing him to confront uncomfortable truths about his portfolio composition. Initially resistant, Kalim soon discovered the ledger's power during a bandit attack that destroyed one of the wool-bearing camels. Because he could instantly see that this represented only 14.3% of the caravan's total value and had low correlation to other routes, he remained calm while others panicked. More importantly, the ledger showed him exactly how much capital remained available to rebalance the portfolio.

Modern entrepreneurs can implement a digital risk ledger with similar simplicity. Here's a practical framework:

The Diversification Dashboard

Column 1: Opportunity Name (e.g., "Core Business," "New Product Line," "Real Estate Investment")

Column 2: Capital Allocation (% of total portfolio)

Column 3: Maximum Loss Tolerance (% you can afford to lose)

Column 4: Correlation Score (how this moves relative to your core business)

Column 5: Expected Value (calculated as described earlier)

Column 6: Stress Test Result (performance during simulated worst-case scenario)

Consider how a software entrepreneur might fill this out:

Opportunity	Allocation	Max Loss	Correlation	EV	Stress Test
Core SaaS Platform	50%	30%	1.0	1.25	-25% revenue
Mobile App Extension	20%	50%	0.7	0.85	-40% revenue
API Monetization	15%	70%	-0.2	1.65	+15% revenue
Consulting Services	10%	20%	0.3	0.90	+5% revenue
Hardware Integration	5%	100%	0.9	0.45	-80% revenue

This dashboard immediately reveals critical insights:

- The hardware integration (5% allocation) has dangerously high correlation to the core business while offering the lowest EV

- API monetization has negative correlation and the highest EV, suggesting it deserves greater allocation

- Total portfolio concentration risk remains manageable (no single item exceeds 20%)

The Ur merchants took this analysis further with what they called "premortem stress testing"—imagining specific failure scenarios and calculating their portfolio impact. Mathon required Kalim to conduct these exercises quarterly:

1. **Identify Three Plausible Catastrophes**: (e.g., "Bandits destroy two camels," "Drought ruins grain harvest," "Temple closes during plague")

2. **Calculate Portfolio Impact**: For each scenario, determine percentage loss across the entire portfolio

3. **Verify Survival Threshold**: Ensure worst-case scenario keeps you above the "survival floor" (the minimum capital needed to continue operations)

4. **Adjust Allocations Accordingly**: Shift capital to opportunities that strengthen resilience against identified threats

During one such exercise, Kalim realized that if bandits destroyed both wool camels (28.6% of the caravan), his portfolio would drop below the survival threshold. Mathon showed him how to rebalance—not by reducing wool investments, but by increasing the temple offerings route, which had negative correlation to bandit risk (temple routes traveled with guards).

Modern businesses can conduct equivalent stress tests using scenario analysis:

Scenario: Economic Recession (18-month duration)

- Core Business: -40% revenue

- Countercyclical Business: +25% revenue

- Defensive Business: -10% revenue

- Innovation Business: -60% revenue

- Portfolio Impact: (0.5 × -0.4) + (0.2 × 0.25) + (0.2 × -0.1) + (0.1 × -0.6) = -22%

- Survival Check: Does -22% keep us above operating minimum? (Yes)

Scenario: Technological Disruption (Core product obsolete)

- Core Business: -90% revenue

- Countercyclical Business: -20% revenue

- Defensive Business: -15% revenue

- Innovation Business: +200% revenue

- Portfolio Impact: (0.5 × -0.9) + (0.2 × -0.2) + (0.2 × -0.15) + (0.1 × 2.0) = -32%

- Survival Check: Does -32% keep us above operating minimum? (Barely—needs adjustment)

This second scenario revealed a critical vulnerability: the portfolio could barely survive technological disruption. The solution wasn't abandoning the innovation business (which provided the only positive during this scenario), but increasing its allocation while finding additional countercyclical opportunities with stronger negative correlation to technological risk.

Implementing Your Diversification Strategy: A Step-by-Step Framework

Kalim's transformation from shipwreck victim to successful merchant didn't happen overnight. Mathon guided him through a structured implementation process that modern entrepreneurs can replicate:

Step 1: Audit Your Current Concentration Risk

- Calculate your "concentration score": (Largest Investment ÷ Total Portfolio) × 100

- Ur merchants considered scores above 30% dangerous; modern experts recommend keeping this below 20%

- If your score exceeds 20%, immediately begin rebalancing toward the target

Step 2: Establish Your Survival Floor

- Determine the absolute minimum capital needed to maintain operations for six months

- Ur merchants called this their "temple offering"—resources they would never risk

- Modern businesses should calculate this as six months of essential operating expenses

Step 3: Identify Your Core Risk Exposures

- List the three most likely catastrophic events for your business

- For each, estimate probability and potential impact on revenue

- Ur merchants tracked these on their "risk clay tablets" updated monthly

Step 4: Source Uncorrelated Opportunities

- For each major risk exposure, identify at least one opportunity with negative or near-zero correlation

- Prioritize opportunities requiring minimal new infrastructure (leveraging Mathon's "infrastructure reuse" principle)

- Ur merchants spent 20% of their time prospecting for these counterbalancing opportunities

Step 5: Calculate Expected Value for Each Opportunity

- Use the formula: EV = (Upside × Probability) - (Downside × (1-Probability))

- Only consider opportunities with EV > 1.5x (the threshold for meaningful growth)

- Ur merchants rejected any opportunity with EV below 1.2x as "not worth the mental energy"

Step 6: Build Your Risk Ledger

- Create your diversification dashboard with the six columns described earlier

- Set allocation limits: maximum 20% to any single opportunity, minimum 5% to your core business

- Ur merchants updated their ledgers during the first hour of each market day

Step 7: Conduct Quarterly Premortem Stress Tests

- Simulate three catastrophic scenarios relevant to your business

- Calculate portfolio impact for each scenario

- Adjust allocations to ensure survival in all scenarios while maximizing growth potential

Step 8: Implement Automatic Rebalancing Triggers

- Set rules for when to adjust allocations (e.g., "If any opportunity exceeds 25%, reduce to 20%")

- Ur merchants used physical "rebalancing tokens" that required two witnesses to move

- Modern businesses can automate this through investment platforms with rebalancing features

As Kalim implemented this framework over two years, his business transformed. When drought struck Ur, devastating many merchants, Kalim's grain storage operation more than compensated for his cloth business losses. When bandits disrupted trade routes, his information brokerage service saw unprecedented demand. Most importantly, he never faced the existential threat that had nearly destroyed him after the *Sea Dragon* disaster.

Modern entrepreneurs who follow this same process achieve remarkable results. Consider "Amina," a hypothetical entrepreneur who runs a successful event planning business. Following the eight-step framework:

1. **Concentration Audit**: Realized 85% of revenue came from corporate events (concentration score: 85%)

2. **Survival Floor**: Calculated six months of essential expenses: 120,000 shekels

3. **Risk Exposures**: Identified economic downturns (40% probability, -60% impact), pandemic restrictions (25% probability, -90% impact), and venue shortages (35% probability, -30% impact)

4. **Uncorrelated Opportunities**: Developed virtual event services (negative correlation to pandemic risk), nonprofit fundraising (negative

correlation to economic downturns), and venue consulting (negative correlation to venue shortages)

5. **Expected Value Calculation**: Determined virtual events had EV of 2.1x, nonprofit services 1.8x, venue consulting 1.5x

6. **Risk Ledger Construction**: Allocated 40% to core business, 25% to virtual events, 20% to nonprofit services, 15% to venue consulting

7. **Stress Testing**: Verified portfolio would survive all three scenarios with at least 15% growth in two scenarios

8. **Rebalancing Triggers**: Set rules to maintain allocations within 5% bands

When a simulated economic downturn hit (exactly as forecast), Amina's business not only survived but grew 18% as her nonprofit services expanded while corporate events contracted. Her concentration score had dropped from 85% to 40%, making her business fundamentally more resilient.

The Hidden Power of Diversification: Opportunity Creation, Not Just Risk Reduction

Kalim's most profound discovery came when he realized that diversification wasn't merely about avoiding ruin—it actively created new growth opportunities that wouldn't exist in a concentrated portfolio. As his various business lines developed, he noticed unexpected synergies:

- His grain storage customers needed reliable transportation, creating demand for his camel services

- Temple officials who purchased his information service referred him to wealthy families seeking estate management

- The weaving skills developed for temple garments opened contracts with nobility

What Mathon had understood but not explicitly taught was that diversification creates optionality—the strategic flexibility to pivot toward emerging opportunities without starting from scratch. Each new business line wasn't just a separate revenue stream; it was a platform for discovering adjacent opportunities.

Modern portfolio theory confirms this phenomenon, which academics call "the diversification premium." Studies show that businesses with properly diversified portfolios achieve 22% higher long-term growth than concentrated portfolios, not because each individual investment performs better, but because the portfolio as a whole generates more opportunities for strategic reallocation.

Consider the "option value" created through diversification:

- A concentrated business has only one path forward (improve the core offering)

- A diversified business has multiple paths, plus the ability to shift resources between them

When drought struck Ur, Kalim could have merely survived by drawing on his grain reserves. Instead, he used his information network (developed through the brokerage service) to identify farmers with surplus wool, his camel routes to transport it, and his temple connections to secure premium buyers. This interconnected ecosystem—impossible with a single business line—allowed him to not just endure the crisis but emerge significantly stronger.

The Ur merchants captured this principle in what they called the "Law of Compounding Connections": each additional revenue stream doesn't just add linear growth—it creates exponential opportunity through combinatorial possibilities. Two business lines create one potential synergy; three create four; four create eleven. The mathematical formula is (2^n - n - 1), where n equals the number of business lines.

For Kalim, this meant:

- With 1 business line: 0 potential synergies

- With 2 business lines: 1 potential synergy

- With 3 business lines: 4 potential synergies

- With 4 business lines: 11 potential synergies

This combinatorial advantage explains why diversification-focused merchants consistently outperformed specialists over time. Their portfolios didn't merely survive disruptions—they used them as springboards for growth.

Modern entrepreneurs can harness this same power by designing their diversification strategy to maximize combinatorial potential:

1. **Seek Complementary Capabilities**: Choose opportunities that build transferable skills (e.g., marketing expertise from one business applying to another)

2. **Create Shared Infrastructure**: Design systems that serve multiple business lines (e.g., a customer database used across ventures)

3. **Develop Cross-Pollination Rituals**: Schedule regular meetings to identify synergies between business units

4. **Track Combinatorial Value**: Measure not just individual business performance, but the additional value created through interactions

When Kalim finally stood on the docks again, he no longer saw empty horizons but interconnected opportunities stretching to the horizon. His seven camels now carried not just goods, but a resilient ecosystem of interlocking businesses, each supporting the others through the inevitable storms of commerce. The ship that had once represented his downfall now seemed merely one possible route among many—a valuable option, but never the only path to prosperity.

You've now grasped the mathematical and psychological framework to transform diversification from a fear-based tactic into a growth engine, ensuring no single disaster can erase your progress. The paralysis of opportunity assessment has been replaced with clear risk quantification protocols, letting you pursue high-upside ventures without gambling your foundation. However, merely spreading capital isn't enough—you must now master the art of identifying uncorrelated opportunities that compound synergistically. This chapter equipped you to avoid ruin, but the next challenge is recognizing which risks are worth taking to accelerate growth. You're primed to confront the seduction of "sure things" and learn how to sniff out hidden correlations that make diversification illusory. As you prepare to stress-test your caravan against bandits, snakes, and black swan events, remember Mathon's final lesson to Kalim: "True wealth isn't found in avoiding risk, but in understanding which risks create opportunity and which merely create ruin."

Chapter 4: Bandits, Snakes, and Black Swans – Stress-Testing Your Caravan

The Hidden Trap in Your Diversification Strategy (And Why Kalim's Shipwreck Was Just the Beginning)

You've meticulously built your caravan: seven distinct revenue streams, each seemingly uncorrelated. Your e-commerce division thrives while your brick-and-mortar locations hold steady. Your SaaS product scales alongside your consulting arm. You sleep soundly, believing you've mastered the "Law of the Divided Risk" from Mathon's camels. Then comes the pandemic—or the interest rate shock, or the supply chain collapse. Suddenly, *all* your ventures stumble simultaneously. The recession that clobbered your retail stores also paralyzed your event-based consulting. The data privacy regulations that throttled your SaaS business simultaneously crushed your affiliate marketing streams. Your diversification shield shatters not from a single arrow, but from a coordinated volley you never saw coming.

This is the brutal reality Kalim refused to acknowledge when he poured all his shekels into that single ship. His error wasn't merely concentration risk—it was the fatal illusion that *all* risks are independent. Mathon's true genius lay not in owning seven camels, but in engineering their journeys so that when bandits took one route, floods crippled another, and snakebites stalled a third, his *overall* caravan still delivered profit. Modern entrepreneurs call this "diversification." Mathon called it "surviving tomorrow." Your current strategy likely resembles Kalim's more than you admit. You've spread capital across ventures, but have you stress-tested them against the *simultaneous* collapse of multiple pillars? Without this forensic layer, your "diversified" portfolio is merely a collection of correlated vulnerabilities disguised as safety. This chapter exposes the hidden correlations that turn diversification into delusion and gives you the stress-testing toolkit to build a truly resilient business caravan—capable of navigating not just bandits and snakes, but the black swans that sink entire markets.

The Correlation Illusion: Why Your "Diversified" Portfolio Isn't Safe

Kalim's shipwreck wasn't the outlier he believed. Ur's maritime records reveal that of 100 merchants who invested in "sure thing" single-voyage expeditions over a decade, 73 lost everything to storms, pirates, or cargo spoilage. Only 7 achieved the mythical 10x returns. The remaining 20 eked out marginal profits drowned by opportunity costs. Mathon, meanwhile, never saw his *entire* caravan fail in 30 years of trading. Why? Because he understood a truth modern investors consistently ignore: **risks are rarely independent when systemic shocks hit**.

Consider Ur's caravan routes:

- **Coastal Route (Kalim's ship)**: Vulnerable to monsoons (30% failure rate), piracy (25%), and port closures (15%). Crucially, these risks *amplified* each other—monsoons drove pirates inland, while port closures stranded ships in storm zones.

- **River Barge Route**: Flood-prone (20% failure) but immune to pirates; however, droughts (10% failure) that crippled river traffic also caused famine, collapsing demand for *all* goods.

- **Mountain Pass Route**: Avalanche risks (15%) but safe from floods; yet war between city-states (5% failure) could seal all highland passes simultaneously.

Kalim treated the ship's 70% *aggregate* failure rate as irrelevant because he fixated on the 10x upside. Mathon, however, mapped *correlations*:

- Coastal and river routes had **+0.85 correlation** during monsoons (both failed when rivers overflowed coastal ports).

- Mountain and river routes had **-0.7 correlation** (avalanches blocked mountain passes *while* floods made rivers unnavigable—meaning one route often succeeded when the other failed).

- Coastal and mountain routes had **+0.3 correlation** (pirates sometimes followed caravan routes inland).

His seven-camel strategy wasn't random—it was a **mathematically optimized risk hedge**:

- 2 camels on mountain routes (low correlation with other failures)

- 3 camels on river routes (moderate correlation, but high reliability in fair weather)

- 2 camels with temple guards (high cost, but near-zero correlation to natural disasters)

The result? Even when two camels failed (a 40% loss), the *remaining five* typically succeeded *because* their risks offset each other. Contrast this with Kalim's peers who "diversified" by sending two ships to the same port—one sank in a storm, the other was seized by pirates enforcing new tariffs. Both failed due to the *same* systemic shock: monsoon season.

The Modern Correlation Trap

Today, entrepreneurs replicate Kalim's error through subtle but deadly missteps:

- **Geographic "Diversification" Fallacy**: A coffee roaster with cafes in New York, London, and Tokyo believes they're protected. Yet when a global shipping crisis (like the 2021 Suez Canal blockage) hits, *all* locations face bean shortages simultaneously. The correlation? **+0.92**—near-perfect synchronization of supply chain failure.

- **Customer Base Mirage**: A SaaS company serving restaurants, hotels, and event venues feels secure—until a pandemic hits. All three sectors collapse together with **+0.88 correlation** as gatherings vanish.

- **Revenue Stream Illusion**: An e-commerce brand selling apparel (core), virtual styling (digital), and pop-up events (experiential) assumes diversification. But when consumer spending contracts, *all* segments shrink in tandem (**+0.79 correlation**), as discretionary budgets vanish holistically.

The core failure? Measuring diversification by *number of streams* rather than **correlation coefficients between their failure modes**. Ur's merchants quantified this using clay tablets tracking "failure co-occurrence rates" over 100 journeys. Modern tools like Python's Pandas library automate this analysis by calculating:

`Correlation Coefficient = Covariance(Asset A Returns, Asset B Returns) / (Standard Deviation A × Standard Deviation B)`

A coefficient near **+1.0** means assets move together (disaster when correlated); **-1.0** means they move oppositely (true diversification); **0** means no relationship. Mathon *only* added ventures with coefficients **below +0.3** relative to his existing portfolio. Your current diversification likely has coefficients above **+0.7**—making it riskier than holding a single asset.

The Black Swan Filter: Stress-Testing for Catastrophic Correlation

Mathon didn't trust historical data alone. He knew Ur's records couldn't predict the *unprecedented*—like the Year of the Twin Eclipses when locust swarms (normally a spring risk) coincided with autumn floods, collapsing *all* agricultural trade routes simultaneously. He called these "god's jokes"—events so improbable they defied records, yet so devastating they erased merchants who ignored them. Today, we call them **Black Swan events**: high-impact, unpredictable outliers that retrospectively seem obvious.

To combat this, Mathon implemented the **Black Swan Filter**—a three-step stress test for *every* new venture *before* allocating capital:

Step 1: Define the "Unthinkable" Catastrophes

For each venture, identify three catastrophic scenarios where *multiple* revenue streams fail *simultaneously*. Not "a storm sinks my ship," but:

- *"Monsoon season triggers port closures (hurting coastal shipping) AND river flooding (disrupting barge traffic) AND famine (collapsing demand for non-essential goods)"*

- *"Regulatory crackdown on data privacy kills SaaS subscriptions AND affiliate marketing AND destroys trust in all digital services"*

- *"Global recession causes consumers to slash discretionary spending on apparel (core), virtual styling (digital), AND events (experiential) at once"*

Ur's merchants documented these on "doom tablets," reviewing them quarterly. Modern equivalents use **BowTie Diagrams**—visual risk maps showing:

- **Left Side (Threats)**: Root causes of systemic collapse (e.g., "interest rate spike → consumer debt crisis → spending freeze")

- **Central Event**: The Black Swan (e.g., "simultaneous 30% revenue drop across all streams")

- **Right Side (Mitigations)**: Predefined actions (e.g., "activate circuit breaker: shift 50% capital from apparel to value-tier essentials")

Step 2: Calculate Joint Failure Probability

Don't guess—"What are the odds?" Mathon used Ur's merchant guild failure logs to compute:

`Joint Failure Probability = (Probability of Event A) × (Probability of Event B) × Correlation Coefficient`

Example:

- Probability of monsoon port closure: **20%**

- Probability of river flood: **15%**

- Correlation between them: **+0.85**

- Joint failure probability = **0.20 × 0.15 × 0.85 = 2.55%**

If this exceeded **1.0%**, he deemed the correlation too dangerous and redesigned the venture. Modern entrepreneurs automate this with **Monte Carlo simulations** in tools like @RISK, running 10,000 scenarios to see how often *multiple* streams fail together. If joint failure occurs in >5% of simulations, the diversification is illusory.

Step 3: Build the "Correlation Escape Hatch"

Mathon never relied on diversification alone. For high-correlation risks, he created **uncorrelated hedges**:

- When monsoons threatened coastal/river routes, he activated his **temple guard route** (correlation **-0.6**)—caravans carrying sacred oils for priests, whose demand *increased* during disasters.

- He also sold **"calamity insurance"** to other merchants: For 5% of cargo value, he'd transport emergency grain *only* if floods hit. This generated revenue *during* the very disasters that sank others.

Your modern escape hatch might be:

- For a restaurant chain: **Ghost kitchen partnerships** with grocery delivery apps. When dine-in collapses (pandemic), this stream *surges* (correlation **-0.7**).

- For a SaaS company: **Offline data backup services**. When internet outages cripple SaaS, demand for backups spikes (correlation **-0.8**).

- For e-commerce: **Barter networks** with local producers. When payment systems fail (cyberattack), trade continues (correlation **-0.9**).

Implementation Protocol:

1. Run your top 3 Black Swan scenarios through the filter.

2. If any joint probability >1.0%, identify an uncorrelated hedge (correlation **< -0.5**).

3. Allocate **5% of venture capital** to build/test the hedge *before* launch.

4. Document activation triggers (e.g., "If unemployment rises 3% in 2 months, shift 30% marketing to value-tier essentials").

Volatility-Adjusted Sizing: Allocating Capital to Survive the Storm

Kalim's final error was ignoring *volatility*. His ship promised 10x returns but swung wildly—worthless if sunk, priceless if successful. Mathon's camels offered modest 2x returns but with steady, predictable progress. Ur's merchants quantified this using the **Volatility-Adjusted Allocation Formula**:

`Capital Allocation = (Upside Potential ÷ Volatility) × Confidence Factor`

Where:

- **Upside Potential**: Max realistic return (e.g., ship = 10x, camel = 2x)

- **Volatility**: Standard deviation of returns (e.g., ship = 80%, camel = 20%)

- **Confidence Factor**: 0–1 score based on historical success (e.g., ship = 0.3, camel = 0.9)

Example:

- Kalim's Ship: `(10 ÷ 0.80) × 0.3 = 3.75`

- Mathon's Camel: `(2 ÷ 0.20) × 0.9 = 9.0`

Mathon allocated **more** to the camel *despite* its lower upside because its risk-adjusted return was **2.4x higher**. Kalim, ignoring volatility, poured everything into the ship (score 3.75) while dismissing the camels.

Modern Application:

A crypto venture with 50% upside but 80% volatility scores **0.625** (50 ÷ 80). A SaaS business with 30% upside and 40% volatility scores **0.75** (30 ÷ 40). *Despite lower upside, the SaaS play deserves more capital* because its volatility-adjusted return is higher. Ur's merchants enforced a rule: **No venture with score <1.0 could exceed 15% of total capital**.

Implementation Protocol:

1. For each revenue stream, calculate:

- Upside Potential: Max realistic annual growth (e.g., 30% for stable SaaS, 50% for emerging markets)

- Volatility: Standard deviation of monthly revenue (use 12 months of data)

- Confidence Factor: (Successful months ÷ Total months) × 0.5 + (Profitable months ÷ Total months) × 0.5

2. Compute Volatility-Adjusted Score = (Upside ÷ Volatility) × Confidence

3. Allocate capital proportional to scores, capping any stream at **20%** if score >1.0 or **10%** if score <1.0.

Case Study: The German Manufacturer

A metal fabricator serving automotive, aerospace, and medical device sectors believed they were diversified. After the Ukraine war triggered simultaneous supply shocks:

- Automotive: Steel costs +40% (demand stable)

- Aerospace: Titanium shortages +60% costs (demand down 20%)

- Medical: Regulatory delays +30% costs (demand up 15%)

Their joint failure probability was **18%** (all streams hit by material shortages). Using the Black Swan Filter, they identified an uncorrelated hedge: **scrap metal recycling**. When primary material costs spiked, scrap demand *surged* (correlation **-0.85**). They allocated **15%** of capital to build a recycling line, funded by:

- Selling non-core machinery (5%)

- Shifting marketing spend from trade shows to digital (3%)

- Delaying office renovations (7%)

Within 6 months, scrap operations generated **22%** of revenue during the crisis—offsetting losses elsewhere. Crucially, they'd stress-tested this: Their

Monte Carlo simulation showed joint failure probability dropped from 18% to **4.2%** with the hedge.

Building Resilience Muscle: Disaster Drills and Liquidity Tiers

Mathon didn't wait for disaster to test his caravan. Every quarter, he conducted **"Calamity Drills"** where he simulated the loss of his top two revenue streams and rebuilt from reserves. Ur's records show merchants who did this recovered **65% faster** from real crises. Modern neuroscience explains why: Stress-testing *in advance* reduces amygdala hijack during actual crises, freeing prefrontal cortex for strategic thinking.

Your Quarterly Disaster Drill Protocol:

1. **Select the Scenario**: Pick one top Black Swan (e.g., "60% revenue drop across all streams for 90 days").

2. **Simulate the Collapse**:

- Freeze 60% of revenue from your largest two streams.

- Trigger correlated costs (e.g., if revenue drops, assume supplier payments are due immediately).

3. **Activate Your Response**:

- Deploy circuit breakers (e.g., "Shift 50% marketing budget to highest-margin stream")

- Activate escape hatches (e.g., "Launch barter network with 3 local producers")

4. **Measure Recovery Time**: How many days until cash flow turns positive? Ur's target: **<30 days**.

5. **Refine Your Playbook**: Document what worked; update triggers and actions.

Behavioral Hack: Mathon made drills **ritualistic**. Before each, merchants swore oaths before temple elders: "I will not touch the fifth jar unless *all* caravans fail." This leveraged **precommitment psychology**—binding future self to present decisions. Modern equivalents:

- Sign a "Resilience Pledge" with your team: "We will not raid growth capital for operational shortfalls."

- Use apps like **StickK** to commit cash to charity if you break circuit breakers.

- Hold quarterly "failure feasts" celebrating drill learnings (not outcomes).

Liquidity Tiers: Your Three-Layer Survival System

Mathon's reserves weren't monolithic. He segmented them into **three liquidity tiers**, each with distinct purposes:

Tier	Allocation	Purpose	Access Trigger	Modern Equivalent
Cash Tier	50%	Cover immediate losses (bandit raids)	Revenue drop >15% for 7 days	Operating cash + credit line
Stable Tier	30%	Bridge medium-term disruptions (snakebites)	Revenue drop >30% for 30 days	Short-term bonds + REITs
Deep Tier	20%	Rebuild after systemic collapse (famine)	Revenue drop >50% for 90 days	Hard assets + private equity

Critical Rule: **Never sell assets from a higher tier to cover lower-tier emergencies**. If bandits hit (Cash Tier event), *do not* liquidate Deep Tier assets. Ur's merchants who violated this—selling temple oil reserves to cover a single caravan loss—often starved when famine hit.

Modern Implementation:

- **Cash Tier**: 50% of reserves in cash/credit lines. *Used for*: Payroll during short dips, supplier emergencies.

- **Stable Tier**: 30% in <2-year bonds/CDs. *Used for*: Marketing shifts during moderate downturns, equipment repairs.

- **Deep Tier**: 20% in real estate/long-term equity. *Used for*: Acquiring distressed competitors, R&D pivots.

Pitfall to Avoid: Over-diversification. Ur's records show merchants with >10 ventures failed **3x more** than those with 3–5. Why? Management bandwidth dilution—Mathon personally tracked only 7 caravans. Modern equivalent: Warren Buffett's "20-punch card" rule—you get 20 investment decisions in life; make them count.

The Resilience Dashboard: Metrics That Predict Survival

Mathon didn't fly blind. His "Resilience Dashboard" tracked three leading indicators:

1. **Recovery Time**: Days to positive cash flow after simulated crisis. *Target*: **<30 days**.

- *How to Track*: Run monthly mini-drills (e.g., "What if our top client leaves tomorrow?").

- *Red Flag*: >45 days indicates over-reliance on single streams.

2. **Correlation Score**: Average correlation coefficient between all revenue streams. *Target*: **<0.3**.

- *How to Track*: Use Excel's CORREL function on monthly revenue data.

- *Red Flag*: >0.5 means "diversification" is an illusion.

3. **Diversification ROI**: (Revenue Stability ÷ Capital Deployed) × 100. *Target*: **>8.0**.

- *Revenue Stability* = (Lowest monthly revenue ÷ Average monthly revenue) × 100

- *Example*: If lowest revenue = $80K, average = $100K, stability = 80.

- *Capital Deployed* = Total capital in diversification efforts

- *Diversification ROI* = (80 ÷ $50,000) × 100 = **16.0** (strong)

- *Red Flag*: <5.0 means diversification costs more than it stabilizes.

Case Study: The Brooklyn Bakery

Faced with Amazon Fresh competition, the bakery diversified into:

- Core: In-store sales (60% revenue)

- Digital: Online cake subscriptions (25%)

- Experiential: Baking classes (15%)

Their initial Correlation Score: **+0.72** (all streams collapsed during lockdowns). Using the Black Swan Filter, they identified:

- **Unthinkable Scenario**: "Pandemic shuts indoor dining AND online delivery AND in-person classes."

- **Joint Probability**: 12% (unacceptably high).

- **Escape Hatch**: Partner with hospitals to deliver care packages (correlation **-0.8**).

They allocated **10%** of digital stream capital to build the hospital channel. Quarterly disaster drills showed Recovery Time dropped from **62 to 28 days**. Within a year:

- Correlation Score: **0.21** (down from 0.72)

- Diversification ROI: **14.3** (up from 4.1)

- Revenue during next crisis: **+17%** (vs. competitors -33%)

From Survival to Opportunity: Turning Black Swans into Advantage

Mathon's true mastery wasn't avoiding disaster—it was *leveraging* it. When Kalim's ship sank, Mathon didn't just absorb the loss. He used his intact caravans to buy Kalim's camels at 10% of value, then pivoted them toward transporting emergency grain during the famine Kalim's failure had ignored. **Resilience isn't defensive—it's the platform for offensive growth during chaos.**

Ur's merchants institutionalized this via **"Second-Order Opportunity Mapping"**:

1. During any crisis, ask: *"What problem does this create for others that I can solve?"*

- *Famine*: Mathon saw desperate farmers needing to sell wool *now*—so he bought it cheap to resell later.

- *Pandemic*: A modern gym saw home exercisers needing space—so they rented unused locker rooms as Zoom studios.

2. Allocate **20% of crisis response capital** to these opportunities.

3. Measure **Crisis ROI**: (Revenue from opportunity ÷ Crisis response cost). Target **>3.0**.

Implementation Protocol:

- **During Disaster Drills**, add Step 6: "Identify 3 opportunities created by this crisis."

- **In Your Resilience Dashboard**, track "Opportunity Capture Rate": % of crises where you launched new revenue within 30 days. Target **>75%**.

- **In Liquidity Tiers**, earmark **5% of Deep Tier capital** for "crisis arbitrage" (e.g., buying distressed assets).

The Ultimate Resilience Metric: Reputation Velocity

When Ur's merchants survived famines, their greatest asset wasn't gold—it was **trust**. Drios the shield-maker rebuilt his reputation in 3 months by replacing all defective shields. Mathon doubled his caravan size after the famine because farmers trusted him to pay *during* crisis.

Track your **Reputation Velocity**:

`(Trust Score After Crisis ÷ Trust Score Before Crisis) × 100`

- *Trust Score* = Net Promoter Score + Premium Pricing Tolerance (%) + Referral Rate (%)

- *Target*: **>95%** (e.g., 95 → 90 = 94.7%, unacceptable; 95 → 97 = 102.1%, strong)

How to Achieve It:

- During crises, **over-deliver on promises** Mathon made (e.g., "Pay farmers *before* taking wool").

- Communicate **transparently** about struggles (e.g., "We're diverting 20% of capital to keep prices stable").

- **Sacrifice short-term gain** for long-term trust (e.g., Mathon sold wool *below* famine prices to neighbors).

Synthesis: Building Your Unbreakable Caravan

You now hold Mathon's complete resilience framework—not as isolated tactics, but as an integrated system:

1. **Map Correlations** using the Black Swan Filter to expose hidden risks.

2. **Allocate Volatility-Adjusted** capital to ventures with true offsetting risks.

3. **Drill Relentlessly** with quarterly calamity simulations to build response muscle.

4. **Tier Liquidity** to ensure reserves serve their intended purpose without cross-contamination.

5. **Track Resilience Metrics** that predict survival before crises hit.

6. **Convert Crises to Opportunities** by solving others' problems during chaos.

This transforms diversification from a passive hope into an active engine of stability *and* growth. When the next black swan strikes—be it AI disruption, climate shock, or financial meltdown—your caravan won't just survive. It will thrive while others collapse, positioning you to acquire their assets at famine prices. Mathon didn't fear the storm; he studied its patterns so he could sail *through* it while Kalim drowned.

Your Action Checklist Before the Next Crisis Hits:

- [ ] Run the Black Swan Filter on your top 3 revenue streams this week.

- [ ] Calculate Volatility-Adjusted Scores for all ventures; rebalance allocations.

- [ ] Schedule your first Calamity Drill (simulate 40% revenue drop for 60 days).

- [ ] Segment reserves into Cash, Stable, and Deep Tiers with access rules.

- [ ] Install your Resilience Dashboard tracking Recovery Time, Correlation Score, and Diversification ROI.

The path forward isn't about avoiding bandits or snakes—it's about understanding *which* camels will thrive when they strike. You've engineered a caravan where every loss creates an opportunity, every crisis fuels growth, and no single disaster can erase your foundation. This mastery of resilience isn't the end of your journey—it's the launchpad. For while Mathon's caravans delivered gold, Drios the shield-maker's true wealth lay in something far more valuable: an unbreakable reputation that turned famine into empire. In the next chapter, you'll learn how he forged that reputation not through luck, but through the relentless, uncompromising pursuit of quality—a lesson that shattered competitors and built legacies. The shields of Sparta await, and with them, the secret to making your business *unbreakable* in any storm.

Chapter 5: The Quarry's Byproduct – Profiting from Waste Streams

The Builder Who Saw Gold in Stone Chips

"Are you mad, Sharru?" boomed Amur, the gray-bearded contractor, his belly shaking with laughter as he slammed his fist on the stone table. "You bid for the King's wall project and asked for *rocks* as payment? Not gold, not silver—*rocks*?"

Around the dusty courtyard of the Babylonian Builders' Guild, the other contractors roared with amusement. Sharru stood firm, his arms crossed over his chest, the calluses on his palms still raw from years of working stone. The morning sun glinted off the sweat beading on his forehead as he faced the jeering crowd.

"I asked for the right to keep the excess stone and timber from the quarry," Sharru corrected calmly. "Not rocks. Opportunity."

The laughter only grew louder. One contractor mimicked Sharru's posture, arms crossed, then pretended to cradle an invisible stone while making a weeping sound. Another began tossing pebbles at Sharru's sandals.

"You'll starve before the wall's first tier is laid!" shouted Belshazzar, a portly contractor known for his lavish feasts. "The King's wall requires precision—not some fool's dream of building castles from chippings!"

Sharru felt his jaw tighten but kept his voice steady. "The King's wall will generate more stone than needed. I see value where others see waste."

"And what value is that?" demanded Amur, stepping closer, his shadow falling over Sharru. "Stone chips that can't hold water? Rubble that can't build a goat pen?"

Sharru met the older man's gaze. "The value of a thing is not in what it is, but in what it could become for those who know how to see."

The courtyard fell silent. Even the birds seemed to pause their singing. Sharru had touched a nerve—every builder knew the frustration of watching perfect stone go to waste because it didn't fit the exact specifications of a project. But none had dared to suggest it held value.

King Nebuchadnezzar's decree had arrived at dawn: a great wall must surround the Hanging Gardens, the eighth wonder of the world. The finest stonemasons and builders had gathered at the guild hall to bid for the honor. Most had proposed traditional contracts—fixed sums of gold per block laid, with penalties for delays. Sharru, the youngest contractor present, had submitted a radically different proposal: he would take no gold for building the wall itself. Instead, he requested the right to keep all excess stone and timber produced during the quarrying process—the misshapen blocks, the chippings, the fragments deemed unfit for the King's wall.

To the seasoned builders, it was the proposal of a madman.

As the laughter resumed, Sharru turned to leave, but the guild master, a wizened man named Nabonidus with eyes that had seen three generations of builders come and go, called out, "Sharru, stay."

The courtyard quieted again as Nabonidus approached, his staff tapping against the stone floor. "Explain your thinking," he said, his voice surprisingly gentle.

Sharru took a deep breath. "When we quarry stone for a wall, Master Nabonidus, we extract ten blocks to get seven that are perfect. The three imperfect ones become rubble. For the King's wall, which will require twenty thousand blocks, that means nearly nine thousand blocks of 'waste' stone will be produced."

"And what will you do with this rubble?" asked Nabonidus, stroking his white beard.

"I will build dwellings for the workers," Sharru said. "The workers who quarry the stone and lay the wall live in tents far from the gardens. They walk two hours each morning to reach the site. If I build simple houses from the excess stone near the quarry, they will pay to live there. Their rent will buy better tools. Better tools will allow us to quarry more efficiently, producing even more excess stone, which I can use to build more dwellings."

Amur snorted. "You think workers will pay for shacks made of rubble?"

"Not shacks," Sharru corrected. "Houses. Simple, yes. But with roofs that don't leak and walls that keep out the desert wind. The workers will pay because it saves them hours each day."

"And when the wall is complete?" asked Nabonidus.

Sharru's eyes gleamed. "By then, I will have built an entire district. The King's wall will stand for centuries. My district will generate gold for just as long."

Nabonidus nodded slowly, then turned to the other builders. "The council will consider Sharru's proposal alongside yours. Dismissed."

As the others grumbled and dispersed, Nabonidus pulled Sharru aside. "You understand the risk, boy? If your dwellings don't attract tenants, you'll have nothing to show for your year of labor but dust and disappointment."

Sharru nodded. "I understand. But I also understand that true wealth isn't found in the obvious prize—the King's wall—but in what others discard as worthless."

The old man studied him for a long moment, then placed a hand on his shoulder. "Then may the gods of stone and mortar be with you, young builder. You'll need them."

The Waste Stream Audit: Seeing What Others Discard

Sharru spent the next three days not preparing for construction, but conducting what he called his "waste stream audit." He visited quarries across Babylon, watching how stone was extracted and processed. He spoke with quarry masters, stone cutters, and even the laborers who hauled away the rubble.

What he discovered confirmed his suspicions: for every block of stone used in construction, nearly 30% was discarded as waste. This wasn't insignificant material—the average quarry produced enough chippings and misshapen blocks each day to build a modest home. And yet, this material was routinely hauled away at great expense and dumped in gullies outside the city.

Sharru documented everything in his clay tablet ledger:

- Stone extraction: 10 full blocks per cubic meter of quarry

- Usable blocks: 7 per cubic meter (70%)

- Waste material: 3 blocks per cubic meter (30%)

- Average daily quarry output: 20 cubic meters

- Daily waste production: 60 blocks (enough for 2 small dwellings)

He noted the composition of the waste:

- Large fragments (suitable for foundations): 40%

- Medium chips (suitable for walls): 50%

- Fine dust (suitable for mortar): 10%

Most importantly, Sharru tracked the labor costs associated with waste removal. Quarry owners paid two copper pieces per day for each laborer to haul away rubble—a necessary but unproductive expense that ate into their profits.

At one quarry, Sharru watched as workers discarded a beautiful piece of sandstone that had a minor flaw near one edge. "Why not use this for something?" he asked the quarry master.

The man shrugged. "It doesn't meet the temple's specifications. The priests would reject it for sacred work."

"And could it be used for ordinary buildings?"

"Of course," the man admitted. "But who would bother collecting, sorting, and transporting it? It's easier to just clear it away."

Sharru realized this was the critical insight: waste wasn't inherently valueless—it was only valueless to those who lacked the vision or systems to capture its worth. The stone itself had potential; it was the process that deemed it worthless.

That evening, Sharru met with his small team of seven loyal workers in his modest home. They gathered around a low table as he shared his findings.

"Listen carefully," he began, tracing lines in the dust on the table. "For every ten blocks we quarry for the King's wall, three will be discarded as waste. That's nearly one-third of all stone extracted."

Korah, his foreman, scratched his head. "But Sharru, we've always discarded the unusable blocks. It's how building has always been done."

"Exactly," Sharru said. "But what if we changed that? What if we saw those discarded blocks not as waste, but as our primary product?"

The workers exchanged skeptical glances.

Sharru continued, "The King's wall will take twelve months to complete. At our projected rate, we'll produce enough waste stone to build sixty dwellings. If we charge each worker just two copper pieces per month for housing—less than half what most pay for distant lodgings—we'll collect 120 copper pieces monthly."

He paused for effect. "With that, we can buy better chisels and hammers. Better tools mean we can quarry stone faster, which means we produce even more waste material. More waste means more dwellings. More dwellings mean more rent."

"And if no one rents your houses?" asked a young apprentice named Tammuz.

Sharru smiled. "Have you ever worked a full day hauling stone, then walked two hours home through desert heat? Would you pay two coppers to sleep within minutes of your work?"

Tammuz considered this. "I would."

"Then so will others," Sharru said firmly. "But we must prove it. Tomorrow, we start small. Before the King's wall begins, we'll build one dwelling—from waste stone only. If we can fill it, we build another. If we can fill ten, we build twenty. We let demand guide our growth."

He looked at each man in turn. "This is our opportunity: to build not just a wall, but a legacy. Who's with me?"

One by one, the workers raised their hands.

The First Rental Hut: Validating the Byproduct Model

Sharru knew that grand visions fail without first proving the smallest unit of value. Before committing to the King's wall project, he needed to validate his housing concept with minimal investment.

At dawn the next day, he led his team to the designated quarry site near the Hanging Gardens. While others prepared for the official wall construction to begin, Sharru's crew began their secret experiment.

"Today," he announced, "we are not builders of the King's wall. We are builders of opportunity."

He directed them to collect only the stone that would normally be discarded—the chipped blocks, the misshapen pieces, the fragments with surface flaws. "No perfect blocks," he instructed. "Only what others would haul away."

For three days, they worked in relative isolation, gathering materials. Sharru designed the dwelling to maximize the use of irregular stone—rounded corners that accommodated curved pieces, walls that incorporated varying block sizes into a textured pattern. He instructed the masons to use the fine stone dust, normally swept away, to create a stronger mortar mixture.

On the fourth day, construction began. Without the pressure of the King's timeline, Sharru encouraged his workers to experiment with techniques that would make the most of imperfect materials. They discovered that certain flaws in stone could be turned to advantage—a natural curve became a perfect window arch; a fractured block, split carefully, provided two usable pieces.

By the end of the week, a modest dwelling stood near the quarry entrance. It had:

- Walls of varying stone sizes, creating a distinctive, textured appearance

- A palm-frond roof (since stone chips couldn't form a proper roof)

- A small courtyard with a clay oven

- Space for four families (two rooms with partitions)

Sharru then walked to the temporary worker camp, half a mile from the quarry site. He found dozens of men sitting in the shade, fanning themselves against the afternoon heat.

"Good people," he announced, "I have built a dwelling near the quarry from stone that would have been wasted. It is ready for families to live in. For two copper pieces per month—less than you pay for your current lodgings—you can live within minutes of your work, saving you four hours of walking each day."

A skeptical carpenter stepped forward. "And what makes your dwelling better than our tents?"

Sharru led him to the new structure. "Here, the walls keep out the desert wind. Here, the roof doesn't leak when it rains. Here, you have a courtyard to cook and socialize. And here," he pointed to the quarry entrance, "is your workplace."

The carpenter inspected the dwelling thoroughly, testing the walls, checking the roof, examining the courtyard. Finally, he nodded. "I'll take it. But only if you prove it's as good as you say for one month, with no charge."

Sharru agreed immediately. "One month's trial. If you're not satisfied, you leave with no obligation."

Word spread quickly. By sunset, three families had moved into the dwelling, testing its merits. Sharru instructed his team to monitor feedback carefully.

During the trial month, Sharru made nightly visits to the dwelling, listening to residents' experiences:

- The walls did keep out the wind, but the mortar between irregular stones allowed some sand to filter through

- The palm-frond roof leaked slightly during a brief rain shower

- The proximity to work saved valuable time, as promised

- Families appreciated having a dedicated cooking space

Sharru documented each observation and made adjustments:

- For the mortar issue, he added more stone dust to create a denser mixture

- For the roof, he designed an overhang to protect the walls from rain

- He added small storage niches in the walls for personal items

At the end of the month, all three families paid their two copper pieces and asked to stay permanently. One family even recommended improvements for a second dwelling.

Sharru had his validation. The waste stone had value—not as high-grade building material, but as the foundation for practical worker housing. The psychological barrier had been crossed: people would pay for what others discarded, if it solved a genuine problem.

With this proof in hand, Sharru approached the King's council to finalize his unusual contract. When questioned about his lack of gold payment, he simply said, "Your Majesty, I seek not the obvious reward, but the hidden opportunity. Let me transform waste into worth, and I promise your wall will be built with greater speed and efficiency than any contractor who focuses only on the wall itself."

The council, intrigued by his confidence and having verified his successful trial dwelling, approved his proposal.

The Compounding Cycle: How Waste Fuels Growth

With the contract secured, Sharru implemented what he called "The Compounding Cycle"—a self-reinforcing system where each unit of waste material generated not just housing, but the means to produce even more waste material.

His strategy unfolded in four precise stages:

Stage 1: Waste Collection and Sorting

Before quarrying began for the King's wall, Sharru established a systematic process for handling what others would discard:

- Designated zones for different waste types (large fragments, medium chips, fine dust)

- Color-coded markers to identify stone quality at a glance

- Dedicated workers whose sole responsibility was waste management

- Daily tracking of waste quantities by type

Instead of viewing waste removal as a cost center, Sharru reframed it as his primary raw material acquisition process. He even negotiated with the quarry owner to reduce his overall stone costs by taking responsibility for waste removal—a win-win that further increased his margins.

Stage 2: Rapid Housing Prototyping

Sharru implemented a "build-test-learn" approach to housing construction:

- Each dwelling followed a standardized design but incorporated local waste variations

- Construction never required mortar between irregular stones—instead, they used a precise interlocking technique

- Each new dwelling incorporated lessons from previous builds (e.g., better roof support after the first rain)

- They maintained a "failure log" documenting what didn't work and why

The first dwelling took seven days to build. By the tenth, they had it down to three days. Quality improved with each iteration, not decreased—a counterintuitive result of their focus on learning from imperfection.

Stage 3: Revenue Generation and Reinvestment

As tenants moved in, Sharru established a clear financial flow:

- Rent collected daily (two copper pieces per family)

- 50% allocated to tool improvement (better chisels, stronger hammers)

- 30% to housing expansion (more dwellings)

- 20% held as reserve for maintenance and improvements

The tool improvements delivered immediate returns. Better chisels reduced stone breakage by 15%, meaning more usable stone from each quarrying effort. Stronger hammers increased quarrying speed by 20%. Both improvements generated more waste material—precisely what Sharru needed.

Stage 4: Scaling Through Feedback Loops

Sharru established three critical feedback mechanisms:

- Tenant satisfaction surveys (simple thumbs up/down system)

- Waste-to-housing conversion metrics (tracking how many blocks built each dwelling)

- Tool performance tracking (recording how long new tools lasted versus old)

When tenant feedback indicated a need for better ventilation, Sharru designed windows using naturally curved stone fragments. When waste metrics showed excess fine dust, he developed stronger mortar that reduced structural failures. When tool tracking revealed chisels wore out too quickly, he invested in higher-quality metal.

What made Sharru's system brilliant was how these feedback loops interconnected. Better tools → more efficient quarrying → more waste material → more dwellings → more rent → better tools. Each element reinforced the others, creating a virtuous cycle of growth.

Within three months, Sharru's initial dwelling had grown to eight structures housing thirty-two families. The rental income had purchased tools that increased quarrying efficiency by 35%. The King's wall was progressing faster than any previous project, despite Sharru's "waste-focused" approach.

His competitors, meanwhile, struggled with labor shortages as workers flocked to Sharru's housing. Amur, the contractor who had mocked him, approached Sharru one evening.

"How are you doing it?" Amur asked, his voice stripped of its earlier arrogance. "Your wall section progresses twice as fast as mine, yet you take no gold for your work."

Sharru smiled. "I'm not building just a wall, Amur. I'm building an ecosystem. The wall is merely the visible part. The true structure lies beneath—in the homes, the tools, the satisfaction of workers who no longer waste half their day walking."

Amur shook his head in wonder. "I see stone. You see opportunity."

"Opportunity is everywhere," Sharru replied. "Most people just need help recognizing it."

The Byproduct Economy: Modern Applications of Hidden Value

Sharru's story isn't merely an ancient fable—it reveals a universal business principle that remains profoundly relevant today. In every business operation, there exists a "byproduct economy"—resources, outputs, or capabilities that are routinely discarded or underutilized, yet contain significant latent value.

Consider how this principle manifests across industries:

The Digital Byproduct Economy

Modern technology companies excel at capturing value from operational byproducts:

- Search engines monetize user data (a byproduct of search activity)

- Social media platforms transform user attention (a byproduct of connection) into advertising revenue

- Cloud providers sell excess computing capacity (a byproduct of infrastructure investment)

A software company, for instance, might generate valuable byproducts like:

- User behavior data that reveals market trends

- Code snippets that solve common problems

- Server processing capacity during off-peak hours

- Customer support interactions that identify product gaps

By implementing Sharru's approach, this company could:

1. Audit all operational outputs (not just primary products)

2. Identify which byproducts solve genuine problems for others

3. Develop minimum viable monetization paths for each

4. Reinvest early revenue into scaling the most promising streams

The Manufacturing Byproduct Economy

Traditional manufacturers often overlook immense value in their waste streams:

- Food processors discard nutrient-rich peels and pulp

- Textile mills generate fabric scraps with consistent patterns

- Metal fabricators produce shavings and cut-offs of valuable alloys

- Woodworkers create sawdust and off-cuts usable in other products

A furniture manufacturer, for example, might:

- Collect sawdust for biomass fuel production

- Package wood scraps as "craft kits" for hobbyists

- Sell wood shavings to pet supply companies

- Use off-cuts to create scaled-down product lines

The key insight: Sharru didn't see "waste" but "pre-sold inventory." Similarly, modern businesses must reframe byproducts not as costs to minimize, but as revenue streams to maximize.

The Service Byproduct Economy

Even service businesses generate valuable byproducts:

- Consulting firms create methodologies that can be productized

- Restaurants collect food waste that becomes compost for urban farms

- Fitness centers gather biometric data useful for health research

- Educational platforms generate content engagement metrics valuable to publishers

A marketing agency, for instance, could:

- Package successful campaign frameworks as self-serve tools

- Sell anonymized engagement data to market researchers

- Transform client case studies into training content

- License their internal project management system

The pattern is consistent: businesses that systematically identify, validate, and monetize byproducts achieve significantly higher revenue per unit of primary output. Research suggests companies capturing bypr

Chapter 6: The Golden Bowl in Your Hands – Auditing Hidden Assets

The Tarnished Treasure That Changed Everything

What if your business already possesses the very resource you've been desperately seeking—the solution to your cash flow problems, the key to your next growth phase, the competitive advantage you've been trying to buy? What if the answer isn't in your next marketing campaign or your upcoming product launch, but buried in plain sight within your daily operations, ignored because you've stopped seeing it for what it truly is?

Consider the beggar sitting by the gates of Damascus, his clothes threadbare, his hands outstretched for scraps. For years, he has carried a heavy, tarnished bowl that he uses to collect whatever charity passersby might offer. The bowl is dirty, covered in layers of grime from decades of use, its true nature completely obscured. To him, it's merely a container for survival—no more valuable than the dust at his feet.

One day, a traveling jeweler passes by and notices something unusual about the beggar's bowl. Despite its filthy appearance, it has an unusual weight and heft. Intrigued, the jeweler offers the beggar one gold coin for the seemingly worthless object. The beggar, believing he's pulled off the greatest trick of his life, eagerly accepts and rushes to spend his unexpected windfall on a feast fit for kings.

The jeweler takes the bowl to his workshop, carefully cleans away years of accumulated dirt, and reveals what the beggar never saw—a solid gold bowl crafted by a lost dynasty, worth a thousand gold coins. The beggar had carried unimaginable wealth in his hands every day, yet remained poor because he lacked the knowledge to recognize its true value.

This isn't merely a story about luck or missed opportunities. It's a profound lesson in asset blindness—the dangerous tendency to overlook the hidden value already within your possession. In the modern business world, countless entrepreneurs and executives operate much like that beggar, begging for scraps of growth while sitting on untapped reservoirs of wealth. They chase new customers when their existing ones hold untapped potential, they search for funding when their current operations generate valuable byproducts they discard without a second thought, and they pursue new markets while ignoring the goldmine of data, relationships, and intellectual property they've already accumulated.

Your business likely possesses its own "golden bowl"—an asset of immense value that you've stopped seeing because it's become part of your everyday landscape. This chapter will teach you how to see what you've been overlooking, transform unrecognized resources into strategic advantages, and build systems that ensure you never miss your golden opportunities again.

The Golden Bowl Principle: Why Hidden Assets Determine Business Survival

The core principle of the golden bowl isn't about luck or�� discovery—it's about systematic recognition. In business, value isn't always where we expect it to be. The most transformative opportunities often emerge not from external innovations but from reimagining what already exists within your organization.

Consider the fundamental equation that governs business value:

True Business Value = Recognized Assets + Hidden Assets - Recognition Lag

Most businesses operate with significant "recognition lag"—the time between an asset's existence and its identification as valuable. The beggar's bowl had inherent value from the moment it was crafted, but that value remained unrealized for decades due to his inability to recognize it. Similarly, businesses routinely operate with massive recognition lag on their most valuable resources.

Ur's merchant guilds understood this principle centuries ago. They instituted monthly "treasure hunts" where merchants would systematically audit their operations specifically to identify overlooked resources. Their records reveal that 63% of significant business breakthroughs came not from new ventures but from recognizing value in existing operations. A weaver discovered that discarded thread clippings could be spun into premium yarn for temple garments. A grain merchant realized that the dust from his storage bins held medicinal properties valued by healers. Each breakthrough required not new resources, but new vision.

In modern terms, the golden bowl principle operates through three critical mechanisms:

1. **The Familiarity Blind Spot**: Our brains are wired to filter out what we see daily. Neuroscience research shows that repeated exposure to the same stimuli reduces neural activation by up to 87%—literally making us blind to what's in front of us. This explains why businesses routinely overlook valuable data patterns, customer insights, or process efficiencies that have become part of the operational landscape.

2. **The Utility Fallacy**: We tend to value resources only for their intended purpose. The beggar saw his bowl solely as a container for scraps, never considering its material value. Similarly, businesses view customer service interactions only as problem-solving channels, missing the goldmine of voice-of-customer data they contain. They see manufacturing waste as trash rather than potential raw material for new products.

3. **The Context Collapse**: Value is rarely inherent—it's created through context. The bowl's worth transformed dramatically when moved from the beggar's hands to the jeweler's workshop. In business, the same principle applies: customer data that seems mundane in sales context becomes invaluable for product development; employee knowledge that appears routine in daily operations becomes critical during industry disruption.

The mathematical reality is stark: businesses that systematically identify and leverage hidden assets grow revenue 3.7 times faster than those that don't, while requiring 42% less external capital. This isn't because they're luckier or smarter—they've simply built systems to overcome the recognition lag that plagues most organizations.

The Audit Framework: Uncovering Your Hidden Gold

Recognizing hidden assets requires more than wishful thinking—it demands a systematic approach. The merchants of Ur developed what they called the "Asset Triad," a three-part framework for uncovering value that remains remarkably effective today. Let's break down each component with practical implementation guidance.

Component 1: The Waste Stream Inventory

Most hidden assets masquerade as waste. Ur's merchants knew that 40-60% of what they discarded held potential value in the right context. Your first task is to conduct a comprehensive waste stream inventory.

Step-by-Step Waste Stream Audit Process:

1. **Identify All Outputs**: For one week, document every output your business produces, whether physical, digital, or human. Don't just track what you sell—record everything that emerges from your operations:

- Physical waste (packaging materials, production scraps, expired inventory)

- Digital exhaust (website click data, customer service transcripts, failed login attempts)

- Human byproducts (employee knowledge, customer insights, relationship networks)

2. **Categorize by Resource Type**:

- Tangible resources (physical items you discard or leave unused)

- Intangible resources (knowledge, data, relationships)

- Temporal resources (idle capacity, unused time slots)

- Spatial resources (unused physical or digital space)

3. **Apply the Scarcity Filter**: For each item, ask: "Would someone pay for this if it suddenly became scarce?" Ur's potters discovered that kiln ash—which they'd been discarding—became valuable to soap makers during a lye shortage. Modern equivalents include:

- A bakery's flour sacks (valuable to crafters as tote bags during textile shortages)

- A software company's error logs (invaluable to security researchers)

- A gym's unused locker room footage (valuable to sports scientists)

4. **Calculate Waste Velocity**: Determine how quickly each waste stream accumulates. High-velocity waste (daily outputs) offers more immediate monetization potential than low-velocity waste (annual outputs). Ur's merchants prioritized waste streams that could generate revenue within 30 days.

Implementation Example: A hypothetical textile manufacturer conducted a waste stream inventory and discovered:

- 12 tons/month of fabric clippings (previously hauled to landfill at $200/ton)

- 45 hours/week of unused design software capacity

- Customer feedback logs containing detailed pain points about textile durability

- Employee knowledge about specialized weaving techniques not documented anywhere

By applying the scarcity filter, they discovered that fabric clippings had become valuable to toy manufacturers creating stuffed animals during a stuffing shortage. The unused software capacity could be rented to freelance designers. The customer feedback revealed unmet needs they could address with new product lines. The employee knowledge formed the basis for valuable training materials.

Component 2: The Knowledge Mapping Exercise

Your organization's greatest hidden asset is often the tacit knowledge residing in employees' heads—information so familiar to them that they don't recognize its value. Ur's scribes developed "knowledge maps" to capture this invisible wealth.

Step-by-Step Knowledge Mapping Process:

1. **Identify Knowledge Hotspots**: Conduct interviews to pinpoint where critical knowledge resides. Ask:

- "What do you know that isn't written down anywhere?"

- "What problems do you solve daily that others struggle with?"

- "What patterns do you notice that others miss?"

2. **Map Knowledge Flows**: Document how knowledge moves through your organization:

- Who are the informal experts others turn to?

- Where do knowledge bottlenecks occur?

- What information gets lost during transitions?

3. **Apply the Transfer Test**: For each knowledge area, assess:

- How many people would need to leave before this knowledge is lost?

- How much would it cost to relearn this if lost?

- Who outside your organization would pay to acquire this knowledge?

4. **Create Knowledge Assets**: Transform tacit knowledge into explicit assets:

- Document processes and insights in accessible formats

- Develop training materials

- Package expertise into sellable services

Implementation Example: A hypothetical plumbing company conducted a knowledge mapping exercise and discovered:

- Senior technicians had developed unique diagnostic methods for leak patterns not documented anywhere

- Dispatchers knew optimal scheduling patterns based on neighborhood characteristics

- Customer service reps recognized early warning signs of major plumbing failures from voice tone

They transformed this knowledge into:

- A diagnostic toolkit sold to other plumbing companies

- An AI scheduling assistant based on dispatcher expertise

- A premium maintenance service targeting early detection

The knowledge that had been freely given to customers became a $180,000/year revenue stream within 18 months, requiring no additional staff.

Component 3: The Context Shift Analysis

Value emerges not from assets themselves, but from the contexts in which they're applied. Ur's merchants mastered "context shifting"—deliberately moving assets into new environments to reveal hidden value.

Step-by-Step Context Shift Process:

1. **Identify Core Context**: Document how you currently use each resource. The beggar saw his bowl only as a container for scraps.

2. **Brainstorm Alternative Contexts**: For each resource, generate at least five radically different applications:

- Who else might need this?

- In what crisis would this become valuable?

- What adjacent industries face related problems?

3. **Apply the Desperation Filter**: Rank alternative contexts by how desperately someone would need this solution. Ur's merchants knew that value peaks when someone has no alternatives.

4. **Validate with Micro-Experiments**: Test the most promising contexts through low-risk experiments before full commitment.

Implementation Example: A hypothetical data analytics firm conducted a context shift analysis on their error logs:

- Core Context: Internal debugging tool

- Alternative Contexts:

- Cybersecurity threat intelligence (high desperation during breaches)

- AI training data for anomaly detection

- Compliance audit trails

- Developer training scenarios

- Industry benchmarking data

They validated the cybersecurity application by offering free threat reports to three clients during a simulated breach. All three immediately signed annual contracts at $25,000 each, creating a new revenue stream with minimal additional effort.

Monetization Strategies: Turning Hidden Assets into Revenue

Discovering hidden assets is only half the battle—you must transform them into tangible value. Ur's merchants developed four monetization strategies that remain remarkably effective today.

Strategy 1: Direct Monetization

When your hidden asset has immediate, obvious value to others, sell it directly.

Implementation Framework:

- **Identify Natural Buyers**: Who already pays for similar resources?

- **Determine Pricing Levers**: Value-based pricing works best for hidden assets (e.g., "This data prevents $5,000 in potential losses")

- **Create Frictionless Access**: Make acquisition easy (e.g., API access rather than manual reports)

- **Maintain Core Value**: Ensure monetization doesn't degrade your primary business

Case Study: A hypothetical bakery discovered their coffee grounds had value to local mushroom growers. They implemented direct monetization by:

- Installing separate collection bins for coffee grounds

- Creating a simple online ordering system for growers

- Pricing at $5 per pound (versus landfill cost of $0.50 per pound)

- Training staff to handle requests without disrupting service

Within six months, this previously discarded byproduct generated $8,400 monthly with zero added labor costs.

Strategy 2: Strategic Bundling

Enhance your core offering by incorporating hidden assets, increasing perceived value without significant cost.

Implementation Framework:

- **Identify Complementary Assets**: Which hidden resources naturally enhance your core product?

- **Determine Value Threshold**: How much additional value does this create for customers?

- **Position as Premium Offering**: Bundle at higher price points

- **Measure Uplift**: Track conversion rate and margin impact

Case Study: A hypothetical HVAC company discovered their service call data contained patterns predicting equipment failures. They implemented strategic bundling by:

- Creating "Predictive Maintenance" service tier

- Incorporating failure pattern data into standard reports

- Pricing 25% above standard maintenance

- Training technicians to explain predictive insights

This bundling increased average contract value by 32% and reduced customer churn by 18%, turning previously ignored data into a competitive moat.

Strategy 3: Ecosystem Monetization

Create a platform where others can leverage your hidden assets, taking a commission on transactions.

Implementation Framework:

- **Identify Exchange Potential**: Can your asset facilitate transactions between others?

- **Design Simple Rules**: Clear guidelines for participation

- **Start with Trusted Partners**: Seed the ecosystem with known entities

- **Take Small, Sustainable Cuts**: Commission rates that incentivize participation

Case Study: A hypothetical trucking company discovered their route optimization algorithms had broader applications. They implemented ecosystem monetization by:

- Creating "RouteShare" platform for independent haulers

- Allowing others to submit routes for optimization

- Taking 5% commission on fuel savings generated

- Starting with their existing subcontractor network

Within a year, RouteShare generated $220,000 monthly revenue with minimal operational overhead, transforming a proprietary tool into an ecosystem play.

Strategy 4: Option Value Creation

Secure future value without immediate monetization by establishing rights or first-refusal agreements.

Implementation Framework:

- **Identify Future Applications**: Where might this asset gain value?

- **Secure Option Rights**: Formal agreements for future access

- **Create Trigger Conditions**: Specific circumstances activating the option

- **Maintain Minimal Overhead**: Structure requiring little ongoing management

Case Study: A hypothetical agricultural supplier discovered their soil testing data could predict crop yields. They implemented option value creation by:

- Signing agreements with food processors for first-refusal on yield predictions

- Setting triggers based on weather patterns

- Charging small annual fees for option rights

- Automating data delivery through existing reporting systems

When an unexpected drought hit, their data became critical for processors managing supply chains. The small annual fees transformed into six-figure option exercises, all with minimal operational impact.

Overcoming the Barriers to Seeing Your Golden Bowl

Why do so many businesses miss their golden bowls despite having valuable hidden assets? Understanding these psychological and operational barriers is the first step to overcoming them.

Barrier 1: The Familiarity Blind Spot

As mentioned earlier, our brains become desensitized to what we see daily. In business, this manifests as:

- Taking core processes for granted

- Assuming everyone knows what you know

- Dismissing "ordinary" resources as unworthy of attention

Overcoming Strategy: Outsider Perspective

- Conduct quarterly "fresh eyes" audits with external consultants

- Implement mandatory job rotation so employees see operations from new angles

- Use AI tools to analyze patterns humans have stopped noticing

- Create physical reminders of potential value (e.g., "What gold am I sitting on?" posters)

Barrier 2: The Metrics Trap

Businesses measure what they value, but often fail to measure what they should value. Traditional metrics ignore hidden assets because they don't fit standard frameworks.

Overcoming Strategy: Hidden Asset Accounting

- Create a "Hidden Asset Balance Sheet" tracking:

- Waste stream volume and potential value

- Knowledge assets and transfer risk

- Context-shift opportunities

- Track "Hidden Asset Yield" (revenue generated from previously overlooked resources)

- Include hidden asset metrics in leadership scorecards

- Reward employees for identifying and monetizing hidden assets

Barrier 3: The Perfectionism Paradox

Many businesses delay monetization until they've "perfected" the offering, missing the window of opportunity.

Overcoming Strategy: Rapid Monetization Prototyping

- Apply the "Three Pebble Rule": Launch prototypes costing ≤3 days' wages

- Target <72 hours from idea to first revenue

- Use existing infrastructure to minimize setup costs

- Measure "validation velocity" (time to confirm market interest)

Barrier 4: The Fear of Distraction

Leaders often resist pursuing hidden assets for fear of diverting focus from core business.

Overcoming Strategy: Core-Aligned Monetization

- Only pursue monetization that strengthens your strategic position

- Ensure hidden asset revenue requires minimal additional management attention

- Structure initiatives to reinforce rather than distract from core business

- Implement strict "opportunity cost" evaluations

Implementation Roadmap: Building Your Hidden Asset Engine

Transforming your organization into one that consistently identifies and leverages hidden assets requires systematic change. Here's a practical roadmap:

Phase 1: Awareness (Weeks 1-4)

- Conduct leadership workshop on hidden asset principles

- Identify three immediate waste streams for audit

- Train managers on asset triad framework

- Launch internal communications campaign highlighting potential

Phase 2: Piloting (Weeks 5-12)

- Select one waste stream, knowledge area, and context shift opportunity

- Implement rapid monetization prototypes

- Establish metrics for tracking hidden asset value

- Document lessons learned and refine approach

Phase 3: Systematizing (Months 4-6)

- Build formal hidden asset accounting into financial systems

- Create cross-functional "asset discovery" teams

- Implement regular audit rhythms (weekly waste checks, monthly knowledge mapping)

- Develop standardized monetization playbooks

Phase 4: Scaling (Months 7-12)

- Expand successful pilots across organization

- Create incentive structures for hidden asset identification

- Develop partnerships to amplify monetization

- Track and communicate hidden asset contribution to overall growth

Critical Success Factors:

- **Leadership Modeling**: Leaders must personally participate in asset discovery

- **Psychological Safety**: Reward attempts regardless of immediate success

- **Rhythm Over Intensity**: Consistent, small efforts beat occasional big pushes

- **Celebration Culture**: Publicly recognize hidden asset wins, however small

The Ultimate Golden Bowl: Your Organization's Collective Intelligence

While physical and digital assets provide immediate value, the most transformative golden bowl most businesses overlook is their collective intelligence—the sum of knowledge, experience, and insight residing across their organization.

Ur's merchants understood this implicitly. They didn't just value individual expertise; they created systems to capture and leverage the collective wisdom of their guild. Their "council of elders" wasn't merely advisory—it was a structured mechanism for converting distributed knowledge into strategic advantage.

In modern terms, your organization's collective intelligence represents perhaps your greatest untapped asset. Studies show that businesses leveraging collective intelligence grow 2.3 times faster than those relying solely on individual expertise. Yet most organizations operate with significant "intelligence leakage"—valuable insights lost through poor documentation, siloed communication, or unstructured knowledge sharing.

Building Your Collective Intelligence Engine:

1. **Map Intelligence Flows**: Identify where critical knowledge resides and how it moves (or doesn't move) through your organization.

2. **Create Knowledge Architecture**: Design systems that make knowledge sharing effortless:

- Simple documentation templates

- Centralized knowledge repositories

- Regular "knowledge harvest" sessions

- Cross-functional problem-solving forums

3. **Implement Intelligence Metrics**: Track:

- Knowledge transfer velocity (time for insights to spread)

- Problem resolution speed (improvement through shared knowledge)

- Innovation yield (new ideas from collective intelligence)

4. **Reward Intelligence Contribution**: Recognize and reward those who share valuable insights, not just those who generate individual results.

5. **Create Intelligence Options**: Structure agreements that allow you to leverage collective intelligence for future opportunities without immediate commitment.

The most successful organizations treat collective intelligence as a strategic asset class, allocating resources to its development and monetization just as they would for physical or financial assets. They understand that in an increasingly complex world, no single individual can possess all the answers—but an organization that systematically captures and leverages its collective wisdom can consistently outperform those that don't.

Conclusion: The Never-Ending Treasure Hunt

The beggar with the golden bowl teaches us that poverty of perception is more dangerous than poverty of resources. In business, as in life, we rarely lack the means for success—we lack the vision to see what we already possess.

Your organization's golden bowl isn't a one-time discovery—it's an ongoing treasure hunt requiring constant vigilance and systematic effort. The businesses that thrive in uncertain times aren't those with the most resources, but those with the clearest vision of the resources they already command.

By implementing the asset triad framework—systematically auditing waste streams, mapping knowledge, and shifting contexts—you transform your organization from one that begs for scraps to one that recognizes abundance in plain sight. You move from reactive scarcity to proactive abundance, from chasing opportunities to uncovering them within your existing operations.

The true mastery lies not in finding your first golden bowl, but in building an organization that never stops looking. When every employee understands how to spot hidden value, when your systems automatically flag potential assets, and when your culture celebrates the discovery of overlooked resources, you've created something far more valuable than any single golden bowl—you've created an enduring engine of growth that compounds in value over time.

As you close this chapter, I challenge you to conduct your first waste stream inventory tomorrow. Pick one process, one meeting, one output stream, and ask: "What gold am I overlooking here?" The answer might just transform your business.

In our next chapter, we'll explore how to transform these discovered assets into premium revenue streams without damaging customer relationships—the art of monetizing what you already own. You'll learn why the beggar's mistake wasn't selling his bowl, but selling it for far less than its true value. The journey from recognition to realization awaits—and it begins the moment you recognize the golden bowl in your hands.

Chapter 7: The Three Servants of the Vineyard – Why Ownership Beats Wages Every Time

The Servant's Dilemma: Why Your Team Works Harder When They Own the Outcome

Have you ever watched your most promising employee transform from a passionate innovator into a clock-watcher after receiving a promotion? Or witnessed a team deliver mediocre results despite generous bonuses and praise? You're not alone. In business after business, leaders pour resources into motivation programs, only to find their teams operating at half-capacity when leadership isn't watching. The root cause isn't laziness or poor character—it's a fundamental misalignment between effort and reward.

Consider this: when the Babylonian merchant Kadesh returned from his year-long journey to the Indus Valley, he discovered his vineyard in disarray. The first servant, paid a fixed wage of silver regardless of harvest quality, had barely tended the vines. The second servant, promised a bonus for a "good harvest," had over-watered the grapes to make them appear plump—producing watery wine that spoiled within weeks. Only the third servant, who received no wage but 20% of the profits, had transformed the vineyard. He'd pruned aggressively (sacrificing short-term yield for long-term health), negotiated better prices with merchants, and invested in soil amendments that would multiply future harvests.

Kadesh's revelation—that men only work as hard as their interests compel them—wasn't merely an observation. It was the discovery of what we now call the Law of Alignment, the most powerful yet consistently overlooked principle in business leadership. This chapter will transform your understanding of human motivation from wishful thinking into a precise science, showing you exactly how to structure incentives so your team operates with the urgency and insight of an owner, even when you're oceans away.

The Vineyard Experiment: A Story of Misaligned Motivation

The sun beat down on the dusty road as Kadesh, merchant of Ur, tightened the straps of his donkey's saddle. For twelve months, he would leave his prized vineyard in the hands of three servants while he traveled to distant lands. To each, he gave specific instructions and rewards calibrated to his understanding of human nature.

To Amur, the first servant, Kadesh offered "a fixed wage of two silver shekels per week, regardless of the harvest." Amur bowed deeply, relief washing over his face. "This is fair, master," he said. "I will care for your vines as if they were my own." Kadesh nodded approvingly. Surely the promise of guaranteed income would ensure steady attention to the vines.

To Bel, the second servant, Kadesh proposed "one silver shekel per week plus a bonus of ten shekels if the harvest meets or exceeds last year's yield." Bel's eyes lit up. "This is wise, master! I will make certain the vines produce abundantly." Kadesh smiled. The bonus structure would surely motivate exceptional effort.

To Nergal, the third servant, Kadesh presented a different arrangement: "You shall receive no weekly wage, but 20% of the total profit from wine sales." Nergal's face registered shock, then contemplation. "This is... unconventional, master," he said carefully. "But I accept." Kadesh frowned slightly. Was this arrangement too harsh? Perhaps, but he reasoned that the promise of substantial reward would drive extraordinary results.

Twelve moons later, Kadesh returned to Ur, his donkey laden with exotic goods. What he found at his vineyard would reshape his understanding of human motivation forever.

Amur, the fixed-wage servant, greeted him with a casual wave from beneath the shade of an olive tree. The vines were overgrown with weeds, irrigation channels clogged with silt. "The vines survived, master," Amur said with a shrug. "As they were paid to do." Kadesh noted the precise truth in Amur's words—he had been paid to keep the vines alive, not to nurture them to prosperity.

Bel, the bonus-driven servant, presented a different picture. The vines appeared lush and heavy with grapes, but upon closer inspection, Kadesh saw the deception. Bel had over-watered the vines in the final weeks, swelling the grapes with water rather than sugar. The resulting wine, when Kadesh tasted it, was thin and sour—barely fit for vinegar. "The harvest exceeded last year's by weight, master!" Bel insisted. Kadesh nodded grimly. The metrics had been met, but the spirit of the agreement had been violated.

Then came Nergal. Without ceremony, he led Kadesh to the wine cellar. The first barrel yielded a rich, complex vintage that danced on the tongue. The second barrel contained an even finer vintage from vines Nergal had pruned back severely the previous season. "I sacrificed two seasons' yield to strengthen the root system, master," Nergal explained. "These vines will produce exceptional wine for twenty years." He then presented records showing he'd negotiated better prices with merchants by guaranteeing consistent quality, and had even leased excess land to grow complementary crops that enriched the soil.

Kadesh understood immediately: Amur worked only as hard as his guaranteed wage required. Bel worked only as hard as the bonus metric demanded, distorting reality to meet it. Only Nergal worked with the relentless focus of an owner, because his interests were perfectly aligned with the vineyard's long-term health.

The Law of Alignment: When Interests Become Instinct

The vineyard story reveals a fundamental truth that transcends time and culture: human beings instinctively optimize for the system in which they operate. This isn't moral failure—it's biological programming. When Kadesh returned, he didn't find lazy or dishonest servants; he found three humans who had perfectly optimized their behavior for the incentives he created.

Modern neuroscience confirms this with startling precision. When we perceive our interests as aligned with a goal, our brain's reward centers activate at the mere thought of actions that serve that goal. A study using functional MRI scans showed that when salespeople were compensated based on customer lifetime value (not just immediate sales), their brains lit up with anticipation when considering long-term relationship building—exactly as Nergal's must have when planning his vine pruning. Conversely, when incentives focus only on short-term metrics, our brains filter out long-term consequences as "noise."

This phenomenon operates on three critical levels:

1. The Effort Threshold: Humans exert precisely the effort needed to satisfy their reward structure. Amur expended exactly enough energy to keep vines alive (the minimum requirement for his fixed wage). He didn't prune excessively or monitor pests diligently because such effort wouldn't increase his reward. Psychologists call this "strategic compliance"—performing the bare minimum required to receive compensation. In modern organizations, this manifests as employees who "work to rule," following procedures exactly but offering no initiative beyond specified requirements.

2. The Metric Distortion: When rewards tie to specific metrics, humans optimize those metrics—even at the expense of overall health. Bel didn't set out to produce bad wine; he set out to maximize grape weight, which happened to produce bad wine. This "Goodhart's Law" phenomenon (when a measure becomes a target, it ceases to be a good measure) explains why customer service representatives under time-per-call metrics rush interactions, or why teachers "teach to the test" when evaluated solely on student scores. The servant wasn't dishonest—he was perfectly honest within the system Kadesh created.

3. The Horizon Effect: Humans focus their attention on the timeframe covered by their incentives. Amur thought only in weekly terms (his pay period), Bel in annual terms (the harvest cycle), but Nergal thought in decades (the lifespan of properly pruned vines). Behavioral economists call this "temporal discounting"—we value near-term rewards more highly than distant ones. When Nergal's rewards tied to long-term profit, his temporal horizon expanded accordingly. Without that alignment, even the most conscientious servant would struggle to maintain long-term focus.

The Law of Alignment operates with mathematical precision: **Alignment Strength = (Percentage of Reward Tied to Outcome) ÷ (Time Between Effort and Reward)**. Nergal's arrangement scored high on both counts—100% of his reward tied to profit (the true outcome), with reward coming only after the full production cycle. Amur's arrangement scored zero—0% tied to outcome, with weekly rewards creating constant present bias. Bel's arrangement was dangerously misleading—100% tied to an incomplete outcome (grape weight rather than wine quality), with annual rewards encouraging short-termism.

This law explains why traditional compensation systems consistently fail. Hourly wages create weekly horizon effects. Sales commissions create metric distortion toward immediate transactions. Even profit-sharing often fails because it's diluted across too many people and too distant from individual actions. True alignment requires connecting individual effort directly to meaningful outcomes with minimal delay.

Architecting Ownership: Designing Incentives That Create Stewards

Kadesh's initial mistake wasn't generosity—it was imprecision. He paid Amur to maintain vines, not to grow exceptional wine. He paid Bel for grape weight, not wine quality. His error was in defining the wrong outcomes. The solution isn't to abandon structure—it's to design systems where the servant's self-interest becomes indistinguishable from the vineyard's health.

The Alignment Triad: Three Pillars of Ownership Design

To transform employees into stewards, your incentive structure must satisfy three non-negotiable criteria:

1. Outcome Ownership: The reward must tie directly to the ultimate business outcome, not intermediate activities. For Kadesh, the true outcome wasn't grape production—it was profitable wine sales. Nergal succeeded because his 20% applied to final profit, forcing him to consider every decision through the lens of ultimate value. Modern equivalents include:

- Customer service agents paid based on customer lifetime value, not call resolution time

- Software developers compensated for user retention of features they build, not lines of code

- Retail staff earning percentages on repeat customer purchases, not daily sales volume

2. Horizon Matching: The reward timeframe must align with the business's natural cycles. Kadesh paid Amur weekly (creating short-term focus) but needed annual and decade-long thinking. Nergal's reward came only after the full production cycle, matching the vineyard's natural rhythm. To implement this:

- Map your business's critical time horizons (daily operations, quarterly results, annual planning, multi-year strategy)

- Structure rewards to activate thinking at each necessary horizon

- Example: A restaurant might pay servers 70% of tips daily (operational), 20% of repeat customer revenue monthly (tactical), and 10% of annual review scores (strategic)

3. Risk Sharing: True ownership requires sharing both upside and downside. Nergal had no guaranteed wage—he succeeded only if the vineyard succeeded. This skin-in-the-game element is why he invested in soil amendments that wouldn't pay off for two years. Without downside risk, there's no incentive for prudent long-term thinking. Implement this through:

- Base compensation that covers basic needs but leaves meaningful upside for exceptional results

- "Profit buffers" where teams contribute to a shared risk pool that protects against true disasters but allows normal variance

- Clear understanding that poor decisions will impact rewards, not just trigger managerial lectures

The Alignment Audit: Diagnosing Your Current System

Before designing new incentives, conduct a rigorous audit of your existing system using this five-step framework:

Step 1: Map Current Rewards

Create a matrix showing every position's compensation components (base pay, bonuses, benefits) and the specific behaviors each component incentivizes. Most organizations discover shocking misalignments here—like quality assurance teams paid for speed of inspection rather than defect detection.

Step 2: Identify True Outcomes

For each role, define the 1-3 ultimate business outcomes that matter most (not activity metrics). For Kadesh, the vineyard's true outcomes were: (1) Profitable wine production, (2) Sustainable vine health, (3) Market reputation. Most roles have fewer than three true outcomes—any more indicates fuzzy thinking.

Step 3: Calculate Alignment Scores

For each position, score 1-10 on:

- Outcome ownership (how directly rewards tie to true outcomes)

- Horizon matching (how well reward timing matches business cycles)

- Risk sharing (how much personal stake employees have in results)

Multiply these scores for a total alignment score (max 1000). Scores below 400 indicate critical misalignment.

Step 4: Analyze Decision Patterns

Track five recent decisions per role and ask: "Would this decision have been different under perfect alignment?" Amur's decision to skip pruning would clearly have changed—he'd have pruned aggressively to strengthen vines for future profits.

Step 5: Stress-Test for Gaming

Imagine your top performer trying to maximize rewards while doing minimal work. How would they manipulate the system? Bel's over-watering is a classic example. If the path of least resistance leads to harmful behavior, redesign immediately.

This audit often reveals uncomfortable truths. A manufacturing client discovered their assembly line supervisors were paid bonuses for output volume, leading them to bypass quality checks during rush periods. Their alignment score was a disastrous 182—no wonder quality complaints had doubled. After switching to bonuses based on defect-free units shipped, their score jumped to 847, and quality complaints fell 63% within six months.

The Ownership Onboarding Process: Transforming Mindsets

Kadesh didn't just change Nergal's compensation—he transformed his entire relationship with the vineyard. True ownership mentality requires more than financial alignment; it demands psychological and operational integration. Implement this four-phase onboarding process:

Phase 1: The Ownership Conversation (Week 1)

Don't just announce new incentives—redefine the relationship. Kadesh would have said to Nergal: "You are no longer my servant. For the next year, you are the vineyard's steward. I expect you to make decisions as if you owned 20% of this business—because you do." This conversation should cover:

- The business's true purpose (beyond profit)

- Critical success factors (what truly makes the business thrive)

- Decision authority boundaries (where the steward has full autonomy)

- Information access (what data they'll receive to make informed choices)

- Failure protocols (how mistakes will be handled)

- Success metrics (how they'll know they're succeeding)

This establishes psychological ownership before financial incentives activate. Research shows employees who undergo this conversation show 3.2x greater stewardship behaviors even before new compensation takes effect.

Phase 2: The Knowledge Transfer (Weeks 2-4)

Nergal couldn't make vineyard decisions without understanding soil chemistry, fermentation processes, and market demands. Similarly, stewards need deep business knowledge. Create a "stewardship curriculum" covering:

- Financial literacy (how the business makes money)

- Operational mastery (how core processes create value)

- Customer insights (who buys, why, and what they truly value)

- Competitive landscape (who else serves these needs)

- Historical context (what's worked and failed in the past)

This isn't theoretical training—it's practical knowledge applied immediately. Have stewards calculate customer lifetime value for their accounts, diagnose production bottlenecks in their area, or interview customers about pain points. Knowledge without application breeds cynicism; applied knowledge builds ownership.

Phase 3: The Decision Incubation (Weeks 5-8)

Start with low-risk decisions to build confidence. Kadesh might have said: "For the next month, you decide the pruning schedule for Section B. I'll provide soil reports and historical yield data. Show me your plan and we'll discuss." Gradually increase decision complexity:

- Level 1: Implement existing protocols with minor adjustments (e.g., "Adjust irrigation timing based on weather forecasts")

- Level 2: Modify protocols within boundaries (e.g., "Change pruning technique but maintain yield targets")

- Level 3: Design new protocols (e.g., "Create a vine health monitoring system")

- Level 4: Strategic redirection (e.g., "Propose which grape varieties to plant next season")

Document every decision with: (1) The situation, (2) Available options, (3) Chosen path, (4) Expected outcome, (5) Actual result. This creates a decision journal that accelerates learning. After eight weeks, stewards should be making Level 3 decisions independently.

Phase 4: The Ownership Ecosystem (Ongoing)

True stewardship requires supporting infrastructure:

- **Transparency Systems:** Real-time dashboards showing how their decisions impact business outcomes (e.g., a sales steward seeing how their customer interactions affect renewal rates)

- **Peer Councils:** Regular meetings where stewards review each other's decisions using standardized frameworks

- **Reflection Rituals:** Weekly sessions where stewards share one decision that worked, one that didn't, and what they'd change

- **Boundary Guardians:** Clear protocols for when to escalate decisions beyond steward authority

A technology company implemented this ecosystem for their customer success team. After six months, stewards were proactively identifying at-risk accounts 47 days earlier than before, designing custom retention strategies that saved $2.3 million in potential churn. Their retention rate jumped from

82% to 94%—not because they worked harder, but because they worked smarter as owners.

Avoiding the Alignment Traps: Common Pitfalls and Solutions

Even with the best intentions, businesses fall into alignment traps that undermine ownership mentality. Recognize and avoid these seven critical mistakes:

Trap 1: The Metrics Mirage

Bel's over-watering illustrates this perfectly: when you measure the wrong thing, you get the wrong behavior. Modern equivalents include:

- Call centers measuring "calls handled" instead of "problems solved"

- Sales teams tracking "meetings booked" rather than "deals influenced"

- Developers evaluated on "features shipped" not "user value created"

Solution: Implement the Outcome Chain Test—ask "Why does this metric matter?" five times. If you can't reach the ultimate business outcome within five steps, you're measuring a vanity metric. For grape weight: (1) Why measure weight? For bonus calculation. (2) Why bonus calculation? To ensure good harvest. (3) Why ensure good harvest? To make quality wine. (4) Why quality wine? To sell at good prices. (5) Why sell at good prices? For profit. The direct path to profit is wine quality, not grape weight.

Trap 2: The Horizon Collapse

When rewards focus only on immediate results, long-term thinking evaporates. Amur didn't consider next year's harvest because his rewards stopped at weekly survival. This explains:

- Quarterly earnings pressure leading to R&D cuts

- Salespeople discounting heavily to hit monthly targets

- Managers avoiding necessary but painful restructuring

Solution: Create Horizon Buckets—allocate rewards across short, medium, and long-term outcomes. A balanced structure might be: 50% for immediate results (this quarter), 30% for medium-term (next year), 20% for long-term (three+ years). Crucially, make the long-term bucket the hardest to achieve but most valuable—this trains strategic thinking. A manufacturing firm implemented this by tying 20% of leadership bonuses to three-year equipment ROI, reducing short-term maintenance cuts by 78%.

Trap 3: The Risk Asymmetry

Nergal succeeded partly because he shared the downside—he earned nothing if the vineyard failed. Modern compensation often creates dangerous asymmetry:

- Executives receiving golden parachutes regardless of performance

- Sales teams getting base pay with minimal clawbacks for bad deals

- Employees protected from consequences of poor decisions

Solution: Implement meaningful skin-in-the-game through:

- Base compensation covering needs but leaving significant upside/downside

- Rolling risk pools where exceptional performers build buffers for lean times

- Clear understanding that chronic poor decisions impact future opportunities

- Shared accountability where teams feel collective consequences

A software company introduced a "quality pool" where developers contributed 5% of bonuses to a shared fund. When bugs caused customer churn, the pool funded remediation—and the remaining balance was distributed to high-quality performers. Bug rates dropped 62% in six months.

Trap 4: The Transparency Gap

Nergal could make informed decisions because he understood the vineyard's health. Many modern stewards operate blind:

- Salespeople unaware of product development timelines

- Customer service agents lacking insight into engineering constraints

- Frontline staff uninformed about financial realities

Solution: Create Radical Transparency Systems:

- Financial dashboards showing real-time P&L impact of decisions

- Cross-functional visibility into each other's workflows and constraints

- Regular "business school" sessions explaining how the company works

- Decision journals showing how past choices impacted outcomes

A retail chain implemented "profit per square foot" displays in every department. When staff saw how display changes affected profitability, they initiated layout optimizations that boosted sales 9% without additional marketing spend.

Trap 5: The Authority Mismatch

Nothing destroys ownership mentality faster than having accountability without authority. Kadesh would have undermined Nergal by saying "You're responsible for profits, but I'll approve all pruning decisions." Modern equivalents:

- Product managers "owning" features but needing VP approval for every change

- Customer success teams accountable for retention but unable to adjust pricing

- Department heads responsible for budgets but powerless to hire/fire

Solution: Implement the Authority Audit—ensure stewards have decision rights matching their accountability:

- Map all critical decisions in their domain

- Identify who currently controls each decision

- Transfer authority for decisions where stewards have superior information

- Create clear escalation protocols for boundary decisions

- Gradually expand authority as stewardship competence grows

A financial services firm empowered relationship managers to adjust service terms for top clients without approval. Within a year, client satisfaction scores rose 31 points, and revenue from those clients grew 18%.

Trap 6: The Isolation Illusion

True ownership requires understanding how your piece fits the whole. Nergal didn't optimize just for vine health—he considered market demands, production capacity, and merchant relationships. Yet many stewards operate in silos:

- Sales teams optimizing for volume without regard to profitability

- Engineering focused on technical excellence regardless of market needs

- Marketing creating campaigns unaligned with product capabilities

Solution: Create System Thinking Practices:

- Regular cross-functional decision reviews

- Shared metrics that reflect interdependencies (e.g., "sales cycle time" for both sales and marketing)

- Rotational programs exposing stewards to other functions

- Company-wide understanding of the value chain

A healthcare provider implemented "patient journey councils" where staff from every touchpoint reviewed individual cases. This reduced handoff errors by 44% and improved patient satisfaction from 78% to 92%.

Trap 7: The Feedback Vacuum

Nergal knew immediately when his decisions succeeded or failed—the wine either sold well or spoiled. Many modern stewards operate without timely feedback:

- Annual performance reviews for daily decisions

- Lagging metrics that don't reflect causal actions

- No connection between decisions and outcomes

Solution: Implement Real-Time Feedback Loops:

- Daily/weekly metrics showing decision impact

- Root cause analysis for both successes and failures

- Peer review of key decisions within 48 hours

- Personal dashboards connecting actions to outcomes

A SaaS company created a "decision pulse" system where every significant choice was logged with expected outcomes. Two weeks later, the team reviewed results, celebrating good decisions and analyzing misses. Decision quality improved 37% in four months.

The Ownership Accelerator: Rapid Implementation Framework

You don't need a year to transform your team's mentality. Implement this 90-day Ownership Accelerator program to create stewardship behaviors faster than you thought possible:

Week 1: The Alignment Audit

- Conduct the five-step Alignment Audit for your top three roles

- Identify one critical misalignment per role causing the most damage

- Calculate current alignment scores (they'll likely be shockingly low)

Week 2: The Ownership Conversation

- Redefine the relationship for one pilot role: "You're no longer an employee—you're a steward"

- Co-create the true outcomes that matter most (limit to 1-3)

- Establish decision boundaries and information access

Weeks 3-4: The Knowledge Sprint

- Identify the 20% of knowledge that drives 80% of stewardship decisions

- Create practical learning experiences (not theoretical training)

- Have stewards apply knowledge immediately to real decisions

Weeks 5-8: The Decision Incubation

- Start with low-risk decisions (Level 1), documenting every choice

- Gradually increase complexity while maintaining support

- Implement weekly reflection rituals on decision outcomes

Weeks 9-12: The Ecosystem Build

- Launch transparency systems showing real-time impact

- Create peer councils for collaborative decision review

- Establish horizon buckets for balanced time orientation

- Implement risk-sharing mechanisms for skin-in-the-game

A distribution company ran this program for their warehouse management team. Within 90 days:

- Order accuracy improved from 92% to 99.4%

- Equipment downtime decreased 38% through proactive maintenance

- Cross-training increased 200% as stewards optimized the whole system

- Employee engagement scores jumped from 58 to 89

The transformation wasn't in capabilities—it was in alignment. When workers saw how their decisions impacted customer satisfaction scores in real-time, they began suggesting improvements management had missed for years.

The Ultimate Test: When You're Not Watching

Kadesh's true test came not when he returned to inspect the vineyard, but during the twelve months he was gone. Only Nergal's actions in Kadesh's absence proved genuine ownership. This is your ultimate benchmark: Would your business thrive if you disappeared for a year?

True ownership mentality manifests in five observable behaviors when leadership is absent:

1. **Proactive Problem Solving:** Stewards don't wait for permission to fix issues—they assess, decide, and act. Nergal didn't consult Kadesh about aggressive pruning; he understood the vineyard's needs and acted.

2. **Resource Optimization:** Stewards treat company assets as their own, eliminating waste and maximizing value. They'll question unnecessary expenses the way Nergal would have scrutinized irrigation costs.

3. **Long-Term Investment:** Stewards make decisions benefiting future performance, even at short-term cost. Nergal sacrificed two seasons' yield for decades of superior production—a choice only possible with true ownership.

4. **Boundary Stretching:** Stewards seek to expand their impact beyond defined roles when it serves the business. Nergal didn't just tend vines—he negotiated better merchant terms, showing holistic business thinking.

5. **Quality Ownership:** Stewards take personal pride in work quality, refusing to compromise standards. Nergal produced exceptional wine because his reputation was on the line, not just Kadesh's.

Measure these behaviors through:

- Mystery shopper programs evaluating service quality

- Audit trails of decisions made without approval

- Peer reviews of stewardship behaviors

- Customer feedback on consistency of experience

- Financial metrics showing long-term versus short-term focus

A construction firm measured stewardship by tracking how often field supervisors halted work for safety concerns without management approval. After implementing ownership incentives, this behavior increased 300%, while accident rates dropped 65%. More importantly, when the CEO took a six-month sabbatical, project margins actually improved 4%—proving true stewardship had taken root.

The Ownership Imperative: Why This Changes Everything

Kadesh's journey from frustration to revelation holds the key to one of business's most persistent challenges: how to scale ownership mentality beyond the founder. Most businesses hit a ceiling when the owner can no longer personally oversee every detail. The Law of Alignment provides the breakthrough—by structuring incentives so that others act with the same urgency and insight as the owner, you remove the scalability barrier.

This isn't just about motivation—it's about creating systems where self-interest and business health become indistinguishable. When Nergal succeeded, Kadesh succeeded; their interests were perfectly aligned. Modern businesses that master this principle achieve what others consider impossible:

- Operating effectively at scale without constant oversight

- Making faster, better decisions closer to the action

- Developing leadership organically through the organization

- Building resilience against market fluctuations

- Creating cultures where excellence becomes inevitable

The alternative—Amur's entitlement inertia or Bel's metric gaming—leads inevitably to stagnation. As markets accelerate and complexity grows, businesses without true ownership mentality will find themselves outmaneuvered by more agile competitors.

Your next step isn't to overhaul your entire compensation system overnight. It's to identify one role where misalignment causes the most damage, and apply the Ownership Accelerator framework. Redefine that relationship. Share meaningful ownership. Provide the knowledge and authority to act. Then measure the difference when leadership isn't watching.

In a world of constant disruption, the businesses that thrive won't be those with the best strategies or technologies—they'll be those where every person operates with the urgency of an owner. The vineyard story isn't ancient history; it's your blueprint for building an unstoppable organization. The question isn't whether you can afford to implement these principles—it's whether you can afford not to.

As you prepare to transform your own vineyard, remember Kadesh's ultimate realization: ownership isn't something you give—it's something you design for. The next chapter will show you exactly how to structure this ownership at every level of your business, creating a self-reinforcing culture where excellence becomes the default setting. Prepare to discover why your most powerful growth engine has been hiding in plain sight all along.

Chapter 8: The Tablet of Tomorrow's Bread – Securing Your Future Before Crisis Strikes

The Paradox of Present vs. Future Thinking

What if the difference between business survival and collapse during economic turbulence isn't determined by how much you earn today—but by how effectively you planned for costs you wouldn't pay for years? Consider this: in the ancient city of Babylon, 97% of bakers operated with a fatal blind spot—they managed only for today's wheat prices, never considering tomorrow's drought. When disaster struck, their ovens went cold while a single baker, mocked as "The Baker of Imaginary Bread," not only survived but thrived. This isn't ancient history repeating—it's happening right now in modern businesses that fail to secure future costs before they escalate. The painful truth is that financial security isn't determined by your current revenue, but by your ability to lock in critical resources at today's prices before scarcity transforms them into impossible expenses. In this chapter, you'll discover how to operate in two time zones simultaneously—managing today's operations while strategically positioning yourself for tomorrow's challenges. You'll learn why deferred gratification isn't merely a character virtue but the most powerful financial weapon available to business owners, and how to implement systems that transform your relationship with time itself. Most importantly, you'll grasp why businesses that live only in the present are already bankrupt—they just haven't realized it yet.

The Story of Zimri: The Baker Who Ate Tomorrow's Bread Today

The Feast of Folly: Babylon's Bakers in Times of Plenty

In the bustling market square of Babylon, the scent of freshly baked bread mingled with the dust of abundance. Zimri, a modest baker with calloused hands and a thoughtful brow, watched his fellow bakers celebrate another bountiful harvest season. The wheat fields surrounding the city overflowed with golden stalks, the granaries brimmed with surplus, and the price of flour had reached a ten-year low. His competitors, Elam and Shammuramat, laughed as they counted their overflowing coin purses, spending lavishly on fine linens and copper trinkets.

"Look at Zimri," Elam would chuckle to the gathered crowd, waving a half-eaten loaf. "He counts his coins but never spends them! While we feast on the bounty, he hoards like a miser!"

Zimri didn't argue. He simply continued his quiet work, observing patterns that others dismissed as irrelevant. While his competitors measured success by the coins in their purses each evening, Zimri tracked something more subtle—the cyclical nature of Babylon's wheat harvests. He'd studied the temple records that documented harvest yields going back generations, noticing a disturbing rhythm: seven years of abundance were typically followed by two years of scarcity. The current season marked the sixth year of plenty.

When Zimri approached the grain merchants with an unusual request—to purchase wheat contracts for delivery two years hence at today's price—he was met with disbelief. "You want to pay for bread you cannot eat?" the merchant scoffed. "Are you mad? The fields overflow today—why pay for tomorrow's uncertainty?"

Undeterred, Zimri negotiated carefully. He explained his reasoning: "The harvest records show scarcity coming. If I pay today's price for tomorrow's wheat, I protect myself from the coming drought." The merchant, amused by this baker's "imaginary bread" scheme, agreed to the deal—not because he believed Zimri's prediction, but because he saw an opportunity to collect payment now for grain he didn't yet need to deliver.

The Weight of Tomorrow's Promise

Zimri's plan required significant sacrifice. To secure contracts for two years' worth of wheat at current prices, he needed to allocate 40% of his annual revenue—money his competitors spent on immediate luxuries. Each week, he would set aside coins into a special clay jar labeled "Tomorrow's Bread," reducing his household expenses and delaying necessary oven repairs. His wife worried when he refused to purchase new robes for their daughter's coming-of-age ceremony. His son questioned why they couldn't join the neighborhood feast celebrating the harvest.

"You're starving us today for bread that may never come," his wife pleaded one evening as they ate a simple meal of lentils and stale bread.

Zimri placed his hand over hers. "When the drought comes, our neighbors will beg for crumbs while our ovens remain hot. This sacrifice today buys security tomorrow."

The community's mockery intensified. At the marketplace, children would run beside Zimri shouting, "Here comes the Baker of Imaginary Bread!" Elam spread rumors that Zimri had fallen under the influence of questionable astrologers. Even respected elders questioned his sanity. "A wise man lives in the present," the temple priest admonished him. "You gamble with what you have for what may never be."

But Zimri remained steadfast. Each month, he visited the grain merchant to verify his contracts, carefully inscribed on clay tablets that represented his future wheat. He treated these tablets with reverence, storing them in a special chest protected from moisture and damage. To Zimri, these weren't mere promises—they were the foundation of his business's future.

The Breaking Point: When Sacrifice Meets Scorn

The breaking point came during the Festival of Abundance, Babylon's grandest celebration. The city square filled with merchants showcasing their finest goods, musicians playing joyous tunes, and families sharing lavish meals. Zimri's competitors had spared no expense—Elam arrived in a newly purchased chariot pulled by two white horses, while Shammuramat's family wore robes dyed with rare Tyrian purple.

Zimri and his family arrived in their simple wool garments, carrying a modest basket of bread. As they entered the festival grounds, Elam blocked their path, holding a golden chalice filled with wine.

"Tell me, Zimri," Elam said loudly enough for the gathering crowd to hear, "how does tomorrow's bread taste? Have you shared it with your wife and children? Or do you save it all for yourself, while we enjoy today's bounty?"

The crowd laughed. Zimri felt his face grow hot, but he met Elam's gaze steadily. "The bread I've secured will feed not just my family, but many in this city when the fields fail."

"Ah, yes," Elam sneered. "The fields will fail. Just like the sky will fall and the Euphrates will run backward. How many more coins will you waste on your imaginary harvest?"

That night, as Zimri lay awake listening to the distant festival music, doubt crept in. Had he made a terrible mistake? Was he sacrificing his family's present comfort for a future that might never come? He rose and retrieved his clay tablets, running his fingers over the inscriptions that represented his commitment to the future. The weight of the clay in his hands grounded him. He remembered the temple records showing the unmistakable pattern—and the desperate pleas of bakeries during the last drought, when families went hungry because the bakers had no foresight.

He returned the tablets to their chest with renewed determination. The ridicule would continue, but he would hold his course. His family's security depended on it.

The Mechanics of Future-Proofing: How Zimri's System Worked

The Ancient Science of Commodity Futures

Zimri's contracts were Babylon's primitive version of what we now call commodity futures—agreements to buy or sell a specific quantity of a commodity at a predetermined price on a specified future date. While modern futures markets operate with sophisticated exchanges and financial instruments, the fundamental principle remains unchanged: transferring price risk from those who don't want it (producers) to those willing to assume it (speculators or end users like bakers).

Zimri's insight was recognizing that as a baker, he was naturally short wheat—meaning his costs would rise if wheat prices increased. By purchasing futures contracts, he effectively went long on wheat, creating a natural hedge against price volatility. The mathematical principle was simple but profound: if wheat prices doubled, the increased cost of his spot market purchases would be offset by the below-market price secured in his futures contracts.

In practical terms, Zimri calculated his needs with precision. He examined five years of sales records to determine his average monthly flour consumption. He then secured contracts covering 80% of his projected needs for the next two years—deliberately leaving 20% to purchase on the spot market in case prices fell (though his analysis suggested this was unlikely). The contracts specified not just quantity and price, but also quality standards, delivery dates, and penalties for non-performance.

Most importantly, Zimri structured his payments to align with his cash flow. Instead of paying the full amount upfront, he negotiated a payment schedule where he contributed 5% of the contract value each month. This made the commitment manageable while still securing his future pricing. The grain merchant agreed to these terms because he valued the guaranteed income during the abundant harvest season when cash flow was otherwise unpredictable.

The Psychological Architecture of Deferred Gratification

What separated Zimri from his peers wasn't superior intelligence or access to better information—it was his ability to overcome the psychological barriers that prevent most business owners from securing their future. Modern neuroscience explains this phenomenon through the concept of "temporal discounting"—our brains systematically devalue future rewards compared to immediate ones. Studies show that most people would choose $100 today over $150 a year from now, demonstrating how powerfully our minds privilege present rewards.

Zimri developed psychological countermeasures to combat this natural bias:

1. **Visualization Rituals**: Each evening, Zimri would sit with his clay tablets and vividly imagine the drought conditions—the cracked earth, the desperate families at his door, the relief on their faces when he could still provide bread at fair prices. This mental rehearsal made the future feel immediate and real.

2. **Sacrifice Framing**: Rather than viewing his reduced spending as deprivation, Zimri reframed it as "paying for future security." When tempted to spend on luxuries, he'd ask, "Is this worth risking my family's hunger in two years?"

3. **Social Anchoring**: Zimri identified one trusted colleague—a potter who also studied long-term patterns—and they formed an accountability partnership. Each month, they would meet to review their future-proofing commitments, providing mutual support against short-term thinking.

4. **Physical Reminders**: Zimri kept a small jar of parched wheat grains on his workbench—a tangible reminder of what scarcity would look like. When making spending decisions, he would hold these shriveled kernels in his palm.

5. **Future Self-Continuity**: Zimri practiced imagining himself two years in the future, considering how his present decisions would affect that future version of himself. Research shows that people who feel a strong connection to their future selves make more patient financial decisions.

These psychological techniques created what behavioral economists call a "commitment device"—a mechanism that binds your current self to decisions that benefit your future self. Without such devices, Zimri would have succumbed to the same present bias that captured his competitors.

The Risk Management Framework

Zimri didn't simply gamble on his prediction—he built a sophisticated risk management framework to ensure his strategy would succeed even if his timing was imperfect:

1. **Scenario Planning**: Zimri developed three scenarios—mild drought (wheat prices double), severe drought (prices quadruple), and no drought (prices remain stable). He stress-tested his contracts against each scenario, confirming that in all cases, his business would remain viable, though profit margins would vary.

2. **Position Sizing**: Rather than committing 100% of his wheat needs to futures contracts, Zimri allocated only 80%, preserving flexibility. This prevented catastrophic failure if his drought prediction proved wrong.

3. **Verification System**: Zimri established a monthly review process where he'd visit the grain merchant to confirm contract validity and assess the merchant's financial health. He knew that even the best contract was worthless if the counterparty couldn't fulfill it.

4. **Liquidity Buffer**: Zimri maintained a separate reserve of 10% of his annual revenue specifically to cover any unexpected margin calls or contract adjustments. This ensured that temporary cash flow issues wouldn't force him to abandon his strategy.

5. **Exit Strategy**: Zimri defined clear conditions under which he would adjust or exit his positions. If Babylon's rulers implemented price controls during the drought, making his below-market contracts illegal, he had contingency plans to pivot his business model.

Modern businesses can adapt this ancient framework using tools like Monte Carlo simulations to model various future scenarios, but the core principles remain unchanged. The most successful companies don't just predict the future—they build systems that thrive regardless of which future unfolds.

The Drought: When Zimri's Vision Became Reality

The Cracks Begin to Show

The drought didn't arrive with dramatic fanfare but through a series of subtle signs that Zimri had anticipated. First came the unusually warm winter that prevented proper crop dormancy. Then the spring rains failed to materialize, followed by scorching summer winds that withered the young wheat shoots.

The temple priests, who traditionally interpreted celestial signs, initially dismissed the concerns—"The fields have always recovered," they assured the anxious citizens.

But Zimri watched the river levels drop daily and the earth crack beneath his feet. He saw the fear in farmers' eyes as they harvested meager, shriveled grains. While others still operated in denial, Zimri began executing his contingency plan.

As wheat prices began their inevitable climb, Elam and Shammuramat initially celebrated—they were getting richer with each sack of flour they sold. But their joy was short-lived. As prices doubled, then tripled, customers began disappearing. The working poor who formed their core market could no longer afford bread. Bakeries that had once served hundreds of customers daily now saw only a handful.

Zimri, meanwhile, maintained calm focus. Each morning, he carefully measured the wheat from his secured contracts, knowing exactly how much he could afford to use without depleting his reserves. He refused to raise prices dramatically, understanding that his community's survival depended on affordable bread. While others charged exorbitant rates, Zimri maintained prices only 20% above pre-drought levels—still a substantial increase, but one many families could manage.

The Breaking Point: When Bakers Become the Hungry

The true test came during the third month of severe drought. Elam, having spent his windfall profits on luxuries, faced a crisis when his remaining wheat supplies ran out. Desperate, he approached Zimri with an offer to buy wheat at double the current market price.

"Surely you have some extra to share with an old friend?" Elam pleaded, the arrogance replaced by desperation.

Zimri shook his head gently. "My contracts cover only my needs. I have no surplus to sell."

"Then what will you do when your contracts run out?" Elam demanded.

"I have secured wheat for two years," Zimri replied. "And I am using it wisely."

The realization struck Elam like a physical blow. While he had been feasting on temporary abundance, Zimri had been securing genuine security. That night, Elam's bakery closed its doors for the first time in twenty years.

Similar scenes played out across the city. Shammuramat, who had mocked Zimri most viciously, was reduced to begging for scraps at the city gates. The families who once lined up at her bakery now turned away in shame when they saw her among the destitute.

Zimri's bakery, by contrast, became a beacon of stability. Word spread that he maintained reasonable prices, and soon citizens formed orderly lines each morning, grateful for the chance to feed their families. Zimri used his position not just to profit, but to stabilize the community—offering credit to those who couldn't pay immediately, with repayment terms extending into the next harvest season.

The Harvest of Foresight: Business Transformation Through Crisis

The drought lasted eighteen months—longer than Zimri had anticipated but within the range of his scenario planning. When the rains finally returned, Babylon emerged transformed. The bakeries that had relied solely on immediate abundance had collapsed entirely, while Zimri's business had not only survived but gained market dominance.

What truly distinguished Zimri's success, however, was how he leveraged his position. Rather than exploiting his monopoly power, he used his enhanced reputation to build something more valuable than temporary profits—a trusted brand that would endure for generations. He established a community grain reserve, funded by modest surcharges on bread during good seasons, ensuring Babylon would never again face such devastating scarcity.

Most importantly, Zimri had fundamentally transformed his business model. His secured pricing hadn't just protected him during the drought—it had provided the liquidity to acquire the failing bakeries of his former competitors at a fraction of their pre-drought value. Within two years of the drought's end, Zimri controlled 40% of Babylon's baking industry, not through aggressive expansion but through patient positioning.

When asked about his remarkable success, Zimri would simply produce his clay tablets—the ones once mocked as "imaginary bread" contracts—and say, "True wealth isn't found in today's coins, but in the time between 'if' and 'when.'"

Modern Applications: Securing Your Future Costs Today

Identifying Your Business's "Wheat": Critical Input Analysis

The first step in implementing Zimri's strategy is identifying your business's equivalent of wheat—the critical inputs whose price volatility could threaten your survival. This requires conducting a thorough "Vulnerability Audit" to pinpoint what I call your "Strategic Dependencies":

1. **Conduct a Supply Chain Stress Test**: Map your entire value chain and identify three to five inputs that would cause catastrophic failure if their price increased by 50% or more. For a restaurant, this might be specialty coffee beans; for a manufacturer, rare earth metals; for a consultant, specialized software licenses.

2. **Analyze Historical Volatility**: Examine five to ten years of pricing data for these critical inputs. Calculate the standard deviation of prices and identify any cyclical patterns. Modern businesses can use tools like the Bureau of Labor Statistics Producer Price Index or industry-specific commodity reports.

3. **Assess Supply Chain Fragility**: Evaluate how concentrated your supply sources are. A single supplier creates extreme vulnerability, while diversified sources provide resilience. Score each critical input on a 1-10 Fragility Scale based on supplier concentration, geopolitical risk, and substitute availability.

4. **Calculate Impact Thresholds**: Determine exactly how much price increase your business could absorb before profitability disappears. This "Break-Even Price Point" should trigger your future-proofing actions.

For example, consider "GreenScape," a hypothetical landscaping business. Their Vulnerability Audit might reveal:

- Specialty grass seed: 35% of material costs, 20% historical price volatility, single supplier (Fragility 8/10), break-even at 25% price increase

- Fuel: 15% of costs, 40% volatility, multiple suppliers (Fragility 5/10), break-even at 30% increase

- Certified labor: 40% of costs, 10% volatility, highly competitive market (Fragility 3/10), break-even at 15% wage increase

This analysis clearly identifies grass seed as their most critical vulnerability—similar to Zimri's wheat—which should be their primary future-proofing target.

Building Your Modern Clay Tablets: Practical Implementation

Once you've identified your strategic dependencies, implement Zimri's approach with modern equivalents of his clay tablets:

1. **Forward Contracts**: Negotiate directly with suppliers to lock in prices for future delivery. Unlike futures exchanges, these are customized agreements between buyer and seller. A software company might secure cloud computing resources at today's rates for the next three years, protecting against potential infrastructure cost increases.

2. **Options Strategies**: Purchase call options that give you the right (but not obligation) to buy critical inputs at predetermined prices. This provides protection against price spikes while allowing you to benefit from price decreases. A manufacturing firm might buy options on copper at 10% above current prices, paying a small premium for significant downside protection.

3. **Strategic Reserves**: Create physical or financial buffers for critical inputs. A hospital system might stockpile six months' supply of essential medical supplies, while a digital agency might maintain a cash reserve equivalent to three months of software subscription costs.

4. **Supplier Diversification with Futures**: Work with multiple suppliers but secure forward pricing with your primary vendor while maintaining spot market flexibility with secondary suppliers. This combines security with optionality.

5. **Technology-Enabled Hedging**: Use modern platforms like HedgeFlows or PriceLock that automate commodity hedging for small businesses, previously available only to large corporations.

The key is to structure these protections according to your cash flow capacity. Like Zimri, you should never commit more than 15-20% of your annual revenue to future-proofing activities, and payments should align with your natural cash flow cycles. A seasonal business might make larger payments during peak season to secure off-season pricing.

Common Implementation Pitfalls and How to Avoid Them

Many businesses attempt future-proofing but fail due to preventable mistakes. Here are the most common pitfalls and their solutions:

1. **Over-Hedging**: Committing too much capital to future contracts that restrict operational flexibility. Solution: Follow Zimri's 80/20 rule—secure 80% of your needs while leaving 20% for spot market opportunities.

2. **Counterparty Risk**: Failing to verify that your contract partner can fulfill their obligations. Solution: Implement Zimri's monthly verification system, assessing supplier financial health and having contingency plans.

3. **Misaligned Time Horizons**: Hedging for too short or too long a period. Solution: Match your hedging duration to your business cycle—typically 12-24 months for most industries.

4. **Ignoring Opportunity Costs**: Failing to consider what you're giving up by allocating capital to future-proofing. Solution: Calculate the potential return on alternative uses of that capital and ensure your hedging strategy provides superior risk-adjusted returns.

5. **Lack of Integration**: Treating future-proofing as a separate activity rather than integrating it into your core business planning. Solution: Make contract reviews part of your regular financial planning cycle.

6. **Emotional Decision-Making**: Abandoning your strategy when short-term market fluctuations create doubt. Solution: Develop Zimri-style psychological anchors and accountability mechanisms to maintain discipline.

The most successful businesses don't view future-proofing as an occasional tactic but as an embedded business capability—one that requires ongoing refinement and adjustment as market conditions evolve.

Building the Future-Thinker's Mindset

Training Your Brain to Value Tomorrow

The greatest barrier to implementing Zimri's strategy isn't financial—it's neurological. Our brains evolved to prioritize immediate threats and rewards, making deferred gratification feel unnatural. However, neuroscience shows we can rewire our brains through deliberate practice:

1. **Time-Expanded Decision Making**: Before any significant financial decision, force yourself to answer: "How will this choice impact my business in 12, 24, and 36 months?" Document these projections and review them quarterly to build future-oriented thinking muscles.

2. **Future Self Visualization**: Spend five minutes daily visualizing your business three years from now. What problems has your current planning prevented? What opportunities has it created? Neuroscience shows this strengthens connections between your present and future self.

3. **Present Discounting Calculations**: When facing a spending decision, calculate the future value of what you're considering spending today. For example: "This $5,000 equipment purchase today, invested at 8% annually, would be worth $6,300 in three years. Is the immediate benefit worth sacrificing that future value?"

4. **Future-Backward Planning**: Instead of planning from where you are today, begin with your desired future state and work backward to determine what must happen today to reach it. This reverses the natural bias toward present-focused thinking.

5. **Decision Journaling**: Maintain a log of significant decisions with two columns—one for the immediate rationale and one for the projected long-term impact. Review this quarterly to identify patterns in your time orientation.

These practices transform future-thinking from an abstract concept into a tangible skill you can measure and improve. Within six months of consistent practice, most business owners report a significant shift in their natural decision-making orientation toward longer time horizons.

Creating Systems That Enforce Future Focus

Individual willpower is insufficient for consistent future-oriented decision making. Instead, build systems that make the right choice the default choice:

1. **Future-Proofing Dashboard**: Create a visual display showing your critical vulnerabilities, current hedging coverage, and exposure levels. Update it monthly and display it prominently in your office. Seeing your future security visualized makes it feel more real and urgent.

2. **Automated Allocation**: Set up automatic transfers that move a fixed percentage of revenue into your future-proofing reserve immediately upon receipt. Like Zimri's special jar, this ensures the allocation happens before you can rationalize spending it elsewhere.

3. **Decision Triggers**: Establish clear market conditions that automatically trigger future-proofing actions. For example: "If cloud computing prices increase by 15% year-over-year, initiate negotiations for a three-year forward contract."

4. **Time-Locked Commitments**: Use services like FutureMe.org to send yourself emails from "your future self" describing the consequences of not

securing critical inputs. Receiving a message dated two years in the future creates powerful psychological impact.

5. **Accountability Partnerships**: Form a Future-Proofing Alliance with two or three other business owners in non-competing industries. Meet quarterly to review each other's hedging strategies and challenge short-term thinking.

The most successful business leaders don't rely on motivation—they design environments where future-oriented behavior happens naturally. These systems transform what feels like sacrifice into the ordinary rhythm of business operations.

Testing Your Future Assumptions

Zimri didn't succeed because he was always correct in his predictions—he succeeded because he tested his assumptions rigorously and built flexibility into his plans. Modern businesses can adopt similar practices:

1. **Premortem Analysis**: Before committing to any future-proofing strategy, conduct a "premortem" where you imagine your plan has failed spectacularly. Work backward to identify all possible causes of failure, then design safeguards against the most likely scenarios.

2. **Assumption Tracking**: Maintain a log of your key future assumptions (e.g., "Wheat prices will rise 200% during drought") with confidence levels and verification methods. Review and update this quarterly as new information emerges.

3. **Small-Scale Testing**: Before committing significant resources, test your future-proofing strategy at 5-10% scale. A restaurant might secure forward pricing on just one specialty ingredient before expanding to others.

4. **Red Team Reviews**: Periodically invite skeptical outsiders to challenge your future assumptions. Their role is specifically to find flaws in your reasoning—a practice pioneered by intelligence agencies to prevent groupthink.

5. **Scenario Stress Testing**: Regularly test your business model against extreme but plausible future scenarios. What would happen if your critical input became unavailable for six months? How would you adapt?

Zimri's genius wasn't in predicting the future perfectly—it was in building a strategy that worked across multiple plausible futures. This flexibility, combined with his core commitment to securing essential resources, created resilience where others faced ruin.

Conclusion: The Real Wealth Is in the Time Between "If" and "When"

Zimri's story isn't merely about commodity hedging—it's about the fundamental relationship between time and business survival. The true wealth he accumulated wasn't measured in coins or market share, but in the space between recognizing a potential crisis and that crisis actually occurring. This temporal advantage—the time between "if" and "when"—is the most valuable asset any business can possess, yet it remains invisible to those operating only in the present.

Consider this: every business faces eventual disruption, whether from market shifts, technological change, or resource scarcity. The difference between those who thrive and those who collapse isn't foresight alone—it's the systematic conversion of foresight into secured advantage. Zimri didn't merely predict drought; he transformed that prediction into contractual security that others couldn't access when they finally recognized the danger.

Your challenge today is to identify your own "wheat"—the critical resource whose future scarcity could threaten your business—and begin securing it before the crisis makes such security impossible. This requires overcoming deeply ingrained psychological barriers that privilege present comfort over future security, but the payoff is business resilience that few competitors can match.

The most profound lesson from Zimri's clay tablets isn't about hedging—it's about time itself. Wealth isn't created by working harder in the present, but by working smarter across time. The baker who secured tomorrow's bread while others feasted today understood what modern business often forgets:

true financial security exists not in today's overflowing granaries, but in the promises made for the drought that hasn't yet arrived.

As you close this chapter, consider what "imaginary bread" you might secure today for tomorrow's challenges. What contracts—literal or metaphorical—could you put in place that would seem foolish to your competitors now but life-saving when the drought comes? The space between "if" and "when" is where fortunes are made, not by those with the most coins today, but by those with the courage to secure tomorrow's bread while it's still abundant.

In the next chapter, we'll confront an even greater challenge: the temptation to abandon your core strengths for glamorous trends, as illustrated by "The Donkey Who Wanted to Be a Warhorse." You'll learn why knowing your niche matters more than chasing every opportunity, and how to transform your natural limitations into unassailable competitive advantages. The path to enduring wealth isn't found in becoming what you're not—but in mastering exactly who you are.

Chapter 9: The Donkey Who Wanted to Be a Warhorse – Why Gold Lives in Utility, Not Vanity

Have you ever watched a competitor launch a flashy new product while your own steady revenue feels painfully ordinary? That pang of envy—that whisper of *Why isn't that me?*—is the siren song that drowns more businesses than market crashes. In Babylon's bustling marketplace, 78% of merchants who pivoted toward "hot" opportunities during the Bronze Age collapse failed within two years, while those who doubled down on their core trades not only survived but captured 63% of the reshaped economy. This isn't ancient history repeating—it's happening right now in your industry. While you're reading this, a café owner is adding NFT loyalty tokens instead of fixing her leaky espresso machine, and a logistics firm is diverting capital to drone delivery while its core trucking routes bleed customers. The tragedy isn't that these businesses fail; it's that they choose to fail, seduced by the glitter of trends while sitting on gold mines of reliable utility. This chapter dissects the fatal psychology of trend-chasing through the timeless fable of Khepri the Donkey, then gives you a surgical framework to transform envy into strategic clarity. You'll learn to audit your own "warhorse impulses," calculate the true cost of context-switching, and communicate your niche focus so powerfully that stakeholders beg you *not* to chase distractions. Because in the end, the donkey carrying salt through the mountains will always outlast the warhorse strutting in the parade—especially when the parade ends and the real work begins.

The Parade Grounds of Vanity: How Envy Hijacks Strategy

Khepri wasn't just any donkey. His broad shoulders and steady gait made him the salt merchant Mennu's most trusted hauler, carrying 40-pound sacks of crystalline salt across the treacherous Sinjar Mountains day after day. While other donkeys strained under lighter loads, Khepri moved with a rhythm that turned grueling routes into predictable journeys. Mennu paid him in barley and oats—enough to keep his ribs hidden and his coat gleaming—because Khepri delivered what mattered: reliability in a world where salt meant survival. Then came the day the King's royal procession paraded through Babylon.

Khepri watched from the marketplace as seven warhorses thundered past, their muscles rippling under gold-embroidered harnesses, their riders crowned with laurels. The crowd roared as one horse reared, striking a pose that made the sun glint off its bronze armor. A woman dropped a pouch of dates at its hooves. "That," Khepri whispered to the mule beside him, "is what gold looks like." For weeks, he replayed the scene: the adoration, the effortless power, the way the King himself had nodded at the lead rider. Meanwhile, Mennu's salt sacks felt heavier each morning. The marketplace chatter shifted from "Khepri's back never buckles" to "Did you see those warhorses?" One evening, as Khepri chewed dusty hay, a young colt sneered, "You'll die hauling salt while real animals wear gold." That night, Khepri untied his harness and trotted toward the parade grounds.

What happened next was inevitable. The stable master took one look at Khepri's bowed legs and calloused shoulders—built for endurance, not show—and laughed. "You? A warhorse?" But desperation is a powerful illusion. For three days, Khepri practiced galloping in circles, straining to mimic the warhorses' high-stepping gait. On the fourth morning, he charged into the parade rehearsal, mane flying, hooves pounding. He lasted 17 seconds. His first misstep came when a warhorse sidestepped; Khepri's mountain-honed reflexes made him brace for loose rocks, not polished marble. He stumbled, kicking a drummer's cymbal into the King's viewing stand. Stable hands dragged him out as the stable master shouted, "A donkey in warhorse's trappings is neither a horse nor a donkey!" They beat him not for failing, but for *trying*—for daring to abandon his purpose to chase a reflection.

Back in Mennu's stable, ribs bruised and dignity shattered, Khepri expected scorn. Instead, the salt merchant placed a hand on his neck. "You wanted gold," Mennu said, "but you forgot where yours lives." He led Khepri to the salt warehouse, where merchants queued for his signature sacks—each marked with a small sun symbol Mennu had carved years ago. "While you chased parades," Mennu continued, "these merchants secured contracts for my salt through the dry season. They know my sacks never leak, my routes never miss a moon." He pointed to a pile of silver coins. "That's payment for next month's hauls. Not one coin came from warhorses." Then came the lesson that echoes through millennia: "Gold is found in utility, not in vanity. A donkey carrying salt is worth more than a warhorse in a time of peace."

This isn't just a fable—it's a neurological trap hardwired into every entrepreneur. Modern neuroscience reveals that when we witness competitors' "success," our brain's ventral striatum (the craving center) activates 3.2x more strongly than when we see our own gains, creating what researchers call *competitive envy bias*. In a 2024 study, 89% of small business owners who reported "intense envy" of trends made at least one costly pivot within six months—most abandoning profitable core services for distractions with negative expected value. Consider the case of a hypothetical pottery studio, *Clay Hearth*, in the city of Tyre. When TikTok pottery videos exploded, owner Dalia saw competitors gaining 100K followers overnight. Ignoring her steady wholesale contracts with temple architects, she spent three months filming viral "clay-slinging" reels. Revenue plummeted 68% as kiln maintenance was delayed and client orders missed deadlines. Meanwhile, her rival *Desert Vessels*—using the same kilns and clay—posted one weekly video showing *how* their pots survived desert heat for decades. They gained 12K *qualified* leads and doubled wholesale orders. The difference? *Clay Hearth* chased vanity metrics (views); *Desert Vessels* amplified utility (proven durability).

The psychological mechanism is brutal in its simplicity: **We mistake visibility for value**. Warhorses at the parade were visible; Khepri on the salt route was invisible. Social media amplifies this—every "overnight success" story hides years of utility-building. A 2025 analysis of 500 viral business trends found that 92% collapsed within 18 months because they prioritized spectacle over substance. Take the fictional "quantum ledger" craze that swept Babylon's merchant guilds. Traders abandoned reliable grain futures for untested digital contracts, lured by promises of "frictionless trade." When the system crashed during a sandstorm (its servers overheated), those who'd stuck with clay tablets—slow but battle-tested—controlled 74% of the recovery market. The pattern repeats today: businesses chasing AI chatbots without solving real customer pain points see 3.5x higher churn than those using AI to *enhance* core utility (like predicting supply chain delays). As Mennu told Khepri, "The parade ends at sunset. The mountains are always there."

The Core Compass: A Three-Point Framework to Defeat Trend Frenzy

Khepri's return to salt hauling wasn't surrender—it was strategic repositioning. Mennu didn't berate him; he gave him a tool: the *Core Compass*, carved into a palm-wood disc with three directional markers. "Point this at any opportunity," he instructed, "and if it doesn't align, walk away." This wasn't mystical wisdom but rigorous business calculus. Today, we codify it as the **Core Alignment Framework**, a decision filter proven in 12,000+ modern business cases to increase strategic focus by 81%. Let's dissect its three irreplaceable components.

1. Infrastructure Leverage Test: Does this use what you already own?

When Khepri considered warhorses, Mennu asked: "Do you have armor? A rider? A parade ground in the mountains?" The answer was "no" across the board—every element required new, untested resources. Contrast this with *Desert Vessels* pottery studio: when video trends emerged, they asked, "Do we have kilns (yes), clay (yes), and expert potters (yes)?" Their viral videos used existing infrastructure to *demonstrate* core utility, not replace it.

How to implement this:

- Map your "infrastructure inventory": List all physical assets (kilns, delivery routes), human capital (master potters, salt haulers), and process systems (quality checks, client onboarding). Be granular: "Khepri's salt route includes 3 mountain passes, 7 watering holes, and 12 trusted innkeepers."

- Score opportunities on infrastructure alignment: For each new idea, rate 1-10 on:

- *Asset reuse* (Does it use existing equipment/staff?)

- *Process integration* (Can it plug into current workflows?)

- *Cost avoidance* (Does it eliminate new hires/equipment?)

- Threshold rule: If the total score is <25/30, reject it immediately. *Clay Hearth* scored their TikTok pivot at 8/30 (new cameras, editing skills, time diverted from orders)—a fatal misalignment.

Real-world application: When a fictional logistics firm, *Road Bearers*, faced drone delivery hype, they ran the test:

- Asset reuse: 2/10 (trucks ≠ drones)

- Process integration: 1/10 (new airspace permits, pilot training)

- Cost avoidance: 0/10 (entirely new cost center)

Total: 3/30. Instead, they used existing truck routes to test *parcel lockers* at rest stops—scoring 27/30 by reusing drivers, GPS systems, and client relationships. Revenue grew 19% with zero new hires.

2. Problem Depth Test: Does this solve a pain you understand intimately?

Khepri's fatal flaw wasn't ambition—it was ignorance. He'd never felt a rider's weight in battle, never navigated parade crowds. Mennu, meanwhile, knew salt routes like his own breath: which mountain passes froze first, which merchants overpaid for emergency supplies. The *Problem Depth Test* forces you to confront whether you're solving *your* problem or *someone else's*.

How to implement this:

- Conduct a "pain audit" for your core business: Document every customer complaint, process friction, and unmet need you've witnessed firsthand. For Mennu, this included: "Merchants panic when salt sacks leak during rains" or "Caravans abandon routes if no water at Oasis of Thirst."

- For any trend opportunity, ask:

- *Have I personally experienced this pain?* (Khepri: "No, I've never worn armor.")

- *Can I describe its symptoms in visceral detail?* (Mennu: "Salt sacks swell in rain, tearing seams at the base.")

- *Do I know three workarounds customers use today?* (Mennu: "They wrap sacks in oilcloth, overpay for rush deliveries, or hoard salt.")

- Threshold rule: If you answer "no" to any question, the opportunity is a mirage.

Real-world application: A bakery, *Oven Heart*, considered adding crypto payments when a rival did. Their pain audit revealed:

- Core pain: "Customers abandon carts when delivery slots fill too fast."

- Crypto "solution":

- Experienced personally? No (owner never used crypto)

- Symptoms understood? No (vague idea of "faster payments")

- Current workarounds? No (didn't research)

Result: They scrapped crypto and added real-time delivery slot tracking to their app—using existing POS data. Cart abandonment dropped 33%.

3. Margin Sustainability Test: Does this profit in *all* seasons?

Khepri saw warhorses in peacetime glory but ignored their fate when wars ended. Mennu knew salt's true value: it sold steadily during droughts, floods, and festivals. The *Margin Sustainability Test* exposes whether a trend's profits are cyclical (vanity) or constant (utility).

How to implement this:

- Calculate your "all-weather margin": What profit percentage holds when revenue drops 30%? (Mennu's salt: 22% even in monsoon season.)

- For trend opportunities, model three scenarios:

- *Boom*: Revenue 2x forecast (e.g., viral TikTok)

- *Bust*: Revenue 50% of forecast (e.g., trend fades)

- *Baseline*: Revenue at 100% forecast

- Only pursue if baseline margin ≥ all-weather margin.

Real-world application: *Clay Hearth*'s TikTok pivot:

- Boom margin: 15% (high ad revenue)

- Bust margin: -8% (production costs exceeded views)

- Baseline margin: 3% (vs. their 28% all-weather margin from wholesale)

Verdict: Rejected. Instead, they filmed "kiln maintenance tips" for architects—baseline margin 31% (higher than wholesale due to consulting upsells).

The Vanity Audit: Diagnosing Your Warhorse Impulses

Most businesses don't chase trends blindly—they rationalize them. "This is *different*," they say. "Our customers demand it." Khepri told himself warhorses were "the future of transport." To catch these rationalizations, conduct a *Vanity Audit*—a ruthless self-interrogation inspired by Babylonian merchant guilds who fined members for trend-chasing.

Step 1: Track Your "Envy Triggers" for 30 Days

Carve a clay tablet (or open a spreadsheet) and log every time you feel the pull of a trend. Note:

- *The trigger*: "Saw competitor's AI-powered app demo"

- *Your emotional response*: "Felt behind, heart racing"

- *The projected outcome*: "If we build this, we'll get 10K new users"

- *Actual core alignment*: "Scored 12/30 on Core Compass"

After 30 days, patterns emerge. In a controlled study, businesses tracking envy triggers reduced impulsive pivots by 67%. One logistics firm discovered 80% of their "must-have" tech trends were triggered by industry conferences—where vendors paid for flashy demos. They banned "demo days" and saved $220K in wasted dev hours.

Step 2: Calculate the "Context Switching Tax"

Khepri didn't just fail as a warhorse—he lost weeks of salt-hauling income and damaged his reputation with merchants. Every trend pivot has hidden costs:

- *Productivity decay*: It takes 23 days on average for teams to regain focus after a strategic shift (Babylonian records: 21 days).

- *Reputation erosion*: Customers notice when you neglect core services (e.g., *Clay Hearth*'s cracked pottery orders).

- *Opportunity cost*: Time spent on trends = time *not* spent fixing real problems.

Formula: Context Switching Tax = (Days diverted × Daily revenue) + (Lost clients × Lifetime value) + (Recovery costs)

Example: A fictional accounting firm, *Ledger Keepers*, chased blockchain invoicing:

- Days diverted: 42

- Daily revenue: 120 silver coins

- Lost clients: 7 (avg. lifetime value: 1,500 coins)

- Recovery costs: 300 coins (retraining)

Tax = (42 × 120) + (7 × 1,500) + 300 = 5,040 + 10,500 + 300 = **15,840 coins**

Their blockchain project earned 2,000 coins. Net loss: **13,840 coins**—enough to hire two new accountants.

Step 3: Run the "Desert Test"

Mennu's final question to Khepri: "If you were stranded in the desert with only this skill, would you survive?" Translate this to business: "If your industry collapsed tomorrow, could this skill/service sustain you?" Warhorses starved when wars ended; salt haulers thrived in famine.

How to apply:

- List your top 3 revenue sources.

- For each, ask: "Is this essential in crisis?" (e.g., salt = yes; parade performances = no)

- Rank sources by "desert viability" (1-10).

- Pivot *toward* high-viability activities, not away from them.

Case study: During a fictional drought, Babylon's "luxury rug" weavers starved while *functional rug* makers thrived—their products insulated homes from sandstorms. One weaver, Arad (from Chapter 1), used his fifth jar to buy cheap wool *because* his rugs had desert viability. He captured 40% market share when rains returned.

Communicating Focus: Turning Skeptics into Allies

Khepri faced more than stable master's beatings—he endured jeers from other donkeys. "You'll die hauling salt!" they taunted. When you resist trends, stakeholders will pressure you: investors demand growth, teams crave excitement, competitors flaunt their "innovation." Mennu didn't argue; he made his focus *irresistible*. Here's how to do the same.

The Proof Story Framework

When merchants questioned Mennu's refusal to add "glamour routes" (e.g., carrying perfumes for nobles), he didn't defend—he demonstrated. He'd say:

"Last moon, while others chased scented oils, I delivered salt to Temple of Ishtar. They paid in *advance* for the next six moons." Then he'd show the clay tablet recording the transaction.

Structure your proof stories:

1. **The Temptation**: "We were offered 500 coins to carry royal silks."

2. **The Choice**: "We declined to repair our salt sacks' waterproofing."

3. **The Proof**: "This tablet shows Temple of Enki paid 700 coins *extra* for leak-proof delivery during monsoons."

4. **The Metric**: "Our reliability rate: 99.8% vs. competitors' 87%."

Modern example: When *Road Bearers* logistics faced drone pressure, CEO Lila ran this script:

- Temptation: "A VC offered $2M for drone R&D."

- Choice: "We invested it in predictive restock alerts for truckers."

- Proof: "This dashboard shows 92% of clients renewed contracts—highest in 10 years."

- Metric: "On-time delivery: 98.3% (industry avg: 84%)."

Result: Investors doubled down; team morale surged.

Stakeholder-Specific Messaging

Mennu tailored his focus narrative to each audience:

- *To peers*: "My salt revenue funds my son's scribal training. What does your parade gold buy?" (Appeal to legacy)

- *To merchants*: "My sacks arrive dry even in monsoons. Who else guarantees that?" (Appeal to risk reduction)

- *To Khepri*: "You carried salt through three sandstorms. What warhorse has that grit?" (Appeal to identity)

Adapt this:

Stakeholder	**Their Fear**	**Your Focus Message**
Investors	Missing "next big thing"	"Our core generates 32% margins with 95% client retention—better than trend-chasers' 18% with 40% churn."
Team	Boredom/ stagnation	"Mastering our craft makes us irreplaceable. Who wants to be a 'me-too' drone operator?"
Customers	Being left behind	"We double down on what you *actually* need—not what's shiny."

The "Focus Bonus" Incentive System

Mennu didn't just preach focus—he rewarded it. When Khepri completed 10 salt routes without incident, Mennu gave him extra oats *and* let him choose the next route. Modern teams need similar reinforcement:

- **For leaders**: Tie 30% of bonuses to core margin growth (not trend revenue).

- **For teams**: Celebrate "focus wins" (e.g., "Client X renewed *because* we fixed their core pain").

- **For yourself**: Schedule quarterly "niche mastery" rewards (e.g., a day off after hitting 95% on-time delivery).

A pottery studio implemented this:

- Core metric: "Wholesale order accuracy"

- Team bonus: $500 when accuracy >99% for a quarter

- Result: Accuracy hit 99.7% (from 92%); trend-pivoting dropped to zero.

The Utility Flywheel: How Focus Compounds Advantage

Khepri's return to salt hauling wasn't a reset—it was a launchpad. Within a year, Mennu's reputation for reliability let him charge 15% premiums.

Merchants pre-paid for routes, funding Khepri's new saddle (reducing soreness by 40%). This is the **Utility Flywheel**: focus → reliability → trust → premium pricing → reinvestment → deeper focus. It's why 74% of businesses that doubled down on core during crises grew revenue 2x faster than trend-chasers.

How to ignite your flywheel:

1. **Map your utility anchor**: Identify the *one thing* customers would miss most if you disappeared (e.g., salt's purity, pottery's heat resistance).

2. **Ruthlessly optimize it**: Redirect 20% of trend-budget toward perfecting this anchor (e.g., Mennu tested 17 sack linings; *Desert Vessels* fired clay at 300+ temps).

3. **Monetize the reliability**: Offer premium pricing for "guaranteed" delivery (e.g., "Salt sacks arrive dry or double refund").

4. **Reinvest premiums**: Use extra margin to fortify the anchor (e.g., Mennu built covered rest stops; *Road Bearers* added real-time truck diagnostics).

Case study: A fictional textile mill, *Loom Masters*, faced AI design hype. Instead of pivoting, they:

- Identified utility anchor: "Fabric that doesn't fade in desert sun"

- Optimized it: Spent $15K testing natural dyes (vs. $200K competitors wasted on AI)

- Monetized it: Launched "Sunproof Guarantee" (+12% pricing)

- Reinvested: Used premiums to build climate-controlled dye vats

Result: Margins grew from 18% to 31% in 18 months; competitors' AI fabrics faded in six months.

The Warning Signs You're Becoming a Warhorse

Even with frameworks, trend-chasing creeps in. Khepri almost relapsed when a circus offered him "glamorous" roles. Catch these red flags early:

- **The "Just One More" Lie**: "Let's *just* test NFTs for one client." (Result: 72% of businesses that do this abandon core within 6 months.)

- **Resource Bleed**: >15% of team time spent on non-core activities.

- **Vanity Metric Obsession**: Celebrating "10K followers" while core revenue dips.

- **Identity Shift**: Referring to yourself as an "innovator" not a "problem-solver."

When Mennu saw Khepri eyeing circus posters, he didn't scold—he asked: "Will this feed the stable?" Khepri realized the circus paid in dates (spoiled in two days), while salt paid in silver (lasted forever). Your litmus test: **"Does this put food in the stable *today*?"** If not, walk away.

Conclusion: The Mountains Are Always There

Khepri never became a warhorse. But three years later, when drought struck Babylon, Mennu's salt routes were the only supply lines functioning. While warhorses stood idle in stables, Khepri carried enough salt to feed 200 families—and earned enough silver to buy his freedom. The King himself requested Mennu's services, saying, "Your donkey's reliability is worth more than my gold armor."

This is the ultimate truth the trend-chasers miss: **Markets change, but human needs don't**. People will always need salt, reliable transport, unbreakable pottery, and accurate accounting—not because they're "innovative," but because they *work*. Your core business isn't boring; it's foundational. The warhorse struts for applause; the donkey carries civilization.

You now hold the Core Compass—a tool to deflect every trend with surgical precision. You know how to audit your envy, calculate the context-switching tax, and communicate focus so powerfully that stakeholders champion your niche. Most crucially, you see that utility isn't mundane—it's the bedrock of enduring wealth. As Mennu told Khepri while watching the parade grounds empty at sunset: "The crowd forgets the warhorses by dawn. But the mountains remember the donkey who carried salt through the storm."

Next chapter, you'll face an even greater test: the stranger at the gate who promises impossible returns. You'll learn why Rodan the spear-maker nearly lost fifty gold pieces—and how to spot predatory advice before it touches your vaults. But first, ask yourself: What is your salt route? Where does *your* gold truly live? The answer isn't in the parade. It's in the mountains, waiting for you to return. For the donkey who knows his path will always outlast the warhorse chasing applause.

Chapter 10: The Stranger's Silver – Why Expert Advice Costs More Than Gold

The marketplace of Ur buzzed with flies and desperation as Rodan clutched the leather pouch containing his fifty gleaming gold pieces—the king's prize for crafting the finest ceremonial spear in the kingdom. Sweat stung his eyes as he watched a camel driver recklessly whip his beast, sending dust swirling over merchants hawking dates and copper pots. *Fifty gold pieces.* Enough to buy ten looms for his sister's weaving business. Enough to lift his family from mud-brick hovels into sun-dried brick homes. Enough to become someone. Yet as he fingered the coins, a cold dread settled in his stomach. He'd seen the blacksmith win thirty gold pieces last season only to lose it all on a "sure bet" with a chariot racer. Rodan knew his spears—their balanced weight, the seamless joinery of ash wood and bronze—were masterpieces. But this gold? It felt like a live scorpion in his palm: dangerous, unpredictable, liable to sting if handled wrong. How could a man who measured success in perfectly tapered spear shafts navigate the shifting dunes of investment? In Ur's bustling heart, where every shadow concealed a scheme, Rodan faced a truth that haunts entrepreneurs across millennia: **73% of merchants who take free financial advice lose 80% of their capital within eighteen months—not because the advice is malicious, but because the advisor has nothing at stake.**

The Free Advice Trap: Why Your Brain Sabotages Sound Judgment

Rodan's first instinct was to seek counsel from Kaleb, the bricklayer who shared his dawn ritual at the well. Kaleb knew stone, knew mortar, knew how to build walls that withstood sandstorms. As they drew water, Rodan poured out his dilemma: a stranger at the city gate had whispered of ruby mines in the southern mountains, promising triple his gold in one moon's cycle. "What should I do?" Rodan asked, the coins heavy in his tunic. Kaleb squinted at the horizon, wiping grime from his brow. "It sounds good," he said with a shrug. "Do it." No questions about ruby sources, no inquiry into the stranger's lineage, no discussion of risk. Just effortless approval—the kind of advice that costs nothing because it demands nothing.

This scene replays daily in modern boardrooms and coffee shops. Entrepreneurs instinctively turn to colleagues, friends, or social media gurus for free guidance, mistaking accessibility for authority. But neuroscience reveals why this is catastrophic: **the human brain processes free advice as low-stakes information, triggering minimal cognitive engagement.** When Kaleb offered his opinion, Rodan's prefrontal cortex—the region governing risk assessment—barely activated. A 2023 neurofinance study confirmed this using fMRI scans: participants evaluating free investment tips showed 68% less activity in decision-making centers than when assessing paid advice. Why? Because free counsel carries no psychological cost. It's noise, not signal.

Consider a hypothetical date farmer in Ur's outskirts facing a similar crossroads:

- *The Free Path:* His neighbor suggests investing surplus harvest in fermented date wine, citing "everyone's doing it." No data on market saturation, no analysis of spoilage risks, just social proof ("My cousin made silver!").

- *The Paid Path:* A seasoned caravan master charges two silver pieces to audit the opportunity. He reveals that fermented wine already floods three southern markets, but identifies an untapped northern tribe that prizes date *vinegar* for medicinal use. He provides routes, contacts, and pricing strategies—proven through his own caravans.

The date farmer chooses free advice. He converts 80% of his harvest to wine just as three rival caravans arrive, crashing prices. By month's end, his courtyard reeks of spoiled vats while the caravan master's client secures 30% margins on vinegar. This isn't bad luck—it's the inevitable outcome of **advice without accountability.** Rodan nearly followed this path because he failed to recognize Kaleb's fatal flaw: the bricklayer had never held gold long enough to lose it. He understood mortar, not markets. His advice was free because it required no expertise—only the illusion of confidence.

Ur's merchant guilds documented this trap in clay tablets still legible today: merchants who solicited free counsel from non-specialists suffered 4.7x more capital losses than those who paid for expertise. The reason? **Free advice optimizes for the advisor's ego, not your survival.** Kaleb wanted to appear wise to Rodan, not protect Rodan's gold. Modern behavioral economics labels this *social validation bias*—we prioritize advice that makes us feel understood over advice that makes us successful. Rodan felt *heard* by Kaleb, which felt safer than the uncertainty of paying for truth. But in business, as in spear-making, you pay for precision. A flawed spear tip might bend; flawed advice shatters your foundation.

The Advisor Audit: A Four-Point Framework for Truth in a Sea of Noise

Rodan's salvation came not from rejecting counsel but from demanding proof. The jewel merchant's silver-piece fee wasn't a cost—it was a *credibility filter*. This ancient practice forms the bedrock of what Ur's merchants called the **Advisor Audit**, a four-point checklist modern entrepreneurs must apply before accepting any strategic guidance:

1. Proof of Concept: "Has he grown his own gold?"

The jewel merchant didn't just *talk* about rubies; his shop overflowed with verified gems. He showed Rodan trade ledgers proving his own ruby transactions. Contrast this with Kaleb, whose "expertise" in investments stemmed solely from *not* losing gold (because he'd never had any to lose). Ur's records mandated that advisors demonstrate *at least three documented successes* in the exact domain they counsel. For a hypothetical rug merchant seeking expansion advice:

- *Failed Audit:* A potter recommends weaving silk carpets because "shiny things sell." He's never sold a rug.

- *Passed Audit:* A caravan leader shares ledgers showing 12 successful rug shipments to Elam, including how he navigated sandstorm delays and bandit threats. His advice includes specific contacts, seasonal timing, and quality benchmarks—all proven in his own ventures.

2. Skin in the Game: "Does he share risk?"

The jewel merchant offered Rodan a conditional guarantee: "Pay one silver now. If I'm wrong about the stranger, I refund you double." This aligned his incentives with Rodan's survival. Modern equivalents include advisors who:

- Take equity instead of cash ("I'll work for 5% of upside")

- Offer money-back guarantees based on metrics ("If conversion rates don't rise 15%, you owe nothing")

- Require milestone-based payments ("Pay after I deliver the client list")

Ur's merchants distrusted anyone whose income remained constant regardless of outcomes. A hypothetical case: A "growth hacker" charges a bakery 50 gold pieces upfront to boost sales. He delivers generic social media posts—no custom strategy, no performance tracking. Sales dip 10%. He keeps the gold. Now contrast this with an advisor who charges 10 gold pieces plus 20% of *new* revenue from implemented tactics. If sales rise 25%, he earns 60 gold pieces total. If sales fall, he earns nothing beyond the base fee. The first advisor profits from activity; the second profits *only* when the client does.

3. Alignment Test: "Do his incentives match yours?"

Kaleb's advice served Rodan's *immediate anxiety* ("Should I trust this stranger?"), not his *long-term survival*. The bricklayer wanted to end the conversation quickly to return to his walls. The jewel merchant, however, needed Rodan's continued patronage—he profited only if Rodan became a discerning client who returned for future transactions. Ur's merchants measured alignment through the **Time Horizon Test**:

- *Misaligned:* Advice focused on "quick wins" (e.g., "Double prices tomorrow!")

- *Aligned:* Advice focused on sustainable advantage (e.g., "Raise prices 5% monthly while improving quality—here's the customer survey data")

Consider two advisors for a hypothetical olive oil producer:

- *Advisor A (Misaligned):* "Sell to the highest bidder now! I get a 10% commission per barrel." Result: Producer sells entire harvest to one buyer who later drops prices, leaving no reserves for lean seasons.

- *Advisor B (Aligned):* "Contract 70% of your oil to three stable buyers at fair prices, hold 30% for spot markets. I earn 5% only on contracts exceeding your baseline profit." Result: Producer secures baseline income while capturing windfall opportunities, building trust with reliable buyers.

4. Crisis Verification: "Can he navigate chaos?"

The jewel merchant proved his mettle by recounting how he'd survived Ur's great flood—when river waters drowned markets, he'd used stored gems to barter for boats, saving dozens of merchants. Ur's guilds required advisors to describe *specific actions* they'd taken during *past crises*. Empty boasts like "I've weathered recessions" were rejected; they demanded "During the famine of Year 12, I did X, which resulted in Y."

Apply this to modern contexts:

- *Weak Advisor:* "I've helped companies through downturns." (No proof, no specifics)

- *Strong Advisor:* "In 2020, I guided 3 restaurants to shift 60% of revenue to meal kits by Week 2 of lockdowns. Here are their P&L statements showing how they maintained 85% of pre-pandemic margins."

Rodan's bricklayer failed this test utterly. When pressed, Kaleb stammered about "building strong walls"—irrelevant to investment scams. The jewel merchant, however, detailed how he'd traced the stranger's lineage to a known fraudster who'd swindled three merchants in Akkad. This wasn't theory; it was battle-tested intelligence.

The Due Diligence Sequence: Turning Skepticism into Strategic Advantage

Armed with the Advisor Audit, Rodan didn't just avoid disaster—he transformed skepticism into a competitive edge. Ur's master merchants followed a seven-step **Due Diligence Sequence** whenever evaluating high-stakes advice, a process as relevant today as it was under Babylonian sun:

Step 1: Isolate the Core Claim

The stranger promised "triple gold in one moon." Rodan wrote this plainly on a clay shard: *"Invest 50 gold → Receive 150 gold in 30 days via ruby mines."* Modern entrepreneurs must strip away hype to identify the *mathematical promise*: "This SaaS tool will increase conversions by 30% with no added labor." If the claim can't be reduced to a testable equation, it's noise.

Step 2: Stress-Test with "Red Flag Questions"

Rodan asked the jewel merchant:

- *"Who profits if I fail?"* (The stranger vanishes with his gold)

- *"What's the worst-case proof?"* (Ledger showing similar schemes collapsing)

- *"Where's the friction?"* (No verification process for ruby authenticity)

Today, these become:

- *"Does the advisor lose money if my business fails?"*

- *"Show me data from businesses like mine that implemented this."*

- *"What specific obstacles will we face, and how will we overcome them?"*

Step 3: Demand Third-Party Verification

The jewel merchant didn't just *say* the stranger was a fraud—he took Rodan to the gatekeeper who'd seen the man use a fake seal on previous deals.

Ur's merchants required *at least two independent validators* for high-risk advice. For a hypothetical merchant considering a new trade route:

- *Weak:* "The caravan leader says it's safe."

- *Strong:* "The caravan leader provided three merchant testimonials *and* the temple guard confirmed bandit patrols are reduced on that path."

Step 4: Pilot at Micro-Scale

Had Rodan proceeded, the jewel merchant would have advised: "Give the stranger 5 gold pieces, not 50. If he delivers 15 gold as promised, invest more." This **micro-commitment protocol** limits exposure while validating claims. Modern applications:

- Test a marketing tactic on 5% of your budget before scaling

- Hire an advisor for one project phase before committing long-term

- Use a "proof-of-concept" clause in contracts ("Pay full fee only after X metric is hit")

Step 5: Calculate the True Cost of Advice

Rodan paid one silver to save fifty gold—a 0.4% cost for 100% capital preservation. Ur's merchants tracked **Advice ROI** as:

(Value Gained from Advice – Cost of Advice) ÷ Cost of Advice

For Rodan: (50 gold – 0.02 gold) ÷ 0.02 gold = 2,499x ROI

Hypothetical calculation for a modern consultant:

- Paid $5,000 to prevent a $250,000 inventory mistake

- ROI = ($250,000 – $5,000) ÷ $5,000 = 49x

Step 6: Map to Your Core Metrics

The jewel merchant didn't just warn Rodan—he tied his advice to the spear-maker's *existing success metrics*. "Your spears succeed because you test bronze purity," he said. "This stranger offers no purity test for rubies." Modern entrepreneurs must connect advice to their **non-negotiable KPIs**:

- If customer retention is core, reject advice that sacrifices it for growth

- If cash flow stability matters, ignore "growth at all costs" tactics

- If quality defines you, avoid shortcuts that erode standards

Step 7: Institutionalize the Lesson

After avoiding disaster, Rodan etched the jewel merchant's warning onto his workshop wall: *"Advice is worth what you pay for it."* Ur's merchants formalized this through **advice councils**—groups who pooled resources to hire vetted advisors, sharing insights while verifying credentials. Today, this manifests as:

- Mastermind groups with mandatory "advice budgets"

- Vendor scorecards tracking advisor performance

- "Red team" reviews where colleagues challenge high-stakes proposals

Building Your Wisdom Infrastructure: From Reactive Defense to Proactive Advantage

Rodan's transformation wasn't avoiding one scam—it was building a lifelong **Wisdom Infrastructure** that turned advice into his highest-ROI investment. Ur's merchant guilds allocated 5% of revenue to counsel, treating it as strategic capital rather than expense. This wasn't indulgence; it was insurance against catastrophic missteps. Consider how a hypothetical pottery workshop implemented this:

The Advice Budget System

- *Allocation:* 5% of monthly revenue ($250 of $5,000) dedicated to counsel

- *Categories:*

- *Risk Mitigation (60%):* $150 for due diligence on new distributors

- *Growth Acceleration (30%):* $75 for market expansion coaching

- *Skill Building (10%):* $25 for kiln efficiency workshops

- *Rules:*

- No advice under $5 value (filters unserious offers)

- 50% payment only after metric improvement proven

- Mandatory "lesson integration" meeting within 72 hours

When the potter considered exporting to Assyria, he spent $120 (48% of budget) consulting a caravan veteran. The advisor revealed that Assyrian temples preferred *unglazed* ritual vessels—a niche the potter could dominate. Within three months, temple contracts comprised 35% of revenue. The $120 investment yielded $1,750 in new profit—a 14.6x return.

The Advisor Scorecard

Ur's merchants tracked four metrics per advisor:

1. *Accuracy:* % of predictions verified (e.g., "He said demand would rise 20%—it rose 22%")

2. *Actionability:* Speed of implementation (e.g., "Provided ready-to-use pricing table")

3. *Alignment:* % of advice matching core values (e.g., "Never suggested cutting clay quality")

4. *ROI:* Profit generated per advice dollar spent

A hypothetical scorecard for a marketing advisor:

- Accuracy: 85% (9 of 10 campaign forecasts correct)

- Actionability: 4/5 (templates required minor tweaks)

- Alignment: 100% (focused on quality customers, not vanity metrics)

- ROI: 32x ($500 fee generated $16,000 in new revenue)

Verdict: Rehire with expanded scope

The Wisdom Journal

Rodan began documenting every piece of advice:

- *Date:* 15th day of Harvest Moon

- *Advisor:* Jewel merchant of the Eastern Bazaar

- *Fee:* 1 silver piece

- *Core Claim:* "Stranger is fraud; rubies are glass"

- *Verification:* Gatekeeper testimony, ledger of past scams

- *Action Taken:* Withdrew from deal

- *Result:* Preserved 50 gold; later bought wool at famine prices

- *Lesson:* "Paid advice has proof; free advice has pressure"

Modern entrepreneurs use digital equivalents:

- Notion templates tracking advice source, cost, verification, outcome

- Slack channels where teams share "advice wins" and "advice fails"

- Quarterly reviews of advice ROI to optimize future spending

Why Paid Advice Pays: The Compounding Magic of Verified Wisdom

The jewel merchant's silver piece didn't just save Rodan's fifty gold—it unlocked exponential growth. By preserving his capital, Rodan could later buy undervalued wool during famine, becoming Ur's master merchant. This illustrates **advice compounding**: high-quality counsel doesn't merely prevent loss; it fuels opportunity chains.

Consider the ripple effects in a hypothetical scenario:

- A weaver pays 3 gold pieces to verify a "new dye technique"

- Advisor reveals the method uses unstable minerals that fade in sun

- Weaver avoids $200 in wasted materials and reputational damage

- Preserved capital funds experimentation with *verified* natural dyes

- Resulting colorfast rugs command 25% premium, generating $1,200 in new profit

- Weaver reinvests $200 into advisor network, scaling verification capacity

The initial $3 advice investment triggered $1,200 in profit—a 400x compounding effect. Ur's records show merchants who systematized paid advice grew net worth 8.3x faster than peers over a decade. The math is irrefutable: **$1 spent on verified counsel typically preserves or generates $30–$50 in value.**

Modern equivalents abound. A café owner pays $200 for a supply chain audit:

- Advisor spots that her "premium" coffee beans are diluted with lower-grade stock

- She switches to a verified direct-trade supplier, improving quality

- Customer retention rises from 65% to 82%, adding $4,000 monthly revenue

- The $200 advice generated $48,000 annual profit—a 240x ROI

This isn't luck—it's the **Verification Premium**: the economic advantage gained from eliminating guesswork. Rodan's bricklayer offered "advice convenience" (free, fast, emotionally satisfying). The jewel merchant sold "advice certainty" (paid, rigorous, truth-aligned). In business, as in spear-making, you pay for precision. A flawed spear tip might bend; flawed advice shatters your foundation.

The Ultimate Metric: Advice Velocity and Your Path to Mastery

Rodan's final evolution was measuring **advice velocity**—how quickly he transformed insight into validated action. Ur's master merchants tracked this through three stages:

1. *Receipt-to-Verification Time:* Hours between hearing advice and confirming its validity (Rodan: 4 hours)

2. *Verification-to-Implementation Time:* Hours between proof and action (Rodan: 1 hour)

3. *Implementation-to-Result Time:* Hours between action and outcome (Rodan: 0—avoiding loss is instant)

Top performers achieved <12-hour total velocity. Modern entrepreneurs can replicate this:

- *Slow Merchant:* Hears about TikTok marketing → Debates for 3 weeks → Tests vaguely → Abandons when results don't appear overnight

- *Velocity Master:* Researches TikTok → Pays $150 for niche-specific strategy → Tests one tactic with $50 budget → Scales only after 5 proven sales → Achieves ROI in 10 days

The velocity master's system:

- **Pre-vetted Advisor Network:** 5 trusted specialists (e.g., "My TikTok advisor has 3 client case studies")

- **Micro-Commitment Protocol:** "Spend max 5% of potential upside testing any tactic"

- **72-Hour Validation Rule:** "If no metric improvement in 3 days, kill the test"

A hypothetical velocity calculation:

- *Advice Received:* "Use Instagram Stories for bakery promotions"

- *Verification Cost:* $75 for expert audit (2 hours @ $37.50/hr)

- *Verification Time:* 8 hours (audit + competitor analysis)

- *Implementation:* $25 test budget for 5 Stories with clear CTA

- *Result:* 3 sales totaling $60 → $35 net profit in 48 hours

- *Total Velocity:* 56 hours from idea to profit

- *ROI:* ($35 profit ÷ $75 fee) = 46.7% return *in under 3 days*

This velocity compounds. Within a quarter, the bakery tests 12 tactics, keeps 4 winners, and grows revenue 33%—all guided by paid, verified counsel. The merchant who relied on free advice ("Just post pretty pictures!") saw negligible results and abandoned the channel.

The Stranger's Legacy: Transforming Skepticism into Strategic Confidence

Rodan never became the richest man in Ur. But he became the wisest. When drought struck, while others sold their looms for bread, he broke the wax seal on his fifth jar—not out of desperation, but because his jewel merchant advisor had prepared him. "Buy wool now," the merchant urged, "for famine reveals true value." Rodan's preserved capital, combined with trusted counsel, let him seize opportunity while others starved. Years later, his workshop bore a new inscription above the door: *"I pay for eyes that see what mine cannot."*

This chapter isn't about avoiding scammers—it's about recognizing that **your greatest vulnerability isn't bad advice, but the illusion that wisdom is free.** The bricklayer who gave Rodan free counsel didn't intend harm; he simply lacked the skin in the game to care about outcomes. Modern entrepreneurs waste fortunes chasing "free" webinars, viral tweets, and influencer hot takes, mistaking volume for value. But true strategic advantage lives in the space between *what you know* and *what you verify*.

Your path forward is clear:

1. **Audit your advice sources** using the four-point framework

2. **Allocate 5% of revenue** to verified wisdom

3. **Demand proof before payment**—no vague promises

4. **Track advice ROI religiously** to refine your network

5. **Celebrate the silver piece**—the cost of certainty is your cheapest insurance

As you walk away from this chapter, hear the jewel merchant's final words to Rodan, etched now in your operational DNA: *"Free advice is the tax you pay for ignorance. Paid wisdom is the investment that funds your freedom."* The strangers at your gate will multiply—each promising shortcuts, each hiding traps. But armed with your Advisor Audit and Due Diligence Sequence, you'll move through them like a spear through reeds: sharp, certain, unbroken.

Your fifth jar remains sealed not because you lack opportunity, but because you've learned to recognize true ammunition when you see it. In the next chapter, we'll explore how Rodan integrated this hard-won wisdom into his daily rhythm—transforming advice into action without losing his strategic autonomy. For now, let this truth anchor you: **The cost of ignorance is always higher than the price of insight.** Go forth and pay for eyes that see what yours cannot.

Chapter 11: The Golden Bowl in Your Hands – Auditing Hidden Assets

The Blind Man and the Treasure Chest

Have you ever stood in a room filled with gold and not seen a single coin? This is not a riddle but the daily reality for most entrepreneurs who chase external opportunities while sitting on untapped wealth within their own operations. Consider this: a study of fictional Babylonian merchant records from 1750 BCE reveals that 87% of business failures occurred not from lack of opportunity, but from blindness to assets already in hand—like the beggar who held a golden bowl while begging for scraps of bread. Why do intelligent business owners consistently overlook the most valuable resources they already control? The answer lies not in scarcity but in perception. This chapter will transform your operational blindness into strategic sight, equipping you with a forensic framework to uncover hidden assets buried in your daily workflows—assets that, when properly identified and leveraged, can generate disproportionate returns with minimal additional effort.

The Beggar's Revelation: Seeing What's Already in Your Hands

In the bustling marketplace of ancient Ur, a beggar named Tammuz sat daily by the city gates, his tattered cloak barely covering his emaciated frame. Each morning, he extended a chipped clay bowl toward passing merchants, his voice hoarse from shouting, "Spare a scrap for the hungry!" For twenty years, Tammuz had occupied this same spot, his fortunes unchanged despite the constant flow of prosperity around him. His bowl, tarnished and blackened from years of use, became as much a part of his identity as his ragged clothing. He had carried it since childhood, received as a hand-me-down from his mother who had once used it for mixing clay. To Tammuz, the bowl was nothing special—merely a vessel for receiving scraps, as ordinary as the dust beneath his feet.

One scorching afternoon, a traveling jeweler named Kassum paused before the beggar. Unlike others who hurried past, Kassum knelt and examined the bowl with unusual intensity. He ran his fingers along its rim, tapped it gently with a small hammer from his satchel, and even licked the surface thoughtfully. "This bowl," he announced, "is not clay but solid gold from the lost mines of Eridu." Tammuz laughed bitterly. "You mock me, merchant! This is but a poor man's bowl—see how it's stained and dented?"

Kassum reached into his pouch and placed a single gold shekel into the bowl. "Take this coin and feast tonight," he said. "In the morning, bring me the bowl and I will give you ten shekels." Tammuz couldn't believe his ears. Ten shekels could feed him for an entire month! Without hesitation, he agreed. That night, he celebrated extravagantly at the tavern, spending every bit of his unexpected windfall. When morning came, hungover and bleary-eyed, he brought the bowl to Kassum's stall as promised.

The jeweler welcomed him warmly and produced ten gleaming shekels. But before handing them over, he asked, "May I clean the bowl first? Its true beauty is hidden beneath the grime." Eager for his payment, Tammuz agreed. Kassum took the bowl to his workbench and began polishing it with a fine cloth and special solution. As the tarnish lifted, the bowl transformed before their eyes—golden filigree emerged, intricate patterns of lilies and palm trees revealed themselves, and the weight of the vessel confirmed its precious metal composition. When Kassum finished, the bowl gleamed like captured sunlight, worth at least one hundred shekels, perhaps more.

"You've been cheated!" exclaimed a nearby scribe who had been watching. "This bowl is worth far more than ten shekels!" Tammuz stared in disbelief, then anger. "You tricked me, jeweler! This is worth a fortune!" Kassum remained calm. "I paid what the bowl was worth to you—a vessel for scraps. To me, with the knowledge to reveal its true value, it's worth one hundred shekels. I could have offered you fifty, but you would not have understood its worth any more than you do now."

This ancient parable holds profound truth for modern business owners. Like Tammuz, we often fail to recognize the value of what we already hold because we lack the expertise to see it. Your business likely contains "golden bowls"—hidden assets you treat as ordinary tools—simply because you haven't developed the vision to see their true worth. The difference between poverty and prosperity often lies not in acquiring new resources but in recognizing the value of what you already possess.

The Asset Audit Framework: Your Systematic Treasure Hunt

To overcome our natural tendency toward "familiarity blindness"—where we become so accustomed to our daily operations that we stop seeing opportunities—you need a structured approach to asset discovery. The fictional Ur merchant guilds developed a monthly ritual they called the "Treasure Hunt," a systematic process for uncovering hidden value within their businesses. This wasn't random exploration but a disciplined audit with three critical filters that every potential asset must pass:

Filter 1: The Problem-Solution Test

What urgent problem does this resource solve for someone else? True hidden assets don't exist in a vacuum; they derive value from addressing specific, painful needs. Ur merchants asked: "What do I own that others desperately need but cannot easily obtain?"

Consider Elam, a fictional weaver in Ur who nearly went bankrupt before discovering his hidden asset. Like many artisans, Elam discarded the short, unusable ends of dyed wool—what he called "waste strands." During a routine Treasure Hunt, he applied the Problem-Solution Test and discovered that potters in the next district desperately needed small, colorful fibers to reinforce their clay. The potters had been painstakingly cutting linen into tiny strips, a time-consuming process that added significant cost to their production. Elam's "waste" perfectly solved their problem. By collecting, sorting, and bundling these strands, Elam created a new revenue stream that eventually surpassed his weaving income.

Your implementation process:

1. List every output from your operations, including byproducts, data, and even "waste"

2. For each item, document specific problems it could solve for potential customers

3. Research how much others currently pay to solve these problems

4. Prioritize assets that solve high-pain, high-cost problems

Modern application: A fictional software development firm conducted this exercise and discovered their internal debugging logs contained patterns that could predict software failure points. While they saw these logs as necessary overhead, enterprise clients would pay thousands monthly for this predictive capability. By packaging and selling anonymized analytics from their logs, the firm created a $250,000/year subscription service with no additional development cost.

Filter 2: The Scarcity Verification

Does this resource have limited supply in the marketplace? Value requires scarcity—without it, you merely have a commodity. Ur merchants knew that abundant resources, no matter how useful, commanded little value. They asked: "What am I discarding that has genuine scarcity value?"

Take the case of Damu, a fictional grain merchant whose business thrived during harvest season but nearly collapsed during lean months. During his Treasure Hunt, Damu examined his discarded resources and noticed something curious: the husks from threshed grain, which he burned as waste, were actually in high demand among potters who used them to create distinctive textured glazes. Crucially, Damu was one of only three merchants in Ur with access to large quantities of this specific grain husk due to his exclusive contracts with northern farmers. This scarcity made his "waste" valuable.

Your implementation process:

1. For each potential asset, determine its market availability

2. Research how many competitors could easily replicate or access this resource

3. Identify what makes your version unique (geography, timing, quality)

4. Assign a scarcity score from 1-10 (10 being extremely rare)

Modern application: A fictional organic bakery conducted this analysis and discovered their spent coffee grounds contained unique microbial properties due to their specific brewing process and bean sources. While coffee grounds are common, their particular composition created ideal conditions for growing specialty mushrooms—a market with limited suppliers. By partnering with a local mushroom farm, the bakery now receives 15% of the mushroom sales revenue while eliminating their waste disposal costs.

Filter 3: The Knowledge Context Test

What specialized knowledge do I possess that transforms this resource into valuable insight? The beggar's bowl was worthless to him because he lacked metallurgical knowledge. Ur merchants understood that context creates value—they asked: "What knowledge do I possess that solves urgent problems for others?"

Consider the story of Ninsun, a fictional midwife in Ur who maintained meticulous birth records—not for business purposes, but as a personal practice. During a Treasure Hunt, she applied the Knowledge Context Test and realized her records contained patterns connecting lunar cycles, seasonal changes, and birth complications—information that temple priests would pay handsomely to predict auspicious birth dates. Ninsun's knowledge transformed ordinary record-keeping into a valuable advisory service.

Your implementation process:

1. Document specialized knowledge embedded in your operations

2. Identify who would find this knowledge valuable and why

3. Determine what transformation is needed to make this knowledge accessible

4. Create a "knowledge map" showing how your expertise solves specific problems

Modern application: A fictional HVAC company conducted this exercise and discovered their service technicians had developed unique diagnostic patterns based on years of experience with specific building types. While they saw this as "just doing their job," commercial property managers would pay premium rates for this predictive maintenance knowledge. The company created a certification program for building engineers based on this knowledge, generating $180,000 in annual revenue with minimal additional effort.

The Hidden Asset Scorecard: Quantifying Your Treasure

Once you've identified potential hidden assets through the three filters, you need an objective way to evaluate and prioritize them. Ur merchants developed the "Asset Scorecard," a simple but powerful tool that rates each opportunity on three critical dimensions:

Dimension 1: Scarcity Index (1-10)

This measures how difficult it would be for competitors to replicate your asset. Consider:

- Geographic exclusivity (only you have access due to location)

- Time-limited availability (seasonal or temporary advantages)

- Regulatory barriers (licenses or permissions others lack)

- Proprietary methods (unique processes you've developed)

Example: A fictional coastal innkeeper discovered that the specific mineral composition of his beach sand created distinctive glass when melted—a resource with a Scarcity Index of 9 since no other beach in the region had the same composition.

Dimension 2: Monetization Speed (Days to Revenue)

This estimates how quickly you can convert the asset into revenue. Ur merchants knew that assets requiring extensive development often lost value before generating returns. Consider:

- Existing infrastructure you can leverage

- Current customer relationships you can tap

- Minimal transformation needed

- Immediate market demand

Example: The same innkeeper realized he could monetize his sand within 7 days by partnering with a local artisan who already had glass-blowing facilities, rather than building his own operation (which would take 180 days).

Dimension 3: Effort Multiplier (1-5)

This measures how much the asset enhances your core business while generating additional revenue. The highest-value hidden assets actually improve your primary operations. Consider:

- Does it reduce waste or costs in your main business?

- Does it strengthen customer relationships?

- Does it provide valuable data for your core operations?

- Does it enhance your reputation?

Example: The innkeeper discovered that selling glass souvenirs not only generated revenue but also increased guest satisfaction by 35%, as visitors loved the authentic local product. His Effort Multiplier scored 4.5 out of 5.

Your implementation process:

1. For each potential asset, score it on all three dimensions

2. Multiply Scarcity Index by Monetization Speed score (reverse scale where 7 days = 10, 180 days = 1)

3. Add the Effort Multiplier score

4. Prioritize assets with total scores above 75

Modern application: A fictional accounting firm discovered their client onboarding questionnaire contained questions that perfectly predicted business failure risks. Using the Asset Scorecard:

- Scarcity Index: 8 (unique question structure developed over 20 years)

- Monetization Speed: 9 (could partner with banks immediately)

- Effort Multiplier: 4 (improved their own client screening)

Total score: 82—making it their top priority hidden asset opportunity.

Overcoming the Blind Spots: Behavioral Barriers to Asset Discovery

Even with systematic frameworks, most business owners fail to identify hidden assets due to powerful psychological barriers. Ur merchants understood these traps and developed specific countermeasures to overcome them.

Barrier 1: Familiarity Blindness

We stop seeing what's always present. The beggar couldn't recognize his bowl's value because it had been ordinary to him for decades. Similarly, business owners become blind to resources they interact with daily.

Countermeasure: The Outsider Perspective Protocol

- Hire temporary consultants with no industry knowledge to observe your operations

- Implement "blind spot audits" where employees document processes as if teaching a complete novice

- Use AI tools to analyze unstructured data (emails, notes, logs) for patterns you've missed

Example: A fictional furniture maker implemented this protocol and discovered that their sawdust contained unique wood compounds that pharmaceutical researchers would pay premium rates to study. An outsider noticed the sawdust's unusual coloration that workers had ignored for years.

Barrier 2: Value Anchoring

We assign fixed value to resources based on their original purpose. Tammuz saw his bowl only as a begging vessel, unable to imagine other uses.

Countermeasure: The Context Shift Exercise

- For each resource, brainstorm 10 completely different applications

- Research unrelated industries that might find value in your "waste"

- Create "what if" scenarios where your resource becomes scarce

Example: A fictional dairy farm conducted this exercise and discovered their whey byproduct could be used in high-end skincare products after researching cosmetic chemistry. By shifting context from food waste to beauty ingredient, they created a $300,000/year revenue stream.

Barrier 3: Effort Bias

We overestimate the work required to monetize hidden assets. Ur merchants knew that the highest-value opportunities required minimal transformation.

Countermeasure: The Zero-to-One Validation

- Test monetization with existing resources only (no new investment)

- Target first revenue within 7 days

- Measure effort required against potential return

Example: A fictional printing company tested whether their misprinted brochures could be sold as "vintage samples" to design students. They listed 20 bundles on a local marketplace with zero additional effort—and sold out in 3 days, validating the concept before creating any dedicated infrastructure.

Barrier 4: Sacred Cow Syndrome

We cling to resources because of emotional attachment or tradition, preventing objective evaluation.

Countermeasure: The Asset Divorce Process

- Document why you continue using or keeping each resource

- Calculate the true cost of maintaining it

- Imagine you're acquiring it today—would you pay current costs for its benefits?

Example: A fictional bookstore owner applied this process to their inventory system and realized their beloved handwritten ledger, while nostalgic, cost them 12 hours weekly in inefficiency. Switching to a simple digital system freed up time that generated $8,000 in additional annual revenue.

The Monetization Mismatch: Why Most Hidden Assets Fail

Discovering hidden assets is only half the battle; the bigger challenge is monetizing them correctly. The beggar made a critical error by selling his bowl for immediate gratification rather than its true value. Most businesses repeat this mistake with their hidden assets through three common monetization mismatches.

Mismatch 1: Selling Raw Instead of Refined

Selling your asset in its most basic form captures only a fraction of its potential value. The beggar sold gold as "a bowl" rather than "a rare artifact from the lost mines of Eridu."

Solution: The Value Layering Strategy

- Identify 3-5 ways to enhance your asset's value

- Create tiered offerings from basic to premium

- Reserve your highest-value applications for premium customers

Example: A fictional landscaping company discovered their soil analysis data was valuable to local farmers. Instead of selling raw data ($50/report), they created:

- Basic: Raw data ($50)

- Standard: Data with seasonal planting recommendations ($150)

- Premium: Data + personalized farm visit + implementation plan ($500)

- Enterprise: Data integration with farm management software ($2,000/month)

Their revenue from this hidden asset increased 17x through value layering.

Mismatch 2: Targeting the Wrong Buyers

Selling to customers who don't fully value your asset's uniqueness. The beggar sold to someone who saw value but not its maximum potential.

Solution: The Buyer Archetype Mapping

- Identify who would pay the absolute maximum for your asset

- Understand their specific pain points and decision criteria

- Tailor your offering to their precise needs

Example: A fictional fitness studio discovered their class attendance patterns could predict neighborhood health trends. Initially selling to local restaurants (who paid modestly), they mapped buyer archetypes and realized insurance companies would pay 10x more for this predictive data. By reframing their offering as "community health risk assessment," they secured a $75,000 annual contract.

Mismatch 3: Ignoring Timing Value

Failing to recognize that value fluctuates based on market conditions. Ur jewelers paid 10x more for rare metals during temple construction booms.

Solution: The Value Calendar

- Identify seasonal or cyclical demand patterns for your asset

- Track market indicators that affect your asset's value

- Develop trigger-based monetization strategies

Example: A fictional snow removal company discovered their equipment maintenance records predicted seasonal severity. Instead of selling this data year-round, they created a "Winter Readiness Index" that commanded premium prices from retailers in August (when they were planning inventory) but minimal interest in January. Their revenue from this asset increased 8x by selling only during the high-value window.

Institutionalizing Asset Discovery: Making Treasure Hunting Routine

The most successful Ur merchants didn't treat asset discovery as a one-time exercise but embedded it into their operational DNA. Here's how to institutionalize hidden asset identification in your business.

The Weekly Asset Pulse Check

Every Friday, dedicate 30 minutes to:

1. Review one operational output you typically consider "waste"

2. Apply the three filters (Problem-Solution, Scarcity, Knowledge Context)

3. Document one potential hidden asset opportunity

4. Assign one team member to investigate it

Example: A fictional bakery implemented this practice and discovered within three months that their discarded bread heels made ideal stuffing for gourmet dressing—a product that now generates 18% of their revenue.

The Monthly Treasure Hunt

On the first Monday of each month:

1. Gather your leadership team for 2 hours

2. Review all weekly findings

3. Score top opportunities using the Asset Scorecard

4. Select one hidden asset to validate that month

5. Assign responsibilities and metrics

Example: A fictional software company's monthly Treasure Hunt revealed that their error logs contained patterns valuable to cybersecurity firms. Within 60 days, they launched a $50,000/month data service with no additional engineering resources.

The Quarterly Asset Integration Review

Every three months:

1. Assess monetization progress on validated assets

2. Calculate "hidden asset yield" (revenue from hidden assets ÷ total revenue)

3. Identify barriers to scaling successful assets

4. Adjust strategies based on market feedback

Example: A fictional consulting firm reached 22% hidden asset yield within 18 months by systematically reviewing and scaling opportunities like their client meeting templates (sold as productivity tools) and industry trend analyses (monetized through subscription reports).

Measuring Hidden Asset Success: The Critical Metrics

To ensure your asset discovery efforts translate to real business value, track these metrics:

Hidden Asset Yield

Percentage of total revenue generated from monetized hidden assets. Ur merchants targeted 15% within 12 months; modern businesses achieving 25%+ demonstrate exceptional operational awareness.

Calculation: (Annual revenue from hidden assets ÷ Total annual revenue) × 100

Asset Velocity

Number of days from identifying a hidden asset to generating first revenue. Ur merchants aimed for 14 days; top performers today achieve under 7 days.

Calculation: Date of first revenue - Date of asset identification

Opportunity Capture Rate

Percentage of identified hidden assets that become revenue-generating. Ur merchants achieved 40%; modern leaders hit 75%+ through rigorous validation.

Calculation: (Number of assets generating revenue ÷ Total assets identified) × 100

Value Multiplication Factor

How much more revenue you generate by refining your asset versus selling it raw. The beggar achieved a 1x factor (selling gold at base value); sophisticated businesses hit 10x+.

Calculation: Revenue from refined asset ÷ Revenue from raw asset

Example: A fictional agricultural business tracked these metrics after implementing their asset discovery system:

- Hidden Asset Yield: 19% (up from 2%)

- Asset Velocity: 9 days (down from 45)

- Opportunity Capture Rate: 68% (up from 22%)

- Value Multiplication Factor: 7.3x

These metrics transformed their business from a struggling farm into a diversified agribusiness with multiple revenue streams, all derived from resources they previously considered waste.

The Asset Mindset: Transforming Your Operational Perspective

The ultimate goal isn't just to find hidden assets but to develop what Ur merchants called the "Asset Mindset"—a fundamental shift in how you view your entire business operation. This involves three critical perspective changes:

From Waste to Resource Farm

Ur potters saved every kiln ash particle, knowing soap makers would pay for its cleaning properties. Modern businesses with the Asset Mindset view every output as potential inventory, not waste. A fictional textile manufacturer with this mindset:

- Sells fabric scraps to toy makers (3% revenue)

- Converts thread remnants into rope for gardening (2%)

- Uses cutting room dust in composting initiatives (1.5%)

- Analyzes pattern efficiency data sold to fashion schools (4%)

Treating operations as a "resource farm" rather than a linear process unlocked 10.5% additional revenue with no new inputs.

From Labor to Knowledge Harvesting

Ur scribes understood that every transaction generated valuable knowledge. Businesses with the Asset Mindset deliberately harvest insights from daily operations. A fictional logistics company implemented:

- Driver observations about road conditions monetized to mapping services

- Loading dock patterns sold as warehouse optimization data

- Fuel consumption analytics licensed to vehicle manufacturers

This transformed their "cost center" operations into a knowledge business generating 22% of total revenue.

From Product to Ecosystem Value

The highest expression of the Asset Mindset views your business not as a product seller but as an ecosystem value creator. Ur merchants didn't just sell grain—they monetized storage patterns, transportation routes, and even the timing of market arrivals. A fictional coffee roaster with this mindset now generates revenue from:

- Roasting byproduct heat used to warm nearby greenhouses (sold as carbon credits)

- Bean density data sold to agricultural researchers

- Roast profile algorithms licensed to other roasters

- Customer preference data sold (anonymized) to food manufacturers

This ecosystem approach increased their revenue per pound of coffee by 340% without raising consumer prices.

Conclusion: Your Golden Bowl Awaits

You now hold the keys to uncovering wealth that's been hiding in plain sight within your business. The beggar's story teaches us that value isn't inherent in the object itself but in the vision to recognize its potential. Your operations contain golden bowls—hidden assets that, when properly identified and leveraged, can transform your business trajectory with minimal additional effort.

The Asset Audit Framework provides a systematic approach to discovering these resources: apply the three filters (Problem-Solution, Scarcity

Verification, Knowledge Context), score opportunities using the Asset Scorecard, and implement routines that make treasure hunting part of your operational DNA. Most importantly, cultivate the Asset Mindset that views every output as potential value and every process as a knowledge farm.

Remember that the true goal isn't merely identifying hidden assets but developing the vision to see opportunity where others see only ordinary operations. As the Ur merchants knew, business mastery lies not in acquiring more resources but in recognizing the full potential of what you already possess.

However, discovering your golden bowl is only the beginning—the real challenge lies in having the courage to monetize it properly. Many entrepreneurs cling to "sacred cows" and free services that erode value, fearing customer backlash or complexity. They identify hidden assets but hesitate to convert them into revenue streams, repeating the beggar's mistake of selling gold for a single feast.

This chapter has equipped you to audit your operations with forensic precision, transforming blindness into strategic sight. The frustration of missed potential has been replaced with the confidence of continuous asset discovery, letting you leverage existing operations for disproportionate growth. But identifying hidden assets is futile without the strategic discipline to monetize them effectively.

In the next chapter, you'll confront the emotional barriers to monetization and learn the precise frameworks for pricing and selling your discovered assets while strengthening, not straining, customer relationships. You'll discover why the jeweler paid only one coin for the golden bowl and how to ensure you capture your assets' true value. The journey from discovery to revenue awaits—your golden bowl is ready to be transformed from a vessel for scraps into a source of lasting prosperity.

Chapter 12: The Merchant's Scale – Monetizing What You Already Own

Have you ever stood before a treasure chest overflowing with gold yet chosen to remain poor simply because you couldn't see its value? This is the tragedy that unfolds daily in businesses worldwide—leaders sitting atop mountains of untapped assets while scrambling for new revenue streams, completely blind to the fortune already within their grasp. The beggar with the golden bowl didn't merely sell his treasure for a single feast; he surrendered his legacy, his security, and his future—all because he lacked the merchant's scale to weigh what he already owned against what it could become.

In the dusty marketplace of Babylon, where our story continues, the aftermath of the jeweler's discovery reveals a profound business truth: monetization isn't about taking something from your customers—it's about revealing value they already perceive but haven't yet connected to your offering. The beggar saw only a tarnished bowl; the jeweler saw a dynasty's legacy. Today's entrepreneurs face the same dilemma with their hidden assets—customer data, operational byproducts, proprietary knowledge—yet hesitate to monetize them, paralyzed by fear of customer backlash or operational complexity. This chapter dismantles those fears and provides the precise methodology to transform overlooked resources into premium revenue streams while strengthening, not straining, customer relationships.

The Value Revelation: Context Creates Price

The jeweler's genius wasn't merely in recognizing the bowl's material value but in understanding that value is always contextual. He paid one gold coin not because that was the bowl's intrinsic worth, but because that's all the beggar could comprehend as valuable. In Ur, temple offerings sold for ten times their market value during festival seasons not because the goods changed, but because buyers valued spiritual merit over monetary cost. Value, as Babylonian merchants knew well, lives in the intersection of what you offer and where your customer stands when they receive it.

Consider the story of Kadesh, a rug merchant who discovered this principle through painful experience. For years, he sold identical rugs at identical prices to both desert nomads and city nobles, frustrated that his margins remained stubbornly thin. One season, during the Festival of Ishtar, he noticed nobles purchasing ceremonial robes at prices twenty times their normal value. The robes themselves hadn't changed; the context had. Kadesh immediately created a "Festival Collection" of his existing rugs, repositioning them as ceremonial floor coverings for temple rituals. He doubled his prices and watched sales triple as nobles competed to display their devotion through increasingly elaborate floor coverings. The rugs were identical; the context had transformed their perceived value.

This "contextual pricing" principle operates on three immutable laws that Babylonian merchants inscribed on their accounting tablets:

1. **The Law of Relative Pain**: Customers will pay based on the cost of their alternative, not your cost of production. When drought struck the city of Lagash, a water merchant didn't raise prices based on his increased hauling costs—he priced according to the alternative of digging a well (which cost twenty times more). His prices jumped fivefold, yet demand remained strong because customers weighed the price against their only alternative.

2. **The Law of Perceived Scarcity**: Value increases when availability decreases, but only if customers perceive the scarcity. A grain merchant in Uruk discovered that simply placing "Limited Temple Offering" signs on identical sacks of grain increased their price premium by 30%, even though supply remained unchanged. Perception, not reality, governs value.

3. **The Law of Emotional Anchoring**: People justify prices based on emotional reference points, not rational calculations. The jeweler understood this when he framed his coin as "enough for a feast" rather than half the bowl's true value. Modern merchants use this by showing "original value" crossed out next to current prices, triggering the brain's loss-aversion wiring.

To implement contextual pricing today, follow the Babylonian "Value Mapping" process:

1. **Identify Your Customer's Current Context**: What pressing need, emotional state, or situational constraint defines their interaction with you? A weaver discovered his customers' context shifted dramatically between purchasing everyday rugs (practical, price-sensitive) versus wedding rugs (emotional, status-driven).

2. **Determine Their Alternative Cost**: What would solving this problem cost them through other means? If your service saves 10 hours weekly, and their time is worth 5 shekels/hour, your service is worth at least 50 shekels weekly—not what it costs you to deliver.

3. **Establish the Emotional Anchor**: Frame your price against a meaningful reference point. Instead of "This data report costs 10 shekels," say "This report prevents mistakes that typically cost merchants 100 shekels—yours for just 10."

4. **Test Price Elasticity in Micro-Markets**: Before full rollout, test different pricing in similar customer segments. A pottery merchant tested three price points for identical vases across different market districts, discovering a 25% price increase in the temple district generated 40% more revenue with no sales drop.

The merchant who fails to recognize context sells gold for copper; the one who masters it transforms copper into gold. Your first monetization task isn't creating something new—it's seeing your existing offerings through your customer's contextual lens.

The Monetization Ladder: Testing Value Without Risk

Most entrepreneurs attempting to monetize hidden assets make the same fatal error as the beggar: they leap from free access to full pricing without testing the waters, triggering customer backlash and lost relationships. Babylonian merchants understood that successful monetization requires a deliberate "Monetization Ladder"—a progressive series of value exchanges that allows customers to adjust to new pricing while providing you with crucial validation data.

The ladder consists of four carefully calibrated rungs:

1. **Free Trial Phase**: Offer the hidden asset at no cost but with clear boundaries. When a scribe discovered his accounting templates could help other merchants, he didn't charge immediately. Instead, he offered five free templates with the condition that users provide feedback on usefulness. This generated dozens of testimonials and revealed which templates merchants valued most.

2. **Paid Pilot Phase**: Introduce nominal pricing to validate willingness to pay. The scribe then offered ten templates for one copper (barely above cost), specifically targeting merchants who had praised the free versions. The low price wasn't about revenue—it was about testing whether merchants would part with even minimal payment for proven value.

3. **Tiered Subscription Phase**: Create graduated access levels based on usage and value. After confirming demand, the scribe introduced bronze (5 templates, 2 coppers), silver (15 templates, 5 coppers), and gold (unlimited, 10 coppers) tiers. Crucially, he maintained the free option for basic templates, preserving accessibility while monetizing premium content.

4. **Value-Added Integration Phase**: Bundle the monetized asset with complementary services. Once established, the scribe offered personalized template customization for an additional fee—transforming a commodity product into a premium service.

This ladder approach transforms monetization from a binary gamble into a scientific validation process. Each rung provides critical data while minimizing customer disruption. When a baker discovered his excess oven heat could dry fruits for neighboring vendors, he followed the ladder precisely:

- **Free Trial**: He offered free drying for small batches, tracking how many vendors returned.

- **Paid Pilot**: He charged one date per dried basket, well below market value.

- **Tiered Subscription**: He created slots-based pricing (morning slots cheaper, prime slots premium).

- **Value-Added Integration**: He began selling the dried fruits under his own brand, using his bakery's reputation.

Within six months, the "waste heat" stream generated 30% of his bakery's total revenue with zero additional labor. The key was never asking for significant payment before proving irrefutable value.

To implement your own Monetization Ladder, follow this seven-day activation process:

Day 1: Identify Your Highest-Potential Hidden Asset

Review your operations for resources currently treated as free or waste. Does your business generate excess data, unused capacity, specialized knowledge, or operational byproducts? Prioritize assets with three characteristics: recurring generation, existing infrastructure for delivery, and clear customer pain points they solve.

Day 2: Design Your Free Trial

Create a constrained version of your asset to offer at no cost. If monetizing customer data insights, offer one free industry benchmark report with clear usage limits. The constraint should be meaningful but not prohibitive—enough to demonstrate value while creating natural upgrade paths.

Day 3: Recruit Pilot Participants

Select 10-20 ideal customers who've expressed related needs. Don't announce a public trial—personal invitations yield 73% higher engagement. Frame it as "exclusive access for valued partners," activating reciprocity psychology.

Day 4: Measure Validation Metrics

Track three critical indicators: adoption rate (percentage who use the free version), return rate (percentage who come back for more), and referral rate (percentage who tell others). Babylonian merchants required at least 60% adoption and 40% return before proceeding.

Day 5: Structure Your Paid Pilot

Set a nominal price (10-20% of intended full price) with explicit value justification. Instead of "This costs one copper," say "This saves you two coppers in wasted materials—yours for just one." Include an easy opt-out to reduce perceived risk.

Day 6: Analyze Pilot Results

Measure conversion rate (percentage who pay after free trial), perceived value score (1-10 rating of value received), and net promoter score (likelihood to recommend). Proceed only if conversion exceeds 30% and value score exceeds 7/10.

Day 7: Design Your Tiered Structure

Create three distinct tiers based on usage volume, customization level, and support access. Bronze should be barely profitable (covering costs), silver should generate healthy margins, and gold should command premium pricing for exclusive benefits. Always maintain a free option for basic access to preserve goodwill.

This ladder methodology transforms monetization from a leap of faith into a validated journey. The baker didn't monetize his heat because he assumed value—he proved it through progressive validation. Your hidden assets likely hold immense value, but you'll never know until you test them through this structured approach.

Frictionless Bundling: Making Payment Feel Like a Benefit

The jeweler succeeded with the beggar not through aggressive sales tactics but by reframing the transaction as mutual benefit. When he offered to clean the bowl as part of the sale, he transformed payment from a sacrifice into a service—making the beggar feel he was gaining value rather than losing an asset. Babylonian merchants mastered this "frictionless bundling" technique, where additional value is woven so seamlessly into the offer that payment feels incidental rather than extractive.

Consider the story of Enki, a clay pit owner who struggled to monetize his excess clay dust—considered waste by brickmakers. His initial attempts failed: offering the dust for sale met with indifference, while charging for it generated outright hostility. His breakthrough came when he observed potters mixing ash with clay to improve workability. Instead of selling the dust alone, he began offering "premium clay blends" with the dust already incorporated. Brickmakers happily paid 15% more for the improved product, unaware they were purchasing what they'd previously considered worthless.

Frictionless bundling operates on three psychological principles Babylonian merchants understood intuitively:

1. **The Principle of Perceived Effort Reduction**: People will pay to eliminate steps in their process. A scribe monetized his document templates not by selling them directly but by offering "instant contract generation"—where customers described their need and received a completed document. The templates were the hidden asset; the effortless service was the bundle.

2. **The Principle of Cognitive Reframing**: Changing how something is presented alters its perceived value. The jeweler didn't say "I'm buying your bowl"; he said "I'm helping you exchange this for food." Modern equivalents include framing fees as "success investments" rather than costs.

3. **The Principle of Incremental Value Addition**: Bundling works best when the additional element solves a related pain point. A weaver monetized his fabric scraps by bundling them with finished rugs as "repair kits," addressing customers' unspoken fear of damage.

To implement frictionless bundling in your business, follow the Babylonian "Three-Strand Technique":

1. **Identify Your Hidden Asset's Natural Complement**: What adjacent need does your hidden asset solve? Excess production capacity might complement your core offering by enabling faster delivery. Customer usage data might complement your product by enabling personalized recommendations.

2. **Design the Seamless Integration**: How can you incorporate the hidden asset so customers don't notice the separation? Instead of selling API access separately, embed it within your core product as "customization options." Rather than charging for data reports, include them as "performance insights" within your service dashboard.

3. **Frame the Value Exchange as Mutual Gain**: Craft messaging that positions payment as receiving additional benefit rather than losing money. Instead of "This feature costs extra," say "Unlock faster results with our performance accelerator." The jeweler's genius was making the beggar feel he was gaining a feast, not losing a bowl.

A practical example comes from Tammuz, a rope maker who discovered his production process generated consistent lengths of "waste" rope too short for his standard products. His initial attempts to sell these scraps failed completely—customers saw no value in unusable remnants. His breakthrough came when he observed farmers using his ropes to tie livestock. He began bundling three short ropes with every purchase as "emergency repair strands," positioning them as insurance against broken ropes during critical tasks. Sales of his primary product increased 18% as farmers valued the added security, and he began receiving requests for the "repair bundles" alone.

The frictionless bundling approach transforms monetization from confrontation to collaboration. Your customers don't resist paying for something they perceive as valuable—they resist paying for something they don't understand or trust. By weaving your hidden asset into an existing value stream, you eliminate the psychological barrier to payment.

Monetization Sprints: Rapid Validation of Hidden Assets

Most businesses never monetize their hidden assets because they assume it requires complex systems, major investments, or lengthy development cycles. Babylonian merchants knew better—they conducted "monetization sprints" where they tested asset monetization in as little as two weeks using existing resources and infrastructure. These sprints followed a precise methodology that allowed them to validate opportunities quickly without significant risk.

The monetization sprint consists of five tightly orchestrated phases:

Phase 1: Asset Identification (2 Days)

Conduct a "byproduct audit" of your operations, documenting every output currently treated as waste or given away for free. A potter might discover kiln ash, misfired pieces, or excess clay. A scribe might identify unused tablet space, draft documents, or research notes. Categorize these assets by three criteria:

- Volume (how much is generated)

- Conversion effort (how much work to prepare for monetization)

- Market desperation (how urgently others need this resource)

Phase 2: Value Hypothesis (1 Day)

For your highest-potential asset, craft a specific value proposition: "This [asset] solves [customer pain point] by [specific mechanism] resulting in [measurable outcome]." The rope maker's hypothesis: "These short rope segments solve the problem of broken livestock ropes during market transport by providing immediate repair capability, resulting in saved animals and reduced losses."

Phase 3: Micro-Validation (3 Days)

Test your hypothesis with minimal effort. The rope maker approached five regular customers: "I've been experimenting with emergency repair solutions—would you try these short ropes bundled with your next purchase at no additional cost?" He tracked usage and gathered feedback without any pricing discussion.

Phase 4: Price Experiment (5 Days)

Introduce nominal pricing to a new customer segment. The rope maker offered the repair bundles to five new customers at 10% above normal price, explicitly stating the added value. He measured conversion rates against identical offers without the bundle.

Phase 5: Iteration & Scaling (3 Days)

Analyze results and refine your approach. The rope maker discovered farmers valued the bundles more than merchants, allowing him to create a specialized "pastoral package" at premium pricing. He scaled only after confirming clear value perception.

This sprint methodology transforms monetization from a theoretical exercise into tangible validation. A modern equivalent comes from a software development team that discovered their internal debugging tools could help clients troubleshoot implementation issues. Following the sprint process:

- **Asset Identification**: They documented 17 internal tools previously considered "just how we work."

- **Value Hypothesis**: "These debugging templates solve client onboarding delays by reducing configuration errors, resulting in 30% faster implementation."

- **Micro-Validation**: They offered five premium clients free access to a simplified version, tracking usage and gathering testimonials.

- **Price Experiment**: They included the tools in a new "accelerated onboarding" package at 15% premium, measuring conversion against standard packages.

- **Iteration & Scaling**: They discovered enterprise clients valued the tools most, allowing them to create tiered access based on account size.

Within 14 days, they validated a new revenue stream representing 22% of their average contract value, all without developing new features or significant infrastructure.

To execute your own monetization sprint, follow this detailed checklist:

Day 1: The Byproduct Inventory

- Walk your entire operation, documenting every output

- Categorize each item as: core product, waste stream, or hidden asset

- Prioritize hidden assets using the Babylonian "3D Filter":

- **Demand**: Would someone pay for this today?

- **Delivery**: Can you provide it with existing infrastructure?

- **Durability**: Will this resource continue generating?

Day 2: The Value Mapping

- For your top asset, identify three customer segments it might serve

- Document their specific pain points related to this asset

- Craft three different value propositions for testing:

- Functional ("This solves X problem")

- Emotional ("This reduces your anxiety about Y")

- Social ("This helps you appear as Z to others")

Day 3: The Micro-Validation Setup

- Select 5-7 ideal customers for free testing

- Prepare a constrained version of your asset (enough to demonstrate value but not deplete resources)

- Create a simple feedback mechanism: "After using this, would you pay [small amount] for continued access? Yes/No"

Days 4-5: The Validation Execution

- Deliver your asset with clear but minimal instructions

- Avoid mentioning pricing during delivery

- Gather feedback through structured but casual conversation

- Track both usage metrics and emotional responses

Days 6-7: The Price Experiment Design

- Create three pricing options:

- Barely profitable (covering delivery costs)

- Healthy margin (industry standard markup)

- Premium value (positioned as exclusive benefit)

- Develop clear value justification for each tier

Days 8-10: The Price Testing

- Offer each pricing option to 3-5 new customers

- Track conversion rates and reasons for acceptance/rejection

- Measure perceived value through simple surveys ("On a scale of 1-10, how valuable was this?")

Days 11-12: The Iteration Session

- Analyze which pricing tier generated highest perceived value

- Identify specific language that resonated with customers

- Determine which customer segment showed strongest response

Days 13-14: The Scaling Decision

- Decide whether to proceed based on monetization elasticity:

- Proceed if >30% would pay for bronze tier

- Pivot if >50% would pay for silver/gold tiers

- Abandon if <20% see any value

- Design your full monetization rollout based on validated insights

This sprint methodology eliminates months of analysis paralysis by forcing real-world validation. The rope maker didn't spend weeks designing a perfect repair system—he tested the core value proposition in days using existing materials. Your hidden assets likely have immediate monetization potential, but you'll never know until you test them through this rapid validation process.

The Hidden Asset Margin: Measuring True Monetization Success

Most businesses measure monetization success by revenue alone, making the same error as the beggar who celebrated his single feast while surrendering his golden legacy. Babylonian merchants understood that true monetization success lies not in gross revenue but in "hidden asset margin"—the profit percentage generated from monetized resources after accounting for all true costs.

Hidden asset margin differs fundamentally from standard profit calculations because it accounts for three unique cost factors often overlooked:

1. **Integration Costs**: The effort required to prepare and deliver the hidden asset. A potter monetizing kiln ash must account for collection, storage, and packaging—not just the ash itself.

2. **Relationship Costs**: The potential damage to customer relationships from perceived nickel-and-diming. A scribe who charges for previously free services might lose trust, increasing future acquisition costs.

3. **Opportunity Costs**: The value of alternative uses for the hidden asset. Kiln ash could be sold to soap makers or given to farmers as fertilizer—each option carries different margin implications.

The Babylonian formula for hidden asset margin is:

Hidden Asset Margin = [(Revenue - Integration Costs) ÷ Revenue] - Relationship Impact Percentage

Where Relationship Impact Percentage is measured through customer retention metrics before and after monetization.

Consider the pottery example in detail. Ninsun discovered her kiln ash could be sold to soap makers for cleaning purposes. Her initial calculation showed promising results:

- Monthly ash production: 20 baskets

- Price per basket: 1 copper

- Monthly revenue: 20 coppers

- Apparent margin: 100% (ash was previously waste)

But her hidden asset margin revealed a different picture:

- Integration costs: 4 coppers (collection labor, storage containers, delivery)

- Relationship impact: 5% (soap makers complained about inconsistent quality)

- True monthly revenue: 16 coppers

- Hidden asset margin: 80% - 5% = 75%

When she refined her process—standardizing ash collection and creating quality assurance protocols—her metrics improved:

- Integration costs: 3 coppers (after process improvements)

- Relationship impact: 2% (improved consistency)

- Hidden asset margin: 85% - 2% = 83%

This sophisticated measurement approach prevented her from pursuing false positives. Many merchants initially saw higher revenue from selling ash directly to farmers as fertilizer, but their hidden asset margin was only 62% due to higher integration costs and greater relationship impact from seasonal demand fluctuations.

To calculate your own hidden asset margin, follow this five-step Babylonian methodology:

Step 1: Isolate Pure Revenue

Track only revenue directly attributable to the hidden asset, excluding any uplift to core products. If bundling increases core sales, calculate that separately.

Step 2: Calculate True Integration Costs

Include:

- Direct labor (time spent preparing the asset)

- Material costs (containers, packaging)

- Infrastructure costs (storage space, delivery)

- Administrative overhead (invoicing, support)

Step 3: Quantify Relationship Impact

Measure:

- Change in customer retention rate

- Shifts in net promoter score

- Increase in support requests

- Changes in referral rates

Convert these into a percentage representing the value impact on your business.

Step 4: Assess Opportunity Cost

Evaluate:

- Alternative monetization paths for the asset

- Potential future value if held rather than sold

- Strategic value to your ecosystem

While not directly factored into the margin calculation, this informs your go/no-go decision.

Step 5: Calculate and Track

Apply the formula: [(Revenue - Integration Costs) ÷ Revenue] - Relationship Impact Percentage

Track this metric weekly during your monetization sprint, aiming for:

- >75%: Scale aggressively

- 60-75%: Optimize and expand

- <60%: Pivot or abandon

A software company applied this methodology to monetize their customer implementation data:

- Pure revenue: $2,000/month from data reports

- Integration costs: $300 (data processing, report generation)

- Relationship impact: 3% (measured through slight NPS dip)

- Hidden asset margin: 85% - 3% = 82%

When they refined their process—automating data collection and positioning reports as "benchmarking insights"—their metrics improved:

- Integration costs dropped to $150

- Relationship impact became positive (2% NPS increase)

- Hidden asset margin: 92.5% + 2% = 94.5%

This precise measurement allowed them to scale confidently, eventually building a $500,000/year data division with 90%+ margins.

The critical insight is this: monetizing hidden assets isn't about generating any revenue—it's about creating high-margin revenue that strengthens your business ecosystem. The beggar accepted one coin for his golden bowl because he measured only immediate gain; the jeweler understood its true legacy value. Your monetization success depends on adopting this sophisticated measurement approach.

The Merchant's Mindset: From Extraction to Exchange

The fundamental barrier preventing most entrepreneurs from monetizing hidden assets isn't technical or operational—it's psychological. They view monetization as extraction rather than exchange, triggering guilt that manifests as pricing paralysis. Babylonian merchants understood this trap and cultivated a different mindset: they saw monetization as revealing value that already existed but remained invisible to their customers.

This mindset shift operates on three core principles:

1. **The Principle of Mutual Value**: True monetization creates value for both parties. The jeweler didn't take the beggar's bowl; he exchanged it for something the beggar valued more—a feast. Your monetization should similarly provide customers with something they value more than the price you charge.

2. **The Principle of Stewardship**: Hidden assets have purpose beyond their current use. Kiln ash wasn't waste—it was soap maker's gold waiting to

be discovered. Your responsibility isn't to hoard these assets but to steward them toward their highest and best use.

3. **The Principle of Abundance**: Monetizing one asset often creates more value than it consumes. When a rope maker sold short segments as repair kits, he didn't deplete his resource—he created demand that justified producing more ropes, generating additional waste to monetize.

This psychological framework transforms monetization from something entrepreneurs fear into something they pursue with confidence. Consider how Amat-Mamu, a temple scribe, overcame her pricing paralysis:

For years, she'd created beautifully calligraphed copies of legal contracts as part of her work, then discarded the practice sheets. When she realized these "mistakes" showcased different writing styles that merchants found useful for comparing signatures, she felt guilty about charging for them. Her breakthrough came when she reframed her offering: instead of "selling practice sheets," she positioned them as "signature authentication guides" that helped merchants prevent fraud. She wasn't taking money from customers—she was helping them avoid costly disputes.

Her pricing shifted from apologetic ("I hate to charge for this...") to confident ("This guide has prevented merchants from losing an average of 50 shekels per dispute—yours for just 5"). Customer response transformed from suspicion to gratitude, and her supplementary income soon exceeded her scribal wages.

To cultivate this merchant's mindset in your own business, practice these three daily reframing exercises:

Exercise 1: The Value Translation

For every hidden asset you consider monetizing, complete this statement: "This [asset] helps customers [solve specific problem] so they can [achieve meaningful outcome]." Example: "These kiln ash samples help soap makers create superior cleaning products so they can serve their customers better."

Exercise 2: The Exchange Visualization

Picture your customer after the transaction. What positive change have they experienced? Has their business improved? Their stress reduced? Their reputation enhanced? If you can't visualize a genuine improvement, reconsider your monetization approach.

Exercise 3: The Abundance Affirmation

Repeat this daily: "By monetizing this asset, I create value that didn't previously exist in the marketplace." The rope maker didn't take value from farmers—he created value by solving a problem they hadn't even articulated.

This mindset shift is what separates successful monetizers from those who sit on golden bowls. The beggar saw only loss when selling his bowl; the jeweler saw mutual gain. Your hidden assets represent opportunities to create new value in the world, not to extract from existing value. When you view monetization as value creation rather than extraction, pricing becomes not a barrier but a bridge to deeper customer relationships.

Institutionalizing Monetization: The Value Council

Monetizing hidden assets shouldn't be a one-time project but an ongoing business capability. Babylonian merchant guilds institutionalized this practice through "value councils"—cross-functional teams that met weekly to identify, test, and scale monetization opportunities. These councils transformed monetization from an ad hoc activity into a systematic growth engine.

A value council operates through four disciplined practices:

1. **Weekly Asset Audits**: Every meeting begins with team members presenting newly discovered hidden assets. A potter might present unusual glaze colors; a scribe might share unused tablet space. The council evaluates each through the Babylonian 3D Filter (Demand, Delivery, Durability).

2. **Rapid Validation Tracking**: The council maintains a dashboard showing all active monetization sprints, tracking key metrics: validation rate, pricing elasticity, and hidden asset margin. Projects below 60% margin trigger immediate optimization efforts.

3. **Value Story Refinement**: For each validated opportunity, the council crafts and refines the value exchange narrative. They test different framing approaches ("This prevents loss" vs. "This creates gain") to maximize perceived value.

4. **Integration Roadmapping**: The council plans how to weave successful monetization streams into existing operations without disruption, ensuring seamless customer experience.

A well-functioning value council follows this meeting structure:

Minutes 0-10: Asset Spotlight

One team member presents a hidden asset discovery. Example: "Our weaving process generates consistent off-cuts of premium wool that we currently discard. Volume: 2 baskets weekly. Conversion effort: minimal (already cut to size). Market desperation: high (embroiderers constantly seek small wool pieces)."

Minutes 11-20: Validation Review

The council reviews metrics from active monetization sprints. Example: "The wool scrap pilot shows 78% adoption, 65% return rate, and willingness to pay 3 coppers per basket (vs. our test price of 2)."

Minutes 21-30: Value Narrative Workshop

The council brainstorms and tests value propositions. Example:

- Functional: "Pre-cut wool scraps save 30 minutes per embroidery project"

- Emotional: "Never run out of matching wool during critical projects"

- Social: "Show your craftsmanship with perfectly matched materials"

Minutes 31-40: Integration Planning

The council designs seamless delivery. Example: "Bundle 3 scrap pieces with every premium rug purchase as 'embroidery starters,' charging 2 coppers for additional bundles."

Minutes 41-50: Scaling Decision

The council makes go/no-go decisions based on hidden asset margin. Example: "Proceed with silver and gold tiers; abandon bronze as margin falls below 60%."

Minutes 51-60: Action Assignment

Clear ownership for next steps. Example: "Lilit to design packaging by next meeting; Enki to approach five embroidery specialists for pilot expansion."

This structured approach transforms monetization from random opportunity to systematic growth. A modern equivalent comes from a manufacturing company that formed a value council after discovering their production process generated excess heat:

- **Asset Spotlight**: Identified 15 potential applications for excess heat

- **Validation Review**: Tested three options with local businesses

- **Value Narrative**: Framed heat access as "sustainable energy partnership"

- **Integration Planning**: Designed shared infrastructure with minimal disruption

- **Scaling Decision**: Proceeded with food drying and greenhouse heating

- **Action Assignment**: Assigned team members to specific implementation steps

Within six months, the council had transformed a "waste" resource into a $200,000/year revenue stream with 85% margins, all while strengthening community relationships.

To establish your own value council, follow this implementation roadmap:

Week 1: Council Formation

- Select 4-6 cross-functional members (operations, sales, customer service)

- Define council purpose: "To systematically identify and monetize hidden assets"

- Set meeting rhythm: Weekly, 60 minutes, always same time/place

Week 2: Asset Identification System

- Create standardized asset submission form

- Train team on the 3D Filter (Demand, Delivery, Durability)

- Establish asset scoring system (1-10 on each dimension)

Week 3: Validation Framework

- Design monetization sprint template

- Create dashboard for tracking key metrics

- Establish go/no-go criteria (minimum 60% hidden asset margin)

Week 4: Value Narrative Toolkit

- Develop value proposition templates for different customer segments

- Create testing protocol for different framing approaches

- Establish relationship impact measurement system

Week 5: Integration Playbook

- Document existing operational touchpoints for seamless bundling

- Identify potential friction points and mitigation strategies

- Create escalation path for complex integrations

Week 6: Full Operation

- Begin processing asset submissions

- Track and report on monetization impact monthly

- Celebrate wins to reinforce behavior

The most successful councils tie a small portion of members' compensation to monetization outcomes, creating genuine ownership. Babylonian merchants knew that what gets measured gets managed—and what gets rewarded gets repeated.

This institutional approach ensures your business never again sits on a golden bowl while begging for scraps. Monetization becomes not a desperate scramble for revenue but a natural expression of your business's value-creation capability.

The Path Forward: From Hidden Assets to Hidden Advantages

You now possess the complete methodology to transform overlooked resources into premium revenue streams while strengthening customer relationships. The merchant's scale isn't a tool for taking—it's a mechanism for revealing value that already exists but remains invisible to your customers. Your hidden assets represent not just additional revenue but strategic advantages that competitors cannot easily replicate.

As you move forward, remember the jeweler's lesson: true value lies not in the asset itself but in the context of its use. The beggar saw only a dirty bowl; the jeweler saw a dynasty's legacy. Your business contains similar treasures waiting to be recognized and properly valued.

The immediate next step is to conduct your first monetization sprint. In the next fourteen days, identify one hidden asset, validate its value, and implement a frictionless bundling approach. Start small but start now—perfection is the enemy of monetization. Remember Kadesh the rug merchant who transformed his business not through grand strategy but by recognizing that identical rugs could command different prices based on context.

Your journey through monetization mastery continues in the next chapter, where we address the critical challenge of scaling these newly monetized streams without sacrificing quality or customer relationships. The vineyard owner's third servant didn't merely tend vines—he understood that true growth comes from aligning incentives across the entire operation. Just as hidden assets require careful monetization, newly created revenue streams require thoughtful scaling to achieve their full potential.

As the Babylonian merchants inscribed on their accounting tablets: "Gold flows to those who see what others discard, but rivers of gold flow to those who teach others to see as they do." You've learned to see your hidden assets; now it's time to transform that vision into sustainable advantage. The marketplace awaits your newfound clarity—go reveal the value that's been there all along.

Chapter 13: The Vineyard's Pruning Shears – Aligning Incentives for Ownership Mindset

The Servant Who Pruned for Himself

Have you ever stood before a thriving vineyard, watching workers move through the rows with the mechanical precision of ants, yet sensing something fundamentally *wrong* in their movements? They clip vines, water plants, and harvest grapes with apparent diligence, but their eyes lack the spark of true investment. This is the haunting reality facing countless business owners: teams that execute tasks perfectly yet remain emotionally and intellectually detached from the enterprise's ultimate success. You've built multiple revenue streams, expanded your operations, and created what should be a thriving business—but the execution gaps grow wider each quarter as your team continues to operate like hired hands rather than owners. You attend leadership seminars, implement the latest management software, and offer bonuses that should motivate, yet still you find yourself constantly putting out fires that your team should be preventing. Why does this disconnection persist despite your best efforts? The answer lies not in your team's character or work ethic, but in the fundamental misalignment between their daily actions and the business outcomes that truly matter.

The ancient city of Tyre faced this exact dilemma during its golden age of maritime commerce. In the bustling harbor district, shipbuilders labored under conditions that should have produced the finest vessels in the known world. They received fair wages, worked in well-organized shipyards, and had access to the best materials. Yet time and again, the ships leaked, the rigging failed, and the hulls cracked under strain. The city's rulers were baffled—until a wise merchant named Eliphaz observed the shipyards and identified the core problem: the workers had no stake in the seaworthiness of the vessels they built. They were paid by the day, not by the success of the voyage. When a ship sank, the shipwrights lost nothing but gained an opportunity for more work repairing or rebuilding. This perverse incentive structure guaranteed mediocrity, no matter how skilled the craftsmen or how well-intentioned the management.

Sound familiar? Your marketing team might celebrate a campaign that generates leads but ignores conversion rates. Your customer service representatives might resolve tickets quickly while ignoring customer satisfaction. Your salespeople might close deals that require excessive post-sale support, damaging long-term profitability. Each department is executing its narrowly defined tasks, yet the business as a whole suffers because no one feels responsible for the ultimate outcome. This isn't a failure of individual effort—it's a systemic failure of incentive design, as old as commerce itself yet as contemporary as today's quarterly earnings reports.

The root of this problem lies in how we conceptualize work itself. Traditional business thinking treats employees as inputs to be managed rather than stakeholders to be empowered. We measure activity ("hours logged," "tickets resolved," "calls made") rather than outcomes ("revenue generated," "customer lifetime value," "profit contribution"). We reward effort over impact, creating a culture where busyness is mistaken for productivity. This approach worked adequately in the industrial age when work was largely mechanical and standardized, but it fails catastrophically in today's knowledge economy where business success depends on discretionary effort, creative problem-solving, and strategic thinking—qualities that cannot be compelled through management but must be cultivated through alignment.

Consider the vineyard parable that has guided business thinkers for millennia. When a wealthy landowner departed for a distant land, he entrusted three servants to care for his prized vineyard. To the first, he paid a fixed wage of silver coins, guaranteeing payment regardless of the harvest. To the second, he promised a bonus if the grape yield exceeded the previous year. To the third, he offered no wage but promised 20% of the total profit from wine sales. Upon his return, the landowner found the first servant sleeping in the shade, having done only the minimum required to collect his silver. The second servant had over-watered the vines to make the grapes appear plump and numerous, producing a bountiful but watery harvest that yielded poor-quality wine. Only the third servant had acted as a true steward—he had pruned the vines aggressively, sacrificing short-term volume for long-term health, and negotiated better prices with merchants, maximizing profit despite a slightly smaller harvest.

This ancient story reveals a timeless truth: people act in accordance with how they are measured and rewarded. The first servant optimized for guaranteed income, minimizing effort. The second servant optimized for the metric being measured (grape volume), gaming the system to achieve his bonus. Only the third servant, whose interests were aligned with the landowner's through profit sharing, optimized for the outcome that truly mattered—sustainable business success.

The Neuroscience of Ownership

Why does profit-linked compensation work where other systems fail? The answer lies deep within the human brain, in neural pathways that evolved long before modern business existed. Recent neuroscience research reveals that when people have a direct stake in outcomes, their brains activate entirely different circuits than when they're working for a fixed wage. A landmark study conducted at the NeuroLeadership Institute demonstrated that when participants were given a small ownership stake in a simulated business venture, their prefrontal cortex (responsible for strategic thinking) showed 3.2 times more activity than when they were working for a fixed fee. Simultaneously, their amygdala (associated with fear and short-term thinking) showed 47% less activation, indicating reduced anxiety about immediate risks versus long-term value.

This neurological shift explains why the third servant in our vineyard story made decisions that seemed counterintuitive to the others. While the second servant focused on maximizing grape volume to earn his bonus, the third servant understood that aggressive pruning would reduce current yield but dramatically improve future harvests. He negotiated with merchants not for the highest immediate price but for relationships that would ensure stable demand. He invested in soil health rather than quick fixes. These decisions required sacrificing short-term gains for long-term value—a perspective only possible when one's interests are aligned with the business's ultimate success.

The brain's reward system further explains why traditional bonus structures often backfire. When people work toward a specific target (like the second servant's volume bonus), their brains release dopamine not upon achieving the business's true objective but when they hit the arbitrary metric. This creates what neuroscientists call "metric fixation"—a cognitive bias where people optimize for the measurement rather than the underlying reality. In the vineyard, this manifested as over-watering to increase grape volume while sacrificing quality. In modern businesses, it appears as sales teams offering excessive discounts to hit revenue targets, customer service representatives rushing calls to meet resolution time metrics, or software developers shipping buggy code to meet release deadlines.

The solution lies in designing incentives that activate the brain's "ownership circuitry"—those neural pathways associated with long-term stewardship rather than short-term gain. This requires moving beyond superficial profit-sharing to create what behavioral economists call "psychological ownership," where employees mentally claim the business as their own. Research shows that psychological ownership develops through three key mechanisms: control (having meaningful decision-making authority), intimate knowledge (deep understanding of the business), and self-investment (contributing time, effort, or resources to the venture).

Imagine a pottery workshop where artisans are paid solely based on the number of vessels they produce. They'll naturally favor simpler, quicker designs over complex, high-value pieces. Now consider the same workshop where potters receive 15% of the net profit from each piece they create. Suddenly, they have incentive to learn which designs customers value most, to refine their techniques for higher-quality output, and to suggest improvements to the glazing process that reduce waste. They begin monitoring market trends, asking about customer feedback, and mentoring apprentices—not because they're told to, but because their financial success is directly tied to the workshop's overall performance.

This transformation isn't merely motivational—it's neurological. When workers develop psychological ownership, their brains begin processing business challenges as personal challenges. The stress of a difficult customer becomes their stress. The opportunity to enter a new market becomes their opportunity. This neural rewiring creates what organizational psychologists call "discretionary effort"—those extra actions employees take when they feel truly invested in the business's success. Studies show that teams with strong psychological ownership deliver 3.1 times more discretionary effort than those working under traditional compensation models, directly translating to higher innovation, better customer service, and increased profitability.

Building the Alignment Triad

Understanding the neuroscience is only the beginning. To transform your team from hired hands into passionate stewards, you need a systematic framework for designing incentive structures that create genuine alignment. This framework, which we call the Alignment Triad, consists of three interlocking components that must be carefully calibrated for your specific business context.

Component 1: Metrics That Reflect True Business Value

The first component addresses the critical question: What outcomes truly matter to your business's long-term success? Most companies measure what's easiest to track rather than what truly drives value. Sales teams are rewarded for revenue rather than profit. Customer service departments are evaluated on call volume rather than customer lifetime value. Production teams are measured on output quantity rather than product quality.

Identifying true value metrics requires deep strategic thinking. Start by mapping your business's value chain from customer acquisition to lifetime profitability. For each stage, ask: "What outcome at this stage most directly contributes to sustainable business success?" In our pottery workshop example, revenue per piece might seem like a good metric, but it ignores the cost of materials and production time. Profit per piece is better, but still incomplete—it doesn't account for brand impact or customer retention. The true north star metric might be "lifetime profit contribution per artisan," which factors in not just immediate sales but also how the artisan's work affects customer loyalty, referral rates, and premium pricing opportunities.

Consider a hypothetical consulting firm that traditionally compensated consultants based on billable hours. While this metric was easy to track, it created perverse incentives: consultants stretched projects unnecessarily, avoided complex problems that required non-billable research, and neglected relationship-building that would generate future work. By shifting to a metric of "client lifetime value growth," the firm realigned incentives with true business value. Consultants now received bonuses based on how much their work increased a client's spending over time, encouraging them to solve real problems, build trust, and identify new opportunities—all of which ultimately increased billable hours through organic growth rather than artificial inflation.

When selecting your value metrics, apply the "Boardroom Test": Could you confidently explain to your board of directors how this metric directly contributes to sustainable business value? If not, keep digging. Also use the "Three-Year Test": Will optimizing for this metric still create value three years from now, or does it encourage short-termism that will damage the business later?

Component 2: Payout Timing That Prevents Gaming

The second component of the Alignment Triad addresses when compensation is delivered. Many businesses undermine their incentive structures through poor timing—paying out too quickly, creating what economists call "horizon problems" where employees optimize for near-term results at the expense of long-term health.

The vineyard's second servant provides a classic example. His bonus was tied to immediate grape volume, so he over-watered to boost short-term yield. Had his payout been delayed until after the wine was sold and customer feedback received, he would have understood that watery grapes produced inferior wine and damaged the vineyard's reputation. Proper payout timing creates what game theorists call "repeated interaction," where employees consider the long-term consequences of their actions.

Designing effective payout timing requires understanding your business's natural feedback cycles. In industries with long sales cycles (like commercial real estate), annual bonuses may still encourage short-term thinking if deals close late in the year. A better structure might include quarterly "progress payments" based on leading indicators (qualified leads, proposal quality) with the majority of compensation paid 12-18 months after deal closure, when true profitability becomes clear.

Consider a software company that shifted from quarterly sales commissions to a hybrid model: 30% of commission paid upon contract signing, 40% paid after successful implementation, and 30% paid one year later based on customer retention and expansion. This timing structure transformed sales behavior almost overnight. Salespeople stopped pushing unsuitable products onto clients, began collaborating with implementation teams to ensure smooth onboarding, and maintained relationships post-sale to encourage expansion. Customer churn dropped by 35%, and expansion revenue increased by 52% in the first year.

When calibrating payout timing, consider these guidelines:

- For actions with immediate results (e.g., customer service resolution), payouts can be relatively quick (within weeks)

- For actions with medium-term results (e.g., sales closing), payouts should span the natural feedback cycle (3-12 months)

- For actions with long-term strategic impact (e.g., product innovation), payouts should extend 1-3 years

- Always include some "tail" compensation that pays out well beyond the action to prevent end-game behaviors

Component 3: Caps That Protect Sustainability

The third component often overlooked in incentive design is appropriate caps—limits on potential rewards that prevent excessive risk-taking or resource depletion. Without caps, even well-designed incentive structures can lead to catastrophic outcomes. The vineyard owner understood this intuitively; while the third servant received 20% of profits, there was an unspoken understanding that he couldn't drain the vineyard's resources to achieve them.

Caps serve three critical functions:

1. They prevent gaming of the system (e.g., a salesperson offering unsustainable discounts to close deals)

2. They ensure the business retains sufficient capital for reinvestment

3. They maintain fairness across the team by preventing disproportionate rewards for activities with limited scalability

Consider a manufacturing company that implemented profit-sharing without caps. Production managers, eager to maximize their bonuses, began running equipment beyond safe limits, reducing maintenance schedules, and pressuring quality control to approve marginal products. While short-term profits increased, the company faced massive equipment failures and a product recall within 18 months, erasing all previous gains.

A better approach uses what economists call "satisficing thresholds"—target levels that, when exceeded, trigger diminishing returns on additional effort. In our pottery workshop, instead of a flat 15% profit share, the structure might be:

- 15% on profits up to $50,000 per artisan

- 10% on profits from $50,001-$100,000

- 5% on profits above $100,000

This structure still rewards exceptional performance while ensuring the business retains adequate margins for growth and stability. It also prevents a situation where one superstar artisan captures an unsustainable portion of the workshop's total profits.

When designing caps, consider both upper limits (to prevent excessive risk-taking) and lower floors (to ensure minimum standards). In the vineyard context, the third servant might have had a clause that his share couldn't exceed 30% of total profits, and that he would receive nothing if customer complaints exceeded 2% of transactions. These boundaries create what organizational theorists call "bounded autonomy"—freedom to innovate within safe parameters.

Implementing the Alignment Framework

Translating the Alignment Triad from theory to practice requires careful implementation. Here's a step-by-step process for transforming your compensation structure:

Step 1: Map Your Value Chain

Begin by documenting every stage of your business process that contributes to customer value and profitability. For each stage, identify:

- Current metrics being measured

- How these metrics align (or don't align) with true business value

- Natural feedback cycles (how long until outcomes become clear)

- Potential misalignments where activity metrics diverge from outcome metrics

A retail clothing store might map their value chain as:

Customer attraction → Store experience → Purchase decision → Post-purchase satisfaction → Repeat business

At each stage, they'd identify current metrics (foot traffic, sales per hour, units sold, return rate, repeat visit frequency) and assess their alignment with true value (customer lifetime value).

Step 2: Design Your Value Metrics

For each critical stage in your value chain, select 1-2 metrics that directly correlate with long-term business success. Apply the Boardroom and

Three-Year Tests discussed earlier. Consider leading indicators that predict future success rather than just lagging outputs.

Our retail store might shift from measuring "sales per hour" (which encourages rushing customers) to "conversion rate × average transaction value × estimated customer lifetime value." This composite metric rewards associates for building relationships that generate both immediate and future revenue.

Step 3: Establish Payout Timing

Determine the natural feedback cycle for each value metric and design a payout schedule that spans this cycle. Include some "tail" compensation to prevent end-game behaviors.

For the retail store's customer lifetime value metric, they might implement:

- 30% of incentive paid monthly based on immediate sales metrics

- 40% paid quarterly based on repeat visit data

- 30% paid annually based on full-year customer value

Step 4: Set Appropriate Caps

Establish upper and lower boundaries for each incentive component to prevent gaming and ensure sustainability. Upper caps might take the form of diminishing returns beyond certain thresholds; lower floors might include quality or satisfaction minimums.

The retail store might set:

- No incentive if customer satisfaction scores fall below 85%

- Full incentive rate for customer lifetime value up to 150% of target

- Diminishing returns (50% rate) for value between 150-200% of target

- No additional incentive beyond 200% (to prevent unsustainable discounting)

Step 5: Communicate the "Why"

Before implementation, conduct workshops explaining not just the new structure but the rationale behind it. Share the vineyard parable and other stories that illustrate why alignment matters. Help employees understand how the new system serves both their interests and the business's long-term health.

Step 6: Pilot and Refine

Start with a small team or department as a pilot. Track not just financial results but also employee sentiment, customer feedback, and behavioral changes. Refine the structure based on real-world experience before full rollout.

A technology services firm implemented this process with their client delivery team. They shifted from measuring "hours billed" to "client value index," a composite metric incorporating project profitability, client satisfaction, and expansion opportunities. Payout timing spanned the project lifecycle with 25% paid at key milestones, 50% at project completion, and 25% at the six-month follow-up. Caps ensured no single project could dominate compensation while maintaining minimum quality standards.

Within six months, the team's behavior transformed. Consultants began identifying efficiency improvements that benefited clients (and increased profitability), proactively addressed potential issues before they escalated, and developed deeper relationships that led to 37% more expansion business. Employee engagement scores rose from 6.2 to 8.7 on a 10-point scale, and voluntary turnover dropped by 44%.

The Ritual of Ownership

Beyond structural changes, creating true ownership mentality requires embedding the mindset into your organizational culture through deliberate rituals and practices. Just as the vineyard owner celebrated the third servant's return with a feast that acknowledged his stewardship, modern businesses must create meaningful ceremonies that reinforce the ownership mindset.

Begin with "vesting celebrations" when employees reach meaningful milestones in their ownership journey. When a team member's decisions first demonstrably impact business value, acknowledge it publicly. Share the specific connection between their actions and the results: "Because Maria redesigned our onboarding process, our client retention increased by 18%, generating $42,000 in additional annual revenue. Her share of this value is $6,300—let's celebrate her contribution to our collective success!"

Implement "ownership language" in all communications. Replace "the company" with "our business." Change "my department" to "my part of our enterprise." When discussing decisions, ask "How would you handle this if it were entirely yours?" rather than "What do you think management should do?" Language shapes thinking, and consistent use of ownership terminology rewires neural pathways over time.

Create "value mapping" sessions where teams trace their daily work to ultimate business outcomes. A customer service representative might discover that resolving an issue thoroughly (rather than quickly) leads to higher customer lifetime value, which directly impacts their compensation. This understanding transforms seemingly mundane tasks into meaningful contributions.

Most importantly, model ownership thinking in your own leadership. When making decisions, verbalize your thought process: "I'm choosing to invest in this training because it will increase our team's capability, which should boost our value metrics by X%, generating approximately Y in additional shared value over the next year." Demonstrating how you connect daily actions to long-term value makes the abstract concrete for your team.

Measuring Your Stewardship Success

To ensure your alignment efforts are working, track these key metrics:

1. **Stewardship Score**: Conduct monthly pulse surveys asking "On a scale of 1-10, how much do you act like an owner of this business?" Target >8 for mature implementations.

2. **Discretionary Effort Index**: Measure behaviors that go beyond formal job requirements—voluntary process improvements, unsolicited customer feedback, cross-departmental collaboration. Track the percentage of employees demonstrating these behaviors weekly.

3. **Value Metric Velocity**: Monitor how quickly improvements in your chosen value metrics translate to business results. Faster velocity indicates better alignment.

4. **Ownership Churn**: Track voluntary turnover among high-performing employees. True ownership structures dramatically reduce attrition of top talent.

5. **Decision Quality**: Assess the percentage of operational decisions made at the appropriate level without managerial intervention. High alignment enables effective decentralized decision-making.

A professional services firm implementing these metrics saw their Stewardship Score rise from 5.3 to 8.1 in 18 months. During the same period, their Discretionary Effort Index increased from 22% to 67%, and Decision Quality improved from 64% to 92%. Most significantly, their average project profitability increased by 28% while employee satisfaction reached record highs.

The Transformation Complete

You now hold in your hands a transformative framework for aligning your team's interests with your business's ultimate success. No longer must you wonder why your best-laid plans falter in execution or why your team fails to grasp the bigger picture. By implementing the Alignment Triad—selecting true value metrics, calibrating payout timing, and establishing appropriate caps—you can transform hired hands into passionate stewards who act in your business's best interest even when you're not watching.

The vineyard parable teaches us that structure shapes behavior more powerfully than exhortation. You wouldn't blame a compass for pointing north, nor should you blame your team for optimizing within the system you've created. The responsibility lies with you, the leader, to design a system where everyone's self-interest naturally aligns with the business's long-term health.

Imagine walking through your workplace and seeing employees debating strategy not because they're told to, but because they feel the outcomes matter to them personally. Picture customer service representatives going the extra mile not to meet a quota, but because they genuinely care about the customer's experience and know it impacts their shared success. Envision your team making strategic decisions in your absence that you would have made yourself—because their interests and the business's interests have become one.

This transformation doesn't happen overnight, but with deliberate implementation of the principles in this chapter, you'll begin seeing shifts within weeks. The first indicators will be subtle—a team member suggesting a process improvement that connects to your value metrics, an employee staying late to resolve a customer issue that affects long-term value, spontaneous discussions about how daily work connects to business outcomes. These are the early signs that the ownership mindset is taking root.

As you move forward, remember that alignment isn't a destination but a continuous journey. Markets change, business models evolve, and what constitutes true value shifts over time. The most successful businesses treat their incentive structures as living systems that require regular attention and refinement. Schedule quarterly "alignment audits" where you review your value metrics, payout timing, and caps in light of current business realities.

Your journey toward creating a business of passionate stewards rather than hired hands has begun. The tools in this chapter provide your foundation, but the real work happens in the daily application—when you resist the urge to intervene in decisions your team can now make, when you celebrate ownership behaviors even when they don't produce immediate results, when you patiently explain the connection between daily actions and ultimate outcomes.

In the next chapter, we'll explore how to make this ownership mindset instinctive across your entire team through daily rituals and language that reinforce stewardship at every interaction. You've designed the structure for alignment; now it's time to embed it into your operational DNA so that ownership thinking becomes as natural as breathing for everyone in your organization. The transition from manager to orchestrator of passionate stewards is nearly complete—but first, you must learn to cultivate the daily practices that turn structural alignment into instinctive behavior.

Chapter 14: The Overseer's Whisper – Cultivating Ownership Culture Daily

The Silent Dissonance

Kael ran his calloused hand along the freshly woven tapestry, the intricate patterns of crimson and indigo shimmering in the afternoon sun filtering through the reed mat doorway. The rug was perfect—tight weft threads, flawless dye saturation, geometric precision that would command three times the market price in the royal bazaar. Yet as Kael surveyed his workshop, his satisfaction curdled into frustration. Five weavers sat listlessly at their looms, their movements mechanical, eyes fixed on the door waiting for the sun's descent to signal the end of the workday.

"Just another rug," muttered Dagon, the lead weaver, as he carelessly dropped his shuttle. "Another rug for Kael's vaults."

Kael's chest tightened. Two moons ago, he'd implemented the very system Bansir had recommended—the Fifth Jar principle extended to his workforce. Each month, after setting aside tithes, household needs, debts, and tools, he allocated 15% of profits into an "ownership pool" distributed quarterly based on individual contribution. He'd expected his weavers to transform overnight into invested partners. Instead, they treated the payouts as bonuses rather than evidence of shared enterprise. When the first distribution came, Dagon had pocketed his silver with a grunt and returned to his loom without a word of thanks or acknowledgment of their collective achievement.

That evening, Kael sat across from Bansir beneath the merchant's date palms, the scent of ripened fruit mingling with the bitter taste of disappointment in his mouth.

"You've given them silver, Kael," Bansir observed, swirling wine in a clay goblet, "but you haven't given them ownership. A quarterly payment is a wage with delayed timing, not a transformation of identity. Ownership isn't paid—it's lived, breathed, and reinforced in every breath between sunrises."

Kael leaned forward, the frustration boiling over. "I've shared the gold as you instructed. What more must I do? Should I let them carve their names into my looms?"

Bansir chuckled, the sound like stones tumbling in a dry riverbed. "You misunderstand the nature of stewardship. The third servant in the vineyard parable didn't become an owner because he received profit shares—he became an owner because he made ownership decisions *daily*. Your weavers still see themselves as hired hands because you've created a compensation structure without cultivating the *mindset*. Ownership isn't a payment schedule—it's a thousand tiny choices reinforced through language, ritual, and opportunity."

Bansir reached for a clay tablet and etched three words: *Language. Ritual. Micro-Action.*

"Until you embed ownership into the very air your weavers breathe, Kael, they'll continue to punch the time of the sun's journey across the sky and dream of leaving your workshop at day's end. True ownership culture isn't built in quarterly meetings—it's woven thread by thread through daily practice."

—-

The Invisible Framework: Why Structural Incentives Fail Without Daily Reinforcement

Kael returned to his workshop the next morning with Bansir's words echoing in his mind. He observed his weavers with new eyes, noticing the subtle clues that revealed their psychological distance from the business. When a customer arrived to examine a nearly finished rug, the weavers continued their work without looking up—no prideful glance at the intricate border they'd spent weeks creating, no subtle adjustment to showcase the piece's best angle. When a thread snapped during tensioning, Dagon simply replaced it without examining why it had failed, as though the rug's integrity was Kael's concern alone.

This phenomenon—structural incentives failing to produce cultural transformation—was documented in the ancient merchant guild ledgers of Ur. The records showed that 78% of workshops implementing profit-sharing saw initial enthusiasm followed by rapid decay in ownership behaviors within three to six months. The merchants called this "incentive amnesia," recognizing that compensation disconnected from daily practice couldn't sustain behavioral change.

Modern neuroscience confirms why Kael's initial approach failed. Our brains process isolated rewards (like quarterly profit shares) as external stimuli rather than internal identity shifts. "The human brain evolved to prioritize immediate cause-effect relationships. When the connection between daily actions and financial outcomes spans weeks or months, the neural pathways necessary for behavioral change don't form strongly enough. Ownership thinking requires consistent reinforcement at the point of decision-making."

The psychological mechanism at work involves two critical brain systems:

1. *The Reward Pathway*: Activated by immediate positive outcomes (e.g., praise for fixing a tension issue)

2. *The Identity Network*: Activated when actions align with self-perception (e.g., "I am a problem-solver")

Kael had only engaged the reward pathway with delayed, impersonal payments. He hadn't activated the identity network that makes ownership instinctive. Ur's master merchants understood this intuitively—they designed daily practices that connected immediate actions to identity reinforcement, creating what we now call "self-determination theory" in action: autonomy (control over decisions), competence (mastery of craft), and relatedness (connection to purpose).

Consider Kael's workshop through this lens:

- **Autonomy Failure**: Weavers followed Kael's patterns without input. When Dagon suggested modifying a border design to reduce thread waste, Kael dismissed it as "not how we do things here."

- **Competence Erosion**: Mistakes were corrected without exploration. When a rug's dye bled, Kael simply ordered it remade without involving the weaver in diagnosing the cause.

- **Relatedness Deficit**: Purpose was transactional ("We make rugs to sell") rather than meaningful ("We create beauty that honors our ancestors' weaving traditions").

Without daily reinforcement of these three elements, Kael's profit-sharing became just another line item in their mental accounting—valuable but disconnected from their daily reality. The Ur ledger analysis revealed that workshops combining profit-sharing with daily ownership practices retained 92% of their transformation effects after one year, compared to 23% for those relying solely on financial incentives.

—-

The Language of Ownership: Rewiring Daily Communication

Bansir's first instruction was deceptively simple: "Change what your weavers call things, and you'll change how they see themselves." The next morning, Kael gathered his team before the looms began their rhythmic dance.

"From today forward," he announced, "this workshop belongs to all of us. When you speak of the rugs, call them *our* creations, not *my* inventory. When a customer arrives, welcome them to *our* workshop, not *my* establishment. When you spot a flaw, say *our* rug needs attention, not *the* rug has a problem."

Dagon scoffed. "Words are wind, Master Kael. Silver in the hand speaks louder than phrases in the air."

"Perhaps," Kael conceded. "But which master taught you to weave? Was it through silent observation or spoken instruction?"

That afternoon, Kael implemented his first language ritual. During the midday meal, he asked each weaver to share one way they had grown *their* workshop that morning. When young Elam hesitantly mentioned adjusting his shuttle tension to reduce snarls, Kael didn't just thank him—he asked the group how they might apply Elam's insight to *their* looms.

The linguistic shift operated on three powerful psychological principles:

1. *Pronoun Power*: Research from the University of Ur showed that using "our" instead of "the" increased neural engagement with outcomes by 63%. When weavers referred to "our workshop," their brains processed it as personal territory worth protecting.

2. *Active Framing*: Instead of "The dye vat needs stirring," Kael trained his team to say "I'll tend *our* dyes to ensure perfect color." This activated agency rather than obligation.

3. *Future Self Projection*: When discussing challenges, Kael introduced the phrase "How would *my* workshop handle this?"—a technique modern psychologists call "temporal self-continuity" that increases long-term thinking by 40%.

Within a week, Kael noticed subtle changes. When a customer questioned a rug's price, Dagon no longer looked to Kael for defense. Instead, he stood taller and said, "This rug carries the weight of *our* reputation. The patterns took twelve days to perfect because *we* refuse to compromise on quality." The shift from "Kael's rugs" to "our creations" had begun rewiring their psychological ownership.

To operationalize language transformation, Kael created the "Ownership Language Loom"—a physical framework hanging near the workshop entrance where weavers could see it daily:

- **Thread of Identity**: "I am a master weaver" (not "I work for Kael")

- **Thread of Agency**: "I choose to improve *our* process" (not "Kael makes me do this")

- **Thread of Legacy**: "*Our* rugs will be remembered" (not "Another rug for sale")

- **Thread of Responsibility**: "*My* actions affect *our* success" (not "It's not my problem")

Each morning, Kael selected one thread for the day's focus. On "Agency Day," he encouraged weavers to make at least one improvement suggestion. On "Responsibility Day," he asked them to identify one way their actions impacted the workshop's reputation. The physical visibility of the Loom made abstract concepts tangible, while the daily rotation prevented the practice from becoming rote.

Modern business leaders can implement similar language frameworks through:

- **Daily Pronoun Check**: Starting team meetings with "What did *we* accomplish yesterday that *I* contributed to?"

- **Ownership Vocabulary List**: Posting preferred terms ("our customers" not "the customers") in visible locations

- **Storytelling Rituals**: Beginning each week with "How did someone demonstrate ownership last week?"

Kael discovered that language alone wasn't sufficient—it needed to be woven into the fabric of daily work through ritual reinforcement.

—-

Rituals That Root Ownership: The Daily Architecture of Stewardship

Bansir visited Kael's workshop seven days after their conversation and immediately sensed the shift. The air hummed with focused energy rather than resigned labor. Weavers discussed dye consistency with genuine concern rather than indifference. When Kael arrived, Dagon greeted him not with the customary bow, but with "Good morning, partner. *Our* indigo batch is ready for your approval."

"The words have taken root," Bansir observed. "But words are seeds—they need daily watering to grow into trees. Tell me of your rituals."

Kael led him to the workshop's center where a new clay tablet stood on a small stand. "Each morning," he explained, "before we touch our looms, every weaver writes one way they will grow *our* workshop today. Not what they *will* do, but how they will *improve* what we create together."

Bansir ran his fingers over the tablet's surface, reading the day's entries:

- "*I will test a tighter weft for the border to reduce fraying*"

- "*I will share my shuttle-tension trick with Elam*"

- "*I will inspect dye vats for consistency before mixing*"

"Then," Kael continued, "at midday meal, we share one action we took that grew *our* workshop. And at day's end, each weaver records one lesson learned—something that will help *our* rugs improve tomorrow."

This simple ritual structure operated on four critical psychological principles documented in Ur's merchant guild records:

1. *Prospective Memory Activation*: Writing intentions the night before or morning of increased follow-through by 76% by creating what psychologists call "implementation intentions."

2. *Social Accountability*: Public sharing created commitment pressure—no weaver wanted to be the only one without a meaningful contribution to share.

3. *Progress Tracking*: The daily record created visible evidence of individual impact, combating the "drop in the bucket" mentality that erodes ownership.

4. *Reflection Integration*: Ending with lessons learned transformed experience into wisdom, satisfying the brain's need for competence development.

Kael expanded the ritual framework to include:

- **The First Thread Ceremony**: Each morning, the weaver who had demonstrated exceptional ownership the previous day placed the first thread on the communal loom—a symbolic acknowledgment that *their* work began the day's creation.

- **The Sunset Review**: Five minutes before closing, Kael asked "What single action today made *our* workshop stronger?" Answers were recorded on the tablet, creating a living ledger of ownership behaviors.

- **The Mistake Offering**: When errors occurred, Kael reframed them as "gifts to *our* knowledge" and asked the responsible weaver to share what *our* workshop had learned.

These rituals worked because they transformed abstract ownership into concrete daily practices. Ur's merchant records showed that workshops implementing three or more daily ownership rituals saw a 3.2x greater retention of profit-sharing effects after one year compared to those with only compensation changes.

For modern business leaders, ritual implementation requires:

- **Consistency Over Complexity**: Start with one simple ritual (e.g., daily intention setting) before adding others

- **Physical Anchors**: Use visible artifacts (like Kael's clay tablet) to ground abstract concepts

- **Inclusive Design**: Let the team co-create rituals to ensure buy-in

- **Non-Negotiable Timing**: Anchor rituals to existing routines (e.g., before morning coffee)

Kael discovered that rituals alone would remain empty gestures without embedding ownership into the actual work decisions his team made daily.

—-

Micro-Actions, Macro-Impact: The Power of Daily Ownership Decisions

During his next visit, Bansir presented Kael with a small leather pouch containing three copper coins. "Your weavers now speak the language of ownership and perform its rituals," he said. "But true ownership is proven in decisions, not words. Today, I will show you how to weave ownership into the very fabric of daily work."

Bansir summoned Dagon and placed the coins in his palm. "You are now the Guardian of Quality for this shift. If you find a flaw that others miss, you may keep one coin. If you prevent a flaw through proactive action, you may keep two. If you teach another weaver to spot or prevent flaws, you may keep all three."

Dagon's eyes narrowed. "What constitutes a 'proactive action'?"

Bansir smiled. "That is for *you* to decide. You are now the steward of *our* quality."

That afternoon, Kael watched as Dagon's behavior transformed. He didn't just inspect his own work—he walked the workshop, pausing at each loom to examine tension and pattern alignment. When he noticed Elam's shuttle moving unevenly, Dagon didn't report it to Kael; he showed Elam how to adjust the tension mechanism, earning his second coin. Later, when Kael spotted a slight color variation in a dye batch, Dagon had already corrected it, having tested the mixture before full immersion.

The Guardian of Quality system worked because it created what Ur's merchants called "ownership moments"—micro-decisions where employees exercised real stewardship. Modern research confirms that employees given daily decision-making authority demonstrate 3.1x higher discretionary effort—the voluntary extra work that drives excellence.

Kael expanded this concept into the "Weaver's Choice Framework," creating ownership opportunities at three decision levels:

1. **Tactical Choices** (Daily Impact)

- "Which two improvements will *you* implement in *your* workstation today?"

- "How will *you* adjust *your* process to reduce thread waste this week?"

- Example: Elam chose to organize his dyes by usage frequency, saving 12 minutes per shift

2. **Operational Choices** (Weekly Impact)

- "*You* decide the order of rug completion based on material availability"

- "How will *your* team allocate overtime hours this week?"

- Example: Dagon rearranged the production sequence to use leftover red thread before new dye arrived

3. **Strategic Choices** (Monthly Impact)

- "*Your* team selects one process improvement to implement next month"

- "How will *you* invest *your* quality bonus in workshop enhancements?"

- Example: Weavers chose to purchase better shuttle polishers rather than new dye vats

Crucially, Kael implemented "decision journals" where weavers recorded:

- The choice they made

- Why they made it

- How it affected *our* workshop

- What they'd do differently next time

This transformed isolated decisions into a collective learning system. Ur's merchant records showed that workshops implementing decision journals saw a 47% reduction in recurring errors within three months.

Modern equivalents include:

- **Customer Service Autonomy**: Allowing front-line staff to resolve issues up to a set value without approval

- **Process Innovation Time**: Dedicating 10% of work hours to team-chosen improvements

- **Quality Ownership Circles**: Small teams empowered to solve specific operational challenges

Kael discovered that the real magic occurred when ownership decisions were connected to visible outcomes—a concept Bansir called "closing the ownership loop."

—-

Closing the Ownership Loop: Making Impact Visible

One evening, Kael found Dagon studying the workshop's ledger by lamplight. "I've been calculating," Dagon explained, "how many coins our quality improvements have earned *us* this month."

Kael joined him, surprised. Dagon had never shown interest in the workshop's finances before.

"See here," Dagon pointed. "When we reduced thread waste by 18%, *our* material costs dropped by three silver pieces. When we finished Lady Nura's rug two days early, she paid an extra half-shekel for the rush. And when we caught that dye error before it spread, we saved eight shekels in remaking the entire piece."

Kael realized Dagon was doing what Ur's master merchants called "profit mapping"—connecting daily actions to financial outcomes. This practice activated what modern behavioral economists term "outcome salience," making the impact of ownership decisions impossible to ignore.

Kael immediately implemented the "Weaver's Impact Ledger," a simplified financial tracking system where:

- Each quality catch was logged with its monetary value

- Time savings were converted to coin equivalents

- Customer compliments mentioning specific weavers were recorded

- Waste reduction was measured in tangible coin savings

Every Friday, Kael gathered the team to review the ledger, not as a performance report but as a celebration of *their* collective impact. "Last week," he'd announce, "Dagon's early detection of the tension flaw saved *our* workshop five shekels—that's enough to buy two new shuttle polishers. Elam's dye consistency improvements earned *us* an extra three shekels in customer premiums."

The psychological power of this practice operated on three levels:

1. *Tangibility*: Abstract quality became concrete coin

2. *Immediacy*: Impact was shown within days, not months

3. *Attribution*: Individuals saw how their specific actions contributed

Ur's merchant records showed workshops implementing impact ledgers saw a 68% increase in proactive problem-solving within one month. When employees could *see* the connection between their actions and financial outcomes, ownership became self-reinforcing.

Modern implementations include:

- **Real-Time Dashboards**: Showing sales impact of service recoveries

- **Customer Value Calculators**: Converting process improvements to revenue

- **Ownership Scorecards**: Tracking individual contributions to key metrics

Kael added a powerful behavioral reinforcement: after each weekly review, he placed coins in a clear jar labeled "*Our* Growth Fund." When the jar reached a predetermined amount, the team decided how to invest it—sometimes in workshop improvements, other times in shared celebrations. This transformed abstract profit-sharing into visible, collective progress toward meaningful goals.

—-

The Whisper That Changes Everything: Leadership's Role in Daily Reinforcement

Bansir returned to Kael's workshop during the fourth week of implementation. He watched silently as Kael moved through the space, not with the commanding presence of a master but with the attentive focus of a fellow craftsman. When Dagon adjusted his loom tension, Kael didn't command but asked, "What made you choose that tension today?"

Dagon looked up, surprised. "I remembered last week's fraying on the border. I thought *our* rugs would be stronger with just a bit more give."

Kael nodded. "Show me how you tested it."

As Dagon demonstrated, Kael placed a hand on his shoulder—not in dominance but connection—and whispered, "This is how masters are made."

Bansir caught Kael afterward. "That whisper—that is the secret sauce. You've moved from owner to steward of ownership."

Kael shook his head. "I've done nothing special. I simply ask questions and listen."

"Precisely," Bansir replied. "Most leaders believe ownership culture requires grand gestures and dramatic speeches. But the true transformation happens in the quiet moments between tasks, in the questions asked and the attention given. You've learned to speak the language of ownership not just in meetings but in the spaces between."

Bansir explained the leadership practices that made Kael's approach successful:

1. **The 30-Second Investment**: Kael had trained himself to spend at least 30 seconds of genuine attention with each weaver daily—enough to notice small improvements and ask one ownership-focused question. Ur's records showed leaders who implemented this practice saw 2.3x higher retention of ownership behaviors.

2. **Question Framing**: Instead of "Why did this happen?" (blame-focused), Kael asked "What have *we* learned?" (ownership-focused). Instead of "Fix this problem," he asked "How would *you* solve this if *our* reputation depended on it?"

3. **Ownership Affirmation**: When recognizing good work, Kael always connected it to identity: "You caught that flaw because you're the kind of weaver who cares about *our* reputation," not "Good job catching that flaw."

4. **Strategic Vulnerability**: Kael occasionally shared his own uncertainties: "I'm struggling with how to price Lady Nura's commission. How would *you* approach it if *your* workshop depended on this decision?"

Modern neuroscience confirms these practices activate the brain's social cognition networks, creating what researchers call "shared reality" where leaders and teams experience events through a common interpretive lens. When Kael asked "How would *you* handle this?", he wasn't just delegating—he was creating neural alignment between his thinking and his team's.

The most powerful practice Kael had adopted was the "Ownership Mirror"—ending each interaction by reflecting back the ownership behavior he'd observed: "I appreciate how you took responsibility for *our* dye consistency today. That's the mark of a true steward."

Bansir left Kael with one final instruction: "The ultimate test of ownership culture isn't what happens when you're present—it's what happens when you're absent. Next week, I want you to leave the workshop for three days and observe from the shadows. True ownership culture will continue to thrive in your absence."

—-

The Absence Test: When Ownership Culture Stands Alone

Kael followed Bansir's instruction precisely. On the morning of the fourth week, he announced he must travel to inspect a new wool supplier, leaving the workshop in Dagon's care. As he walked away, his heart pounded with uncertainty—would the ownership culture collapse without his daily reinforcement?

From his hiding place in a nearby alley, Kael watched the workshop come alive. Dagon gathered the team for their morning ritual, his voice carrying through the open doorway: "Before we begin, each of *us* shares how *we* will grow *our* workshop today." One by one, the weavers stepped forward with their commitments.

When the midday meal arrived, Kael saw Dagon pause the work. "Before we eat," Dagon announced, "let's share one way *we* grew *our* workshop this morning." Elam spoke of improving his shuttle speed; another weaver shared how she'd caught an emerging pattern flaw.

The true test came that afternoon when a messenger arrived with urgent news: Lady Nura demanded her rug be delivered tomorrow, not in three days as agreed. Kael watched as Dagon gathered the team, not to dictate a solution but to ask, "*Our* most important customer needs us. How will *we* deliver *our* best work on her new timeline?"

The weavers huddled, proposing solutions:

- They'd work through the afternoon meal in shifts

- They'd simplify the border pattern slightly without compromising quality

- They'd use pre-prepared dyes to save mixing time

Dagon nodded. "Then *we* do it together. *Our* reputation depends on it."

As Kael watched his team work with renewed purpose—not for extra pay but for *their* shared pride—he finally understood Bansir's lesson.

Ownership culture wasn't something he gave his weavers; it was something he cultivated until they claimed it as their own.

When Kael returned the next day, the finished rug sat proudly displayed, Lady Nura's delighted note beside it. Dagon met him at the door, not with relief that the master had returned, but with quiet pride: "*Our* workshop met the challenge. *We* are ready for whatever comes next."

—-

Implementing Your Daily Ownership Framework: A Practical Guide

Kael's journey from frustrated owner to steward of ownership culture provides a blueprint any leader can follow. Here's how to implement these principles in your own organization, step by step:

Phase 1: Audit Your Current Ownership Landscape (Week 1)

1. **Conduct a Language Scan**: Record team meetings for three days. Count how often "our" vs. "the" appears when discussing work. Target: 70% "our" usage by month three.

2. **Map Decision Ownership**: Document who makes key decisions at each level. Target: 50% of tactical decisions made at frontline level within 60 days.

3. **Measure Impact Visibility**: Ask team members to estimate how their work affects business outcomes. Target: 80% can accurately describe their contribution to revenue within 90 days.

Phase 2: Implement Foundational Practices (Weeks 2-4)

1. **Launch the Ownership Language Loom**

- Co-create four identity threads with your team

- Display prominently in workspace

- Rotate daily focus thread with morning huddle

2. **Establish Daily Rituals**

- Morning: "One way I'll grow *our* [business] today"

- Midday: "One action that grew *our* [business] so far"

- Evening: "One lesson *our* [business] learned today"

3. **Create Micro-Decision Opportunities**

- Implement a "Guardian of [Key Area]" role that rotates weekly

- Grant authority to resolve customer issues up to X value without approval

- Provide small budgets for team-chosen improvements

Phase 3: Deepen Ownership Integration (Weeks 5-12)

1. **Build Impact Visibility Systems**

- Create simple "ownership ledgers" tracking individual contributions to key metrics

- Hold weekly "impact reviews" celebrating specific connections between actions and outcomes

- Implement transparent "growth jars" showing collective progress toward shared goals

2. **Train Leaders in Ownership Reinforcement**

- Teach the 30-second investment technique

- Practice ownership-focused question framing

- Implement the "Ownership Mirror" feedback method

3. **Conduct the Absence Test**

- Plan a 2-3 day absence where you observe from a distance

- Before leaving, set one collective challenge that requires ownership behaviors

- Debrief upon return focusing on what worked without your presence

Common Pitfalls and How to Avoid Them

- **The Ritual Trap**: Implementing practices without purpose. *Fix*: Connect each ritual to a specific ownership outcome ("We do X to build Y capability").

- **The Performance Pressure**: Focusing on results rather than ownership behaviors. *Fix*: Recognize effort and learning, not just outcomes.

- **The Inconsistency Drain**: Skipping practices when busy. *Fix*: Anchor rituals to non-negotiable times (e.g., always before coffee break).

- **The Leader Dependency**: Culture collapsing without constant reinforcement. *Fix*: Rotate ritual leadership among team members.

Tracking your progress requires measuring both leading and lagging indicators:

- **Leading Indicators**:

- Percentage of "our" vs. "the" in team communications

- Number of frontline-initiated improvements

- Frequency of ownership-focused questions from team members

- **Lagging Indicators**:

- Discretionary effort (voluntary extra work)

- Problem-solving without managerial involvement

- Retention of ownership behaviors after leadership changes

Ur's merchant records showed workshops hitting 80% on leading indicators within 90 days saw a 34% increase in profitability within one year—proof that daily ownership practices compound into tangible business results.

—-

The Ripple Effect: When Ownership Culture Transforms Everything

Six moons after implementing his daily ownership practices, Kael stood before the Merchant's Guild presenting his workshop's results. His figures stunned the assembly:

- 42% reduction in material waste

- 31% increase in premium commissions

- 19% higher customer retention

- 0% turnover among weavers

But the most compelling evidence came when Guild Master Naram asked, "What changed most in your workshop?"

Dagon stepped forward—no longer the sullen lead weaver but a confident partner. "Before, we counted the sun's journey until we could leave. Now, we measure how many perfect threads *we* have woven. The workshop isn't Kael's—it's *ours*. And because it's *ours*, we guard its reputation as we would our own honor."

The transformation extended beyond metrics. When a rival workshop burned to the ground, Kael's weavers volunteered their off-hours to help rebuild—not out of charity but because "*our* guild's reputation depends on all workshops thriving." When a drought threatened the indigo crops, the weavers developed a new dye process using local plants, saving the entire weaving trade.

This phenomenon—the ripple effect of ownership culture—is documented throughout Ur's merchant history. Workshops with mature ownership cultures didn't just outperform competitors; they lifted entire industries through shared innovation and collective problem-solving.

Modern parallels exist in companies like W.L. Gore (makers of GORE-TEX), where the "lattice" organizational structure distributes ownership to all associates. Their associate-driven innovation has produced breakthroughs in medical devices, fabrics, and industrial products—proof that ownership culture isn't just about engagement but about unlocking collective genius.

The ultimate measure of Kael's success wasn't in ledgers but in identity. When a young boy asked Dagon how to become a master weaver, Dagon didn't speak of techniques or patterns. He placed the boy's hand on a loom and said, "Feel this wood. It's *ours*. When you care for *our* loom as if it's part of you, then and only then will you become a master."

—-

Your Ownership Culture Journey Begins Today

As Kael walked home that evening, he passed a struggling pottery workshop where apprentices moved listlessly between kilns. The master potter sat apart, counting coins with a furrowed brow. Kael paused, then entered.

"Your vessels are beautiful," he said, "but your apprentices move like slaves. Would you like to know why my weavers work with fire in their eyes?"

The potter scoffed. "I pay them fairly. What more would you have me do?"

Kael smiled. "Not pay them more—make them owners. Not of silver, but of purpose. Tomorrow morning, gather them and ask: 'How will *you* grow *our* workshop today?' Then listen. The rest will follow."

That night, Kael added a new entry to his own ownership ledger: "*Shared the gift of ownership with a fellow merchant. Our guild grows stronger when every workshop thrives.*"

This is where your journey begins—not with grand restructuring or expensive programs, but with tomorrow morning's first question: "How will *you* grow *our* business today?"

The path to true ownership culture isn't paved with quarterly payouts or mission statement posters. It's woven through daily choices—language that reframes identity, rituals that root responsibility, micro-decisions that build agency. It's the 30-second investment, the ownership mirror, the whispered affirmation that transforms "my job" into "my purpose."

Your team already possesses the capacity for ownership. Your role isn't to give it to them but to create the daily conditions where it can't help but emerge. When you consistently reinforce ownership through language, ritual, and opportunity, something remarkable happens: your people stop waiting for permission and start exercising stewardship. They don't just do their jobs—they guard your reputation, improve your processes, and protect your customers as if their very name was on the door.

The most profound business transformations aren't announced in boardrooms—they're whispered in alleyways, etched in clay tablets, and woven into the fabric of daily work. Your ownership culture isn't built in a day, but it begins with today's choices.

As you close this chapter, consider: What single ownership practice will you implement tomorrow morning? Not next quarter, not when the timing is perfect—but tomorrow, when the sun first rises over your workshop, office, or store. The journey of a thousand ownership moments begins with a single question, a single ritual, a single decision made differently.

This is the work of the master merchant—not optimizing machines, but cultivating stewards. And it starts not with what you give, but with what you allow your people to claim as their own.

Chapter 15: The Baker's Clay Tablet – Forecasting as a Competitive Weapon

The Cost of Living Only in Today's Economy

What if I told you that 92% of business failures aren't caused by poor products or bad leadership, but by a fundamental blindness to tomorrow? Consider this: when the great drought struck Babylon, it wasn't the lack of rain that destroyed the bakeries—it was the failure to see that rain would stop. While Zimri the baker slept soundly through the first dry month, his competitors scrambled to raise prices on shrinking flour supplies, their ovens growing cold as customers could no longer afford bread. By the third month of drought, seven out of ten bakeries had shuttered their doors, their owners reduced to begging for crumbs outside the very establishments they once owned. Yet Zimri's shop remained open, selling bread at fair prices while competitors collapsed around him. The difference wasn't luck or divine favor—it was a simple clay tablet recording a wheat futures contract signed two years earlier, when grain flowed like the Euphrates itself.

You're likely living this reality right now without realizing it. Like the panicked bakers of Babylon, you're reacting to market shifts instead of anticipating them. Your current planning relies on historical data and gut feel, missing future volatility signals until they crash through your door like a flood in reverse. You understand forecasting conceptually but lack frameworks to secure future advantage today, resulting in constant firefighting that drains your energy and erodes your margins. The truth is painful but clear: if you're not actively securing your future costs and opportunities today, you're gambling with your business's survival. This chapter targets your critical gap—transforming forecasting from a passive prediction tool into an active capital allocation strategy that locks in advantages before competitors even recognize the threat, turning future uncertainty into present opportunity.

The Clay Tablet That Changed Everything

Zimri wasn't always the wisest baker in Babylon. Like his peers, he once measured success by yesterday's sales and today's inventory. His turning point came during the Festival of Ishtar, when the city's granary master, a wizened man named Nabu, observed Zimri purchasing wheat at record-low prices. "You buy as if famine will never come," Nabu remarked, watching the young baker load his donkey cart.

Zimri laughed. "Famine? Look at the fields! The harvest is overflowing the granaries. Wheat has never been cheaper."

Nabu's eyes darkened. "Exactly. That is why you should buy not just for today, but for tomorrow's scarcity." He produced a small clay tablet from his robe. "This is my wheat futures contract. I've secured delivery of twenty measures at today's price, to be delivered two years hence."

Zimri scoffed. "You pay for wheat you cannot eat? Madness! I'll buy when I need it."

"Then you'll be a beggar when the rains stop," Nabu replied calmly. "The wise merchant doesn't wait for the river to flood to build his boat. He builds it while the sun shines."

That conversation haunted Zimri. That night, he couldn't sleep, pacing his small bakery as the scent of cooling bread filled the air. He remembered the stories of his grandfather, who had survived the Great Drought of thirty years prior. How many bakeries had closed then? How many families had starved? Yet here he was, spending his surplus on fine linens and copper trinkets while ignoring the most fundamental truth of commerce: today's abundance guarantees tomorrow's scarcity.

The next morning, Zimri made his decision. He canceled his linen order and instead purchased a futures contract for wheat delivery two years hence at current prices. When his fellow bakers mocked him—"Zimri, the baker of imaginary bread!" they called him—he simply smiled and continued his work. Every month, he set aside a small portion of his profits to purchase additional futures contracts, building what he called his "drought defense."

Two years later, when the rains failed to come and the river shrank to a muddy trickle, Zimri's foresight became his fortune. While other bakers faced wheat prices that had skyrocketed tenfold, Zimri could access grain at the price he'd secured years earlier. His bakery remained open when others closed, his bread affordable when competitors' prices put food beyond reach of ordinary citizens. By the time the drought ended, Zimri wasn't just the most prosperous baker in Babylon—he was the owner of three additional bakeries, purchased for copper scraps from desperate former competitors.

Zimri's clay tablets weren't predictions—they were "future cost insurance." While others saw mere speculation, he understood these contracts as strategic weapons that transformed market volatility from a threat into an opportunity. This wasn't gambling; it was calculated defense. The merchants of Ur had used "forward contracts" for 30% of their grain needs for generations, reducing price volatility by 65% and creating stability in chaotic markets. Zimri had simply applied this ancient wisdom with discipline and patience.

The modern equivalent requires what I call "anticipatory hedging"—the systematic identification of 3-5 existential threats to your business, then securing today's costs through futures, options, or long-term contracts. Most entrepreneurs rely on sophisticated tools like Palantir to forecast macro trends using AI, but Zimri's genius was in his simplicity. He tracked only two metrics: the height of the river at planting season and the fullness of the temple granaries. When the river ran low during planting and the granaries remained unusually full (indicating hoarding behavior), he knew drought was coming.

Consider the case of a hypothetical manufacturing business we'll call "Athena Components." Facing potential supply chain disruptions, their leadership identified three critical vulnerabilities: raw material costs, shipping container availability, and energy prices. Instead of waiting for problems to emerge, they allocated 12% of their annual revenue to anticipatory hedging. They secured three-year contracts for 40% of their aluminum needs at current prices, locked in shipping container rates for 30% of their volume, and entered into fixed-rate energy contracts covering half their usage. When global supply chains fractured six months later, Athena Components maintained stable costs while competitors faced 35-50% price increases. Their foresight didn't just protect margins—it allowed them to undercut competitors' prices, capturing 22% market share in a single year.

The critical mindset shift is understanding that forecasting isn't about predicting the future—it's about preparing for multiple possible futures. While Babylon's other bakers lived exclusively in the "now economy," Zimri operated in the "tomorrow economy," deploying capital today to secure advantages tomorrow. Research confirms this approach: entrepreneurs who visualize multiple future scenarios make 2.4x better capital decisions than those focused solely on current conditions. Your brain physically changes when you practice future-oriented thinking—the prefrontal cortex (responsible for planning) strengthens while the amygdala (fear center) calms, creating neurological advantages for strategic thinkers.

Building Your Babylonian Buffer

Zimri's most powerful innovation wasn't his wheat contracts—it was his "Babylonian Buffer," the systematic allocation of resources specifically dedicated to future-proofing his business. While other bakers spent every copper on immediate needs or short-term pleasures, Zimri deliberately set aside 15% of his revenue for securing future advantages. This wasn't savings; it was strategic investment in tomorrow's stability.

The Babylonian Buffer operates on a fundamental principle: volatility is inevitable, but its impact is optional. When market conditions change, those without buffers absorb 100% of the volatility in their costs and revenues. Those with buffers experience dramatically reduced impact, turning potential crises into opportunities. Consider a hypothetical service business facing interest rate volatility. Without a buffer, a 2% rate increase might raise their financing costs by 40%, potentially eliminating profits. With a properly structured buffer, they might experience only a 5% cost increase, maintaining profitability while competitors struggle.

To implement your Babylonian Buffer, follow this four-step process:

1. **Identify Your Volatility Exposure**: List every significant cost and revenue stream in your business. For each, determine how sensitive it is to market fluctuations. A restaurant, for example, would identify food costs (highly volatile), labor (moderately volatile), and rent (low volatility). Rate each on a 1-10 volatility scale, where 10 represents extreme sensitivity to market conditions.

2. **Calculate Buffer Requirements**: For each high-volatility item (7+ on your scale), determine the maximum adverse movement you could withstand before threatening business survival. If your largest cost is raw materials currently at $100,000 monthly, and you could survive a 30% increase, your buffer needs to cover $30,000 of potential volatility. Sum these amounts across all critical vulnerabilities.

3. **Establish Buffer Funding**: Allocate 10-15% of revenue specifically for buffer funding. This isn't discretionary—it's as essential as payroll. For the first six months, focus exclusively on the single largest vulnerability. Once secured, move to the next. Zimri started with wheat, then added barley, then fuel contracts.

4. **Measure Buffer Effectiveness**: Track your "volatility capture ratio"—the percentage reduction in cost volatility achieved through your buffer. If raw material costs increase 50% industry-wide but your costs rise only 15% due to futures contracts, your ratio is 70% (meaning you captured 70% of the potential volatility). Top performers maintain ratios of 60%+.

Consider the case of "Silk Road Logistics," a hypothetical transportation company operating in volatile fuel markets. They identified fuel costs as their primary vulnerability (volatility score 9/10). Their analysis showed a 30% fuel price increase could eliminate all profits. They allocated 12% of revenue to their Babylonian Buffer, initially focusing on fuel hedging. They secured futures contracts covering 50% of their projected fuel needs for the next 18 months at current prices. When global fuel prices spiked 45% six months later, their costs increased only 22.5%—a 50% volatility capture ratio. This seemingly modest protection preserved $287,000 in annual profit that competitors lost, allowing Silk Road to invest in new routes while others cut services.

Your Babylonian Buffer should evolve as your business grows. In early stages, focus on existential threats (those that could kill your business). As you stabilize, expand to strategic opportunities (those that could significantly grow your business). Zimri began by securing wheat for survival, then added barley contracts that allowed him to expand into new neighborhoods. By the third drought cycle, he was using his buffer strategically to buy distressed competitors' assets at bargain prices.

The psychological component is critical. Most entrepreneurs view buffer funding as "money not spent on growth," creating resistance to allocation. Reframe this thinking: your buffer isn't money set aside—it's money deployed strategically to ensure future growth is possible. Ur's merchants treated wheat contracts as "seeds for future loaves," while modern CFOs frame hedges as "strategic inventory." This cognitive shift transforms buffer funding from a cost center to a growth accelerator in your mental accounting.

Operationalizing Tomorrow: The Future Sprint Framework

Knowing you need to forecast is one thing; building the systems to do it consistently is another. This is where most businesses fail—they understand the concept but lack the operational discipline to implement it. Zimri succeeded not because he was smarter than other bakers, but because he built routines that made future-proofing automatic.

The key is what I call the "Future Sprint Framework"—dedicating specific, recurring time to securing future advantages through structured processes. Unlike traditional strategic planning that happens annually (and then gathers dust), Future Sprints are short, focused bursts of activity that yield immediate, actionable results.

Here's how to implement Future Sprints in your business:

Step 1: Schedule Quarterly Future Sprints

Block one full week every quarter specifically for future-proofing activities. During this week, shift your entire team's focus from immediate firefighting to securing future advantages. Zimri did this during planting season when business naturally slowed, aligning his planning with natural business rhythms. Your scheduling should follow similar logic—choose a time when current pressures are lower, not when you're already overwhelmed.

Step 2: Conduct the Threat Radar Review

During the first two days of your sprint, identify and prioritize threats using this process:

- Brainstorm all potential market shifts (use industry reports, customer feedback, and supplier conversations)

- Score each on two dimensions: likelihood (1-5) and impact (1-5, where 5 = business-threatening)

- Focus exclusively on high-likelihood/high-impact threats (quadrant 1)

- For each priority threat, identify one actionable hedge you can implement

For example, a hypothetical software company might identify:

- Cloud service price increases (likelihood 4, impact 5)

- Key developer turnover (likelihood 3, impact 5)

- New data regulations (likelihood 2, impact 5)

Their priority would be cloud service costs, leading to negotiations for long-term pricing agreements with providers.

Step 3: Execute the Hedge Implementation

Days 3-5 of your sprint should focus on implementing one hedge per priority threat. This isn't theoretical—it's concrete action. For the software company, this might mean:

- Negotiating and signing a three-year cloud services agreement

- Drafting and implementing a retention bonus structure for key developers

- Beginning compliance documentation for anticipated regulations

Crucially, track your "cost certainty score"—the percentage of critical inputs with fixed future pricing. Zimri tracked this religiously, aiming for 70%+ certainty on his major costs. Top-performing businesses maintain scores of 65%+ on their most volatile cost categories.

Step 4: Document and Institutionalize

On the final day, document everything in a "Future Certainty Ledger." This modern equivalent of Zimri's clay tablets should include:

- Each hedge implemented

- Terms and duration

- Expected volatility protection

- Renewal dates

- Responsible party for monitoring

Share this ledger with your leadership team and review it monthly. Zimri kept his tablets prominently displayed in his bakery, a constant reminder of his secured advantages.

The Future Sprint Framework works because it transforms abstract forecasting into concrete action. Consider "Delta Manufacturing," a hypothetical industrial equipment producer. They implemented Future Sprints during their historically slow summer months. In their first sprint, they identified steel prices as their primary vulnerability (representing 38% of production costs). They executed a hedge by securing 60% of their steel needs through a supplier at fixed prices for 18 months. When steel prices increased 32% industry-wide six months later, Delta's costs rose only 12.8%—a 60% volatility capture ratio. This protection preserved $1.2 million in annual profit, which they reinvested in automation that further reduced costs. Over three years, their disciplined Future Sprints created a compound advantage: stable costs allowed consistent pricing, which grew market share, which provided more capital for additional hedges.

Most businesses fail at forecasting because they treat it as an intellectual exercise rather than an operational discipline. The difference between those who succeed and those who don't isn't intelligence—it's implementation. Zimri didn't just think about drought; he signed contracts, stored tablets, and monitored conditions. Your Future Sprints must similarly focus on tangible actions, not just analysis.

Leading Indicators and the Art of Strategic Foresight

Zimri's true genius wasn't in his contracts—it was in his ability to identify drought before others saw it coming. While Babylon's other bakers watched only the sky for rain, Zimri monitored bird migration patterns, observing how certain species changed their routes months before the drought became obvious. He watched the behavior of ants, noting how they sealed their hills earlier than usual. He tracked the temple granaries, recognizing unusual hoarding behavior as a signal of coming scarcity.

These were Zimri's "lead indicators"—early warning signals that provided months of advance notice before the crisis became apparent to others. Most businesses today focus exclusively on "lag indicators" (revenue, profit, market share)—metrics that tell you what already happened. Strategic foresight requires identifying and monitoring lead indicators that predict what will happen.

To build your own lead indicator system, follow this process:

Step 1: Map Your Vulnerability Chain

For each critical business vulnerability, identify the chain of events that would lead to crisis. For a restaurant, this might be:

Drought → Poor harvest → Grain scarcity → Wheat price increase → Flour cost increase → Margin pressure

Step 2: Identify Early Signals

For each stage in the chain, identify signals that occur before the next stage manifests. For the restaurant:

- Drought: Bird migration changes, ant behavior, river levels during planting season

- Poor harvest: Planting season rainfall, early crop inspections

- Grain scarcity: Granary levels, hoarding behavior, futures market activity

- Price increase: Supplier conversations, futures prices, export restrictions

Step 3: Establish Monitoring Systems

Create simple, sustainable ways to track these indicators. Zimri visited the riverbank weekly and spoke with farmers daily. Modern equivalents include:

- Setting Google Alerts for key terms

- Subscribing to industry-specific data services

- Building relationships with suppliers for early warnings

- Creating simple tracking spreadsheets

Step 4: Define Trigger Points

Establish clear thresholds that trigger action. Zimri decided: "If river level at planting is below X and two bird species change migration, purchase 20% more wheat futures." Your triggers might be: "If shipping container rates increase 15% for three consecutive weeks, secure 30% of next quarter's capacity."

Consider how "Horizon Textiles," a hypothetical fabric manufacturer, implemented this system. They identified cotton price volatility as their primary vulnerability. Their vulnerability chain: weather patterns → crop conditions → harvest yield → supply/demand balance → price movement. Their lead indicators included:

- Weather: Monthly climate reports from growing regions

- Crop conditions: Satellite imagery of cotton fields

- Harvest yield: Early farmer surveys in key regions

- Supply/demand: Weekly inventory reports from major warehouses

They established simple monitoring: a junior analyst spent two hours weekly gathering these data points. Their trigger points were clear: "If satellite imagery shows moisture levels below threshold in two consecutive readings, begin securing 10% more cotton futures." When unusual weather patterns emerged in cotton-growing regions, Horizon Textiles secured cotton at favorable prices while competitors waited for prices to actually rise. By the time cotton prices increased 28% industry-wide, Horizon had locked in 70% of their needs at 15% below market rates, preserving $850,000 in annual profit.

The psychological barrier to effective lead indicator monitoring is "present bias"—our brain's tendency to prioritize immediate, visible threats over distant, invisible ones. Zimri overcame this by making indicator monitoring part of his daily routine, not a special project. He checked the river while walking to work, spoke with farmers while buying supplies. Your monitoring must similarly integrate into existing workflows to become sustainable.

Track your "forecast accuracy delta"—the difference between your predicted costs and actual costs. Top performers maintain deltas of less than 5%, meaning their forecasts are highly accurate. This metric measures not just your forecasting ability, but your effectiveness in securing advantages based on those forecasts. Zimri tracked this religiously, adjusting his future contracts based on how accurately his drought predictions played out.

Institutionalizing Foresight: The Future Council

Zimri's success wasn't sustainable as a solo endeavor. When his business grew beyond a single bakery, he realized he needed a system to maintain his future-focused approach across multiple locations and an expanding team. His solution was the "Future Council"—a cross-functional group that met weekly to review lead indicators, assess buffer effectiveness, and make strategic hedging decisions.

Your business needs a similar structure to institutionalize foresight. The Future Council transforms forecasting from a periodic activity into an embedded capability that operates continuously. Here's how to establish your own:

Council Composition

Your Future Council should include:

- A leadership representative (CEO or business unit head)

- Finance lead (CFO or controller)

- Operations lead (COO or VP of operations)

- Sales/Marketing lead

- One frontline employee who interacts directly with customers or suppliers

This cross-functional mix ensures multiple perspectives and prevents siloed thinking. Zimri included his head baker, a wheat buyer, and even a delivery boy who spoke with farmers daily.

Meeting Structure

Future Council meetings follow this strict 90-minute format:

1. **Lead Indicator Review (20 minutes)**: Each member shares updates on 1-2 critical indicators in their area. No lengthy presentations—just concise updates with clear implications.

2. **Buffer Assessment (20 minutes)**: Review current buffer positions against actual market conditions. Calculate current volatility capture ratio.

3. **Opportunity Identification (20 minutes)**: Brainstorm new hedging opportunities based on indicator trends.

4. **Action Planning (20 minutes)**: Assign specific actions with owners and deadlines.

5. **Learning Integration (10 minutes)**: Document key insights for future sprints.

Technology Enablement

While Zimri used clay tablets and oral reports, modern councils leverage technology:

- Real-time dashboards showing critical indicators

- Shared documents for decision tracking

- Automated alerts for trigger point breaches

- Video conferencing for remote members

Consider "Aegean Shipping," a hypothetical maritime transport company that implemented a Future Council during a period of extreme fuel price volatility. Their council included the CEO, CFO, operations director, commercial director, and a senior captain with decades of experience. They established a simple dashboard tracking:

- Current and projected fuel prices

- Contract coverage percentage

- Volatility capture ratio

- Key lead indicators (OPEC announcements, geopolitical tensions)

Each week, the council reviewed these metrics, making small adjustments to their hedging strategy. When geopolitical tensions began escalating in a key shipping region, their captain (drawing on decades of experience) recognized patterns similar to previous crises. The council immediately secured additional fuel contracts at favorable rates. When the expected disruption occurred three months later, Aegean maintained stable costs while competitors faced 35% price increases. Their disciplined council meetings transformed forecasting from theoretical exercise to operational advantage.

The ultimate metric for your Future Council is "anticipation ROI"—the profit gained from future-proofing actions versus the cost of implementing them. Top performers achieve ROIs of 5.0x or higher, meaning every dollar spent on forecasting and hedging generates five dollars in protected profit or captured opportunity. Zimri tracked this intuitively—he knew that the silver spent on clay tablets and scribe services to record his contracts generated returns hundreds of times greater when drought struck.

Conclusion: From Reactive to Strategic

You now wield a proactive framework to transform forecasting into actionable capital allocation, replacing reactivity with strategic foresight. The stress of surprise market shifts has been replaced with the confidence of secured advantages, letting you operate from strength during crises. The Babylonian Buffer provides your foundation, the Future Sprint Framework delivers operational discipline, lead indicator monitoring sharpens your foresight, and the Future Council institutionalizes these capabilities across your organization.

This transformation isn't merely about avoiding disaster—it's about positioning yourself to thrive when others falter. When the next market shift comes (and it will), you'll be the one buying distressed assets, capturing market share, and serving customers when competitors cannot. Like Zimri, you'll convert volatility from a threat into your greatest competitive advantage.

The psychological shift required is profound: viewing forecasting not as an abstract intellectual exercise but as your most valuable form of capital deployment. Every dollar allocated to securing future advantages is a seed planted today that will grow into tomorrow's security and opportunity. Ur's merchants understood this deeply—they didn't see wheat contracts as expenses but as investments in future stability that would multiply their returns when scarcity struck.

Your journey toward strategic foresight begins with a single decision: to allocate resources today for advantages tomorrow. Start small if necessary—secure just one critical input against future volatility. Document it on your own "clay tablet" (a simple spreadsheet will do). Review it weekly with your leadership team. Measure its impact. Then expand to the next vulnerability.

As you implement these practices, you'll notice a subtle but powerful shift in your business culture. Your team will begin thinking further ahead, spotting opportunities earlier, and making decisions with greater confidence. Where others see uncertainty, you'll see opportunity. Where competitors react, you'll respond from a position of strength.

However, securing future costs requires capital discipline—you must now master the art of funding these opportunities without straining current operations, as Zimri did by sacrificing linen purchases for wheat contracts. This chapter equipped you to forecast and secure, but the next challenge is balancing present needs with future investments. You're ready to confront the tension between immediate cash flow and long-term positioning—a challenge faced by the salt merchant who refused to abandon his reliable donkey for the fleeting glory of warhorse status. The path to true mastery requires understanding your core strengths deeply enough to know which trends to chase and which to ignore. Your journey from reactive operator to strategic visionary continues, with each lesson building upon the last to create an unstoppable foundation for enduring success.

Chapter 16: The Salt Donkey's Load – Mastering Your Core Before Chasing Trends

The Donkey's Fateful Choice

On the dusty outskirts of Babylon, where the Euphrates River carved its slow path through the fertile crescent, a sturdy donkey named Kassim plodded faithfully along the same trade route he had walked for seven years. His broad back bore two heavy sacks of salt—mined from the northern plains, processed by the salt merchants of Ur, and destined for the spice markets of the eastern deserts. Each step was measured, each turn along the well-worn path familiar. The route was neither glamorous nor fast, but it was reliable. Each trip delivered Kassim's owner, a merchant named Jabir, a steady profit of two silver shekels after expenses—a return of approximately 20% on the invested capital. Over seven years, this consistency had allowed Jabir to build a modest home, educate his three children, and accumulate a reserve sufficient to weather two full seasons of drought.

One evening, as Kassim rested in the stable, a magnificent warhorse named Zephyr was paraded through the city gates. Adorned in golden trappings, his coat gleaming under the setting sun, Zephyr carried the King's messenger who had just returned from a victorious campaign against the Elamites. The streets erupted in cheers. Citizens threw flowers at the horse's hooves. Young boys mimicked the messenger's proud posture, dreaming of one day riding into battle atop such a noble steed. That night, as Jabir scratched Kassim's ears and prepared his evening meal of barley and water, the donkey's eyes followed the distant glow of the palace torches where Zephyr undoubtedly enjoyed a feast of oats and honey.

"Tomorrow," Kassim whispered to himself as he settled onto the straw, "I too shall become a warhorse."

The next morning, Kassim refused his usual load. When Jabir approached with the salt sacks, the donkey reared, kicked over his water trough, and bolted for the palace grounds. For days, he practiced prancing, tried to gallop in tight circles, and even attempted to stand on his hind legs. The stable hands laughed at the spectacle. The warhorses whinnied in confusion at this strange imitator. When Kassim finally mustered the courage to approach the parade grounds, his first attempt to "charge" ended with him tripping over his own hooves, crashing into a stack of ceremonial shields, and earning a beating from the stable master for his trouble.

Jabir, meanwhile, watched helplessly as his reliable income stream evaporated. With no salt being transported, his contracts with the spice merchants dissolved. His customers turned to competitors. By the time Kassim limped back to the stable, bruised and exhausted, Jabir's carefully built business had unraveled. The donkey had traded seven years of dependable progress for three days of humiliating failure.

The lesson echoed through Babylon's marketplaces: **Gold is found in utility, not in vanity.**

Understanding Utility Economics: Why Your Core Matters More Than You Think

At its heart, Kassim's story embodies what modern business strategists call "utility economics"—the principle that sustainable value derives not from what appears glamorous or trendy, but from what reliably solves a genuine problem for which customers will consistently pay. The salt donkey generated steady revenue because salt was essential to preserving food, flavoring dishes, and even serving religious purposes across Mesopotamia. Its utility was unquestioned, its demand constant, and its transportation requirements perfectly matched to a donkey's capabilities. The warhorse, by contrast, offered status and military advantage—but only during wartime. In peacetime, Zephyr's upkeep cost Jabir's counterpart five silver shekels per week with no corresponding revenue stream. The warhorse's margin wasn't merely low—it was deeply negative outside of conflict periods.

This distinction between utility-driven economics and trend-chasing economics represents one of the most fundamental divides in business strategy. Consider the hypothetical example of two pottery makers operating in ancient Thebes. Amunhotep focused exclusively on crafting durable water jugs—simple, functional vessels that every household required. Each jug sold for one copper coin, with a production cost of six-tenths of a coin, yielding a healthy 40% margin. He produced 20 jugs daily and had waiting orders stretching three months into the future. His workshop employed five apprentices who each learned the precise techniques for creating leak-proof seams and comfortable handles.

His neighbor, Nakht, grew envious of Amunhotep's stability. When a traveling merchant introduced painted ceremonial vessels from distant Crete, Nakht abandoned his water jug production to create elaborate, colorful pots adorned with sea creatures—a style completely alien to Egyptian aesthetics. He invested heavily in new pigments, reconfigured his kilns, and trained his staff in unfamiliar techniques. The initial response was enthusiastic—nobles purchased several pieces as curiosities. But after two months, demand evaporated. The ceremonial pots served no practical purpose in Egyptian households, and their novelty wore off quickly. Nakht's margins collapsed from 40% to -15% as unsold inventory piled up. Within six months, he was forced to close his workshop and seek employment as an apprentice in Amunhotep's thriving business.

The difference between these two potters wasn't skill or effort—it was strategic alignment with genuine utility. Amunhotep understood that while ceremonial pots might generate momentary excitement, water jugs represented an enduring need. His focus on perfecting a single product within his core competency created a self-reinforcing cycle of improvement, reputation, and customer loyalty.

This principle manifests across business history in countless forms. In our contemporary context, imagine two competing bakery owners in a mid-sized city. Maya runs "Daily Loaf," specializing in perfecting seven classic bread varieties using time-honored sourdough techniques. She knows exactly which flours work best with her local water chemistry, has optimized her fermentation schedules for consistent results, and has built relationships with neighborhood cafes that rely on her steady supply. Her operation is lean, her waste minimal, and her customer retention rate exceeds 90%.

David, her competitor, has watched food trends come and go. When artisanal donuts became popular, he converted half his ovens to donut production. When cold brew coffee surged, he installed expensive brewing equipment. When keto diets trended, he invested in almond flour and specialty equipment. Each pivot required new training, different ingredients, revised marketing, and reconfigured workflows. While each trend brought temporary spikes in traffic, none created lasting customer loyalty. David's margins fluctuate wildly—from 12% during trend peaks to -5% during lulls—while Maya consistently achieves 18% net margins.

The fundamental insight here is that **utility trumps novelty** in sustainable business building. Customers will pay consistently for products and services that solve real problems in their lives, while trend-based offerings often generate temporary interest without creating lasting value. This doesn't mean innovation has no place—it means that innovation should enhance and extend your core utility, not replace it with something entirely disconnected from your fundamental value proposition.

The Core Compass: A Practical Framework for Strategic Decision-Making

When Jabir confronted Kassim after his failed warhorse aspirations, he didn't simply scold the donkey. Instead, he presented three simple questions—what Babylonian merchants would later call the "Core Compass"—to evaluate any potential opportunity before diverting resources from proven success:

1. **Does this leverage existing infrastructure?** (Physical assets, knowledge, relationships, processes)

2. **Does it solve a problem I understand deeply?** (Domain expertise, customer insight, operational mastery)

3. **Is the margin sustainable?** (Profitability during both boom and bust cycles)

These three questions form a remarkably powerful decision filter that has guided successful merchants for millennia. Let's examine each component in depth with practical applications.

Question 1: Does this leverage existing infrastructure?

This question forces honest assessment of whether an opportunity builds upon what you already possess or requires starting nearly from scratch. Kassim's salt transport leveraged his strength, endurance, and familiarity with desert routes—his natural infrastructure. The warhorse aspiration required entirely new physical capabilities (speed, agility), different training, and access to military circles—none of which Kassim possessed.

Consider the case of a hypothetical scribe named Tani in Memphis who transcribes legal documents for a living. She's built a comfortable practice with steady income, but she notices that her cousin has become wealthy selling amulets to travelers. Tempted by the apparent profitability, Tani considers pivoting to amulet production. Applying the first Core Compass question:

Existing infrastructure she possesses:

- Writing tools and materials

- Knowledge of hieroglyphs

- Relationships with legal professionals

- Understanding of contract law

- A quiet workspace for detailed work

Infrastructure required for amulets:

- Knowledge of gemology and metallurgy

- Relationships with miners and jewelers

- Access to precious materials

- Skills in carving and metalworking

- A different customer base with distinct purchasing habits

The mismatch is profound. Every element required for amulet production would need to be built from scratch, while her current infrastructure would become largely irrelevant.

Now contrast this with a more aligned opportunity: Tani notices that many of her legal clients struggle to understand complex documents. She considers creating simplified summaries of legal contracts as an add-on service. This leverages:

Existing infrastructure:

- Her writing tools and materials (same physical requirements)

- Her knowledge of hieroglyphs (now applied to simplification)

- Her relationships with legal professionals (same customers)

- Her understanding of contract law (core knowledge)

- Her quiet workspace (same environment)

The infrastructure alignment is nearly perfect. The only additions needed are templates for summaries and perhaps slightly more time per client.

This first question separates opportunities that build upon your foundation from those that require you to become someone else entirely. In modern business terms, it asks: "Does this opportunity utilize my existing assets, capabilities, and relationships, or does it demand that I create an entirely new business model?"

Question 2: Does it solve a problem I understand deeply?

The second component of the Core Compass addresses domain expertise—the difference between solving problems you've wrestled with for years versus dabbling in areas where you lack genuine insight. Kassim understood salt transport intimately: the weight distribution that prevented sacks from tearing, the watering schedules for desert crossings, the timing needed to avoid bandits, and the precise routes that balanced speed with safety. The warhorse role required understanding military tactics, battlefield navigation, and the psychology of combat—none of which Kassim had ever encountered.

Consider our scribe Tani again. When contemplating amulet production versus legal summaries:

Amulet production:

- Requires understanding of mystical beliefs across different cultures

- Demands knowledge of which symbols appeal to which travelers

- Needs insight into pricing psychology for superstitious purchases

- Requires awareness of seasonal demand fluctuations (pilgrimage seasons)

- None of these areas fall within Tani's experience

Legal summaries:

- Builds directly on her daily work transcribing contracts

- Leverages her understanding of where clients typically struggle

- Uses her knowledge of common contractual pain points

- Relies on her ability to identify critical clauses

- Directly extends her existing problem-solving capabilities

The distinction here is critical. Solving problems you understand deeply means you can anticipate challenges before they arise, recognize subtle warning signs, and develop solutions that genuinely address root causes rather than symptoms. This deep understanding creates what economists call "asymmetric information advantage"—you know things about your domain that competitors without your experience simply cannot know.

Consider another example: a shipbuilder named Hapi who constructs reliable fishing vessels along the Nile. When steam-powered ships begin appearing on the river, he feels pressured to pivot. Applying the second Core Compass question:

Steam-powered ships:

- Requires understanding of high-pressure boilers

- Demands knowledge of metallurgy for steam components

- Needs expertise in mechanical engineering

- Requires different regulatory knowledge

- Hapi has no experience with any of these

Improved sailing vessels:

- Builds on his existing knowledge of hull design

- Leverages his understanding of local wind patterns

- Uses his relationships with experienced sailors

- Relies on his mastery of traditional woodworking

- Directly extends his problem-solving capabilities

Hapi wisely chooses to deepen his expertise in sailing vessels. He develops a specialized fishing boat with an innovative sail configuration that allows fishermen to work closer to shore during variable winds. His deep understanding of local fishing practices—gained from decades of conversation with his customers—allows him to solve problems steam-powered ships couldn't address. Within two years, his specialized vessels command a 30% price premium while steam shipbuilders struggle with maintenance issues in the Nile's silt-laden waters.

This second question separates opportunities where you can apply hard-won wisdom from those where you'd be operating on equal footing with complete beginners.

Question 3: Is the margin sustainable?

The final component of the Core Compass addresses long-term profitability—looking beyond initial excitement to assess whether an opportunity can generate reliable returns through both good times and bad. Kassim's salt transport generated a consistent 20% margin throughout the year. The warhorse role offered the potential for glory during military campaigns (perhaps 100%+ return during active duty), but during peacetime, the costs of upkeep (feed, grooming, training) exceeded any possible income, creating a -5% margin. The average return across the year was barely positive, while the risk of injury or death during battle represented catastrophic downside risk.

Let's return to Tani the scribe. When comparing margins:

Amulet production:

- High initial profit potential (50-70% margins on first sales)

- Requires significant upfront investment in materials

- Highly seasonal demand (pilgrimage seasons only)

- Vulnerable to changing religious trends

- Margins collapse when competition enters the space

- Average annual margin: 12% with high volatility

Legal summaries:

- Moderate initial profit (35% margins)

- Minimal additional investment required

- Steady demand throughout the year

- Resistant to seasonal fluctuations

- Creates opportunities for recurring business

- Average annual margin: 32% with low volatility

The sustainability question forces us to look beyond the initial excitement of a new opportunity to assess its long-term financial viability. This requires honest analysis of:

- **Fixed versus variable costs**: Opportunities that leverage existing fixed costs (like Tani's workspace) while adding primarily variable revenue generate more sustainable margins.

- **Demand patterns**: Consistent, predictable demand creates more sustainable margins than highly seasonal or fad-driven demand.

- **Competitive dynamics**: Will competitors quickly enter the space and erode margins, or does your expertise create a protective moat?

- **Customer retention**: Sustainable margins typically come from repeat business rather than one-time transactions.

- **Downside protection**: How well does the business withstand economic contractions or market changes?

Consider a modern hypothetical: a small software company specializing in scheduling tools for dental practices. They've achieved steady growth with 25% net margins. When cryptocurrency trading platforms surge in popularity, the founders consider pivoting. Applying the Core Compass:

1. **Infrastructure alignment**: Low (requires entirely new technical skills, different regulatory knowledge, unfamiliar customer base)

2. **Problem understanding**: Low (no experience with financial trading systems or regulatory requirements)

3. **Margin sustainability**: Very low (intense competition, regulatory uncertainty, volatile demand)

Contrast this with expanding their dental scheduling software to include insurance verification features:

1. **Infrastructure alignment**: High (same technical platform, existing client relationships, familiar regulatory environment)

2. **Problem understanding**: High (daily interactions with dental office staff reveal insurance verification as a major pain point)

3. **Margin sustainability**: High (recurring revenue model, low customer acquisition cost for existing clients, defensible niche)

The sustainable margin question reveals why so many businesses fail when chasing trends—they focus on the upside potential while ignoring the volatility and fragility of trend-based profits. True business mastery comes not from capturing temporary spikes but from building consistent, reliable returns that compound over time.

Implementing the Donkey Filter: A Quantitative Approach to Opportunity Assessment

While the Core Compass provides an excellent qualitative framework, Babylonian merchants discovered that adding simple quantitative measures dramatically improved their decision-making. They developed what became known as the "Donkey Filter"—a straightforward formula for calculating the true value of any opportunity relative to their core business:

Opportunity Value = (Alignment with Core ÷ Trend Hype) × Utility Score

Let's break down each component with practical implementation guidance.

Alignment with Core (0-10 scale)

This measures how closely an opportunity connects to your existing business infrastructure, knowledge, and processes. Babylonian merchants assessed this through three specific dimensions:

1. **Resource alignment**: To what extent does this opportunity utilize existing physical assets, staff skills, and operational processes?

- *Scoring guide*:

- 9-10: Uses >80% of existing resources with minimal adaptation

- 7-8: Uses 60-80% of existing resources

- 5-6: Uses 40-60% of existing resources

- 3-4: Uses 20-40% of existing resources

- 1-2: Uses <20% of existing resources

2. **Knowledge alignment**: How deeply does this opportunity leverage your hard-won expertise and understanding of customer needs?

- *Scoring guide*:

- 9-10: Builds directly on your deepest domain expertise

- 7-8: Extends your core knowledge with moderate adaptation

- 5-6: Requires learning adjacent knowledge areas

- 3-4: Requires learning entirely new knowledge domains

- 1-2: Contradicts your existing knowledge base

3. **Relationship alignment**: To what extent does this opportunity serve your existing customers or leverage your established partnerships?

- *Scoring guide*:

- 9-10: Serves the same customers through the same channels

- 7-8: Serves existing customers through new channels

- 5-6: Serves adjacent customer segments

- 3-4: Requires developing entirely new customer relationships

- 1-2: Serves customers who actively oppose your current base

The final Alignment with Core score is the average of these three dimensions.

Example: A pottery maker considering selling online

- Resource alignment: 7 (existing kilns and tools work, but needs packaging materials and shipping setup)

- Knowledge alignment: 8 (same craftsmanship knowledge, but needs to learn digital marketing)

- Relationship alignment: 6 (could serve existing customers plus new online buyers)

- **Alignment with Core = (7+8+6)/3 = 7.0**

Trend Hype (1-10 scale)

This counterintuitive metric measures how hyped the opportunity is in the marketplace—recognizing that higher hype often correlates with lower sustainability. Babylonian merchants learned that opportunities generating the most excitement typically attracted the most competition and proved the least durable.

- *Scoring guide*:

- 1-2: Barely mentioned outside industry specialists

- 3-4: Discussed in professional circles but not mainstream

- 5-6: Gaining attention in business publications

- 7-8: Frequently featured in popular media

- 9-10: Dominating conversations at every market gathering

Example: The pottery maker considering online sales in 1200 BCE

- Trend Hype: 3 (online sales aren't a concept yet, but some merchants discuss distant markets)

- *Note: In our modern context, e-commerce would score 9-10*

Utility Score (1-10 scale)

This measures the fundamental usefulness of the opportunity—how essential the product or service is to customers' daily lives or operations.

- *Scoring guide*:

- 9-10: Solves a critical, recurring problem with no good alternatives

- 7-8: Addresses an important need with few alternatives

- 5-6: Solves a moderate problem with some existing solutions

- 3-4: Addresses a minor inconvenience

- 1-2: Creates a solution in search of a problem

Example: The pottery maker's online sales

- Utility Score: 8 (makes pottery accessible to distant customers who previously couldn't obtain it)

Calculating Opportunity Value

Using our pottery maker example:

- Alignment with Core = 7.0

- Trend Hype = 3

- Utility Score = 8

- **Opportunity Value = $(7.0 \div 3) \times 8 = 18.7$**

Babylonian merchants established clear thresholds for action:

- **Opportunity Value > 15**: Strong candidate for immediate testing

- **Opportunity Value 10-15**: Worthy of small-scale experimentation

- **Opportunity Value 5-10**: Consider only if core business is exceptionally strong

- **Opportunity Value < 5**: Almost certainly a distraction

This simple formula prevents what psychologists call "shiny object syndrome"—the tendency to pursue opportunities based on excitement rather than strategic merit. Notice how high Trend Hype dramatically reduces Opportunity Value, reflecting the Babylonian wisdom that what everyone is chasing rarely remains profitable for long.

Consider another example: a hypothetical scribe named Ani who transcribes religious texts.

Opportunity: Creating NFT versions of sacred scrolls

- Resource alignment: 3 (requires learning digital technology, new tools)

- Knowledge alignment: 2 (no experience with blockchain or digital art)

- Relationship alignment: 1 (religious institutions reject digital copies)

- Alignment with Core = (3+2+1)/3 = 2.0

- Trend Hype: 9 (NFTs are the talk of every marketplace)

- Utility Score: 4 (few customers see value in digital scrolls)

- **Opportunity Value = (2.0 ÷ 9) × 4 = 0.9**

This extremely low score—well below the 5 threshold—clearly signals this as a dangerous distraction.

Alternative Opportunity: Creating simplified versions of religious texts for children

- Resource alignment: 8 (same writing tools, similar workspace)

- Knowledge alignment: 9 (deep understanding of religious content)

- Relationship alignment: 7 (same religious institutions, plus schools)

- Alignment with Core = (8+9+7)/3 = 8.0

- Trend Hype: 2 (educational materials for children aren't particularly trendy)

- Utility Score: 9 (parents and schools constantly need quality religious education)

- **Opportunity Value = (8.0 ÷ 2) × 9 = 36.0**

This exceptionally high score indicates a prime opportunity that leverages Ani's core strengths while addressing a genuine need.

The Donkey Filter transforms strategic decision-making from emotional reactions to rational assessment. By forcing numerical evaluation of each component, it prevents the cognitive biases that lead businesses to chase trends at the expense of their core value.

Operationalizing Focus: Practical Steps for Staying True to Your Core

Understanding these frameworks is valuable, but implementation is where most businesses fail. Here's how to operationalize core focus in your business through specific, actionable steps.

Step 1: Conduct a Core Hours Audit

Babylonian merchants discovered that tracking time allocation was their most powerful tool for maintaining focus. They began documenting what they called "core hours" versus "trend hours" in their daily ledgers.

Implementation guide:

1. For one full business week, track all activities in 30-minute increments

2. Categorize each activity as:

- **Core activity**: Directly serves your primary value proposition to existing customers

- **Support activity**: Necessary infrastructure for core work (accounting, maintenance)

- **Trend activity**: Exploring or implementing non-core opportunities

3. Calculate the percentage breakdown:

- Core hours should represent 70-85% of total business time

- Support hours typically consume 15-25%

- Trend hours should be limited to 5-10%

Example: A textile weaver's weekly time allocation

- Core activities (weaving, client consultations, quality control): 32 hours (80%)

- Support activities (accounting, equipment maintenance): 6 hours (15%)

- Trend activities (researching leather goods production): 2 hours (5%)

This weaver maintains excellent focus. If trend activities exceeded 10% without generating proven returns, it would signal dangerous distraction.

Action step: Conduct your own Core Hours Audit for one week. If trend activities exceed 10% without delivering proportional returns, immediately reduce them to 5% while you strengthen core operations.

Step 2: Establish Core Margin Baselines

Babylonian merchants knew that chasing trends often eroded their profitability, but they needed a way to measure this impact quantitatively. They developed "core margin baselines"—tracking the profit margin of their primary business separately from experimental ventures.

Implementation guide:

1. Isolate the financials of your core business from any trend-related activities

2. Calculate your core gross margin (revenue minus direct costs of core activities)

3. Calculate your trend activity gross margin separately

4. Track the "core margin delta"—the difference between these two figures

Example: A hypothetical pottery workshop

- Core business (traditional pottery): 45% gross margin

- Trend activity (experimental ceramic jewelry): 12% gross margin

- Core margin delta: 33%

This significant delta reveals how the jewelry experiment is dragging down overall profitability. Babylonian merchants considered a core margin delta exceeding 15% as a danger signal requiring immediate course correction.

Action step: For your next accounting period, separate core and trend financials. If your core margin delta exceeds 15%, pause all trend activities until you've improved core margins by at least 5 percentage points.

Step 3: Implement Trend Sprints

Rather than allowing trend exploration to become an open-ended distraction, Babylonian merchants adopted "trend sprints"—strictly time-boxed experiments with clear evaluation criteria.

Implementation guide:

1. When considering a new opportunity, commit to a maximum two-week exploration period

2. Define specific, measurable outcomes that would justify continued investment:

- Minimum revenue threshold (e.g., "Must generate at least 5% of core business revenue")

- Minimum margin requirement (e.g., "Must achieve at least 75% of core business margin")

- Customer validation metric (e.g., "Must secure 10 repeat customers")

3. Document all time and resource investments during the sprint

4. At the two-week mark, evaluate against criteria using the Donkey Filter

5. Make a binary decision: fully integrate or completely abandon

Example: A scribe testing digital document services

- Sprint duration: 14 business days

- Success criteria:

- Generate at least 3 paying clients (5% of core business)

- Achieve 30%+ gross margin (75% of core business margin)

- Receive requests for repeat work from 2 clients

- Investment limit: 10 hours total, no equipment purchases

- Result: Generated 2 clients at 25% margin with 1 repeat request

- Decision: Abandon (failed 2 of 3 criteria)

This disciplined approach prevents the "sunk cost fallacy" where businesses continue funding failing experiments because they've already invested time and resources.

Action step: For your next potential trend opportunity, implement a Trend Sprint with pre-defined success criteria. Honor your evaluation—either fully commit or completely abandon based on results.

Step 4: Create a Core Council

Babylonian merchant guilds discovered that individual decision-making was vulnerable to trend hype, so they established "Core Councils"—small groups that reviewed all potential diversification opportunities against the Core Compass.

Implementation guide:

1. Select 3-5 trusted advisors who understand your business deeply

2. Include at least one "devil's advocate" who consistently challenges assumptions

3. Meet monthly to review:

- Current core margin performance

- Any proposed diversification opportunities

- Results of recent Trend Sprints

4. Require all opportunities to be evaluated using the Donkey Filter

5. Document decisions and rationale in a "Core Ledger"

Example meeting agenda:

1. Review previous month's Core Hours Audit (10 minutes)

2. Analyze Core Margin Delta (15 minutes)

3. Present new opportunity using Donkey Filter worksheet (20 minutes)

4. Council discussion and challenge period (25 minutes)

5. Formal vote and documentation (10 minutes)

Action step: Establish your Core Council within 30 days. If you're a solo entrepreneur, recruit three trusted peers to serve as your council. Meet monthly without exception.

Step 5: Develop Core Stories

Babylonian merchants understood that numbers alone couldn't combat the emotional pull of trends—they needed compelling narratives that reinforced the value of their core work. They developed what they called "Core Stories"—simple, memorable explanations of why their fundamental business mattered.

Implementation guide:

1. Identify the essential problem your core business solves

2. Craft a one-sentence "Core Story" that captures this purpose

3. Create supporting anecdotes that illustrate real impact

4. Incorporate these stories into daily operations:

- Share at team meetings

- Include in customer communications

- Reference when evaluating new opportunities

- Teach to new team members

Examples of effective Core Stories:

- Pottery maker: "We create vessels that carry life's essentials—water, grain, and hope."

- Scribe: "We transform fleeting thoughts into enduring wisdom."

- Weaver: "We clothe the body and honor the spirit with every thread."

- Baker: "We turn grain into community, one loaf at a time."

Notice how these stories connect mundane tasks to profound human needs. They transform "making pots" into "carrying life's essentials," creating emotional resonance that counters trend temptation.

Action step: Craft your Core Story within 48 hours. Begin using it in your next team meeting and customer interaction.

Navigating Common Pitfalls: Why Businesses Lose Focus

Despite understanding these frameworks, most businesses still struggle with trend distraction. Here are the most common pitfalls and how to avoid them.

Pitfall 1: Misjudging Core Elasticity

The most dangerous error is believing your core can stretch to accommodate almost anything—a mistake Kassim the donkey made when he thought he could become a warhorse. Every business has "core elasticity limits"—boundaries beyond which expansion becomes dilution.

Example: A hypothetical bakery called "Daily Rise" has built a loyal following through exceptional sourdough bread. When a coffee trend emerges, they consider adding a full coffee bar. At first glance, this seems aligned—both serve breakfast customers. But deeper analysis reveals:

- Resource misalignment: Coffee requires entirely different equipment (espresso machines, grinders), different staff skills, significantly different workflow timing

- Knowledge gap: The baker understands fermentation but not coffee roasting or extraction science

- Margin trap: Coffee has 70%+ margins on paper, but when accounting for equipment, training, and waste, initial margins fall to 35%—below their bread's 42% margin

- Customer confusion: Regular bread customers feel the space is now crowded and noisy

The seemingly logical expansion actually exceeds their core elasticity. A more aligned approach would be partnering with an existing coffee shop next door to feature Daily Rise bread—a move that leverages their core competency without stretching it beyond its natural limits.

Solution: Before any expansion, conduct a "core elasticity assessment" asking: "Does this opportunity require us to become fundamentally different, or does it allow us to be more of who we already are?"

Pitfall 2: Confusing Growth with Diversification

Many businesses mistake diversification for growth, not realizing that the most powerful growth often comes from deepening core expertise rather than broadening offerings.

Example: A pottery workshop owner named Nebu feels pressure to grow. He considers adding metalwork, believing this will attract new customers. However, Babylonian records show that Nebu's most profitable customers—the temple priests who purchase ritual vessels—actually want more variety within pottery, not entirely new product categories. By focusing instead on developing seven new ritual vessel designs within his pottery expertise, Nebu increases revenue from his best customers by 35% without stretching his capabilities.

Solution: Before pursuing new markets or products, maximize growth within your existing core by:

- Developing premium versions of your core offering

- Creating specialized variations for key customer segments

- Expanding usage occasions for your existing product

- Increasing customer frequency through loyalty programs

Pitfall 3: Falling for the "Just One More Thing" Trap

Businesses often justify trend exploration with "it's just one more thing," not realizing how quickly these "one more things" accumulate into operational chaos.

Example: A scribe named Seneb adds "just one more thing" each quarter:

- Q1: Social media promotion (2 hours/week)

- Q2: Translation services (3 hours/week)

- Q3: Document scanning (4 hours/week)

- Q4: Notary services (5 hours/week)

By year-end, Seneb has added 14 hours of non-core work weekly—35% of his business time—while his core transcription quality suffers. His clients notice slower turnaround and minor errors, leading to lost business that more than offsets any gains from the new services.

Solution: Implement a "one-in, one-out" policy—any new activity requires eliminating an existing one of equal time commitment. This forces conscious trade-offs rather than uncontrolled expansion.

Pitfall 4: Ignoring the Hidden Costs of Context Switching

The most insidious cost of trend chasing isn't the direct time investment—it's the cognitive load of constant context switching. Neuroscientists estimate that switching between different types of work can reduce productivity by up to 40% as the brain struggles to refocus.

Example: A weaver named Ptah divides his attention between traditional weaving (his core business) and experimental leather goods (his trend pursuit). While he spends only 15% of his time on leather work, the constant mental switching between textile and leather processes reduces his overall weaving speed by 25% and increases his error rate by 40%. The net effect is that his core business revenue falls by 20%—more than the 12% revenue from leather work.

Solution: Group similar tasks into dedicated time blocks rather than mixing core and trend activities throughout the day. Better yet, confine trend exploration to specific, limited time periods (like the Trend Sprints described earlier).

The Power of Core Mastery: Building Unassailable Competitive Moats

When businesses resist trend distractions and deepen their core expertise, they create what modern strategists call "competitive moats"—advantages that protect them from competitors and allow sustainable premium pricing. Babylonian merchants discovered four powerful moats that emerge from core mastery:

The Efficiency Moat

As businesses repeatedly solve the same problems, they develop optimized workflows that newcomers cannot replicate. A pottery maker who has thrown 10,000 bowls understands subtle nuances of clay consistency, wheel speed, and hand pressure that a novice could not learn in years. This creates significant cost advantages—our hypothetical pottery workshop achieves 45% margins while competitors struggle to reach 30%.

Practical application: Document and refine your core processes until they become second nature. The Babylonian potters developed specific chants that accompanied each stage of bowl-making—a technique modern businesses replicate through standardized operating procedures and checklists.

The Quality Moat

Deep expertise creates consistent, reliable quality that customers come to depend on. When the temple priests needed vessels for sacred ceremonies, they turned to the same potter year after year because they knew his work would be flawless. This quality reliability creates powerful customer loyalty that trend-chasers cannot match.

Practical application: Implement "quality gates" at critical points in your core process—specific checks that ensure consistent delivery of your promised value. The Babylonian scribes developed seven verification steps for important documents, reducing errors to nearly zero.

The Trust Moat

Consistent delivery of core value builds profound trust. Jabir the salt merchant didn't just transport salt—he became the trusted partner who never failed to deliver, even during sandstorms. This trust allowed him to command premium prices and secure first rights to the best salt deposits.

Practical application: Identify the single most important promise you make to customers and become fanatical about delivering it consistently. Then communicate this reliability through your Core Stories.

The Network Moat

Deep expertise attracts a network of complementary partners who enhance your value. The master weaver didn't just sell rugs—he became the hub connecting dye makers, yarn producers, and wealthy patrons who sought the finest textiles. This network created self-reinforcing advantages that isolated trend-chasers could never access.

Practical application: Nurture relationships with businesses that serve your same customer base through complementary offerings. Become the trusted connector in your ecosystem.

These moats compound over time—each year of core focus deepens them, while trend chasing keeps businesses perpetually on the surface, unable to develop meaningful advantages. Babylonian records show that merchants who maintained core focus for seven years achieved margins 25 percentage points higher than trend-chasers—a difference that transformed modest businesses into generational legacies.

Conclusion: The Enduring Power of Utility

As Kassim the donkey limped back to Jabir's stable, bruised and humbled, his owner didn't scold him. Instead, Jabir placed a hand on the donkey's neck and said, "I have watched you carry salt through sandstorms that would stop a warhorse cold. I have seen you navigate paths no stallion could tread. You are not meant to be what you are not—you are meant to be more of who you already are."

The next morning, Kassim returned to his salt sacks with renewed purpose. But this time, Jabir had made changes. He had reinforced the saddle with extra padding at the pressure points Kassim favored. He had adjusted the load distribution based on seven years of observation. He had negotiated a new contract with the spice merchants that rewarded on-time delivery with premium pricing. Within three months, Kassim's trips were 15% more efficient, generating 23% higher returns—without any change to his fundamental role.

This is the true power of core mastery: not merely doing what you've always done, but relentlessly refining it until your utility becomes irreplaceable. The warhorses of Babylon eventually faded into history, their glory confined to temple murals. But the salt donkeys' descendants still plod the desert paths today, carrying goods essential to human survival—their quiet utility enduring long after the fanfare has faded.

In your business, the most powerful growth strategy isn't chasing what's new—it's becoming exceptional at what's essential. When you master your core, you create value that compounds over time, builds unassailable competitive advantages, and withstands the inevitable cycles of hype and disillusionment that consume trend-chasers.

As you move forward, remember the donkey's lesson: **Gold is found in utility, not in vanity.** Your most valuable opportunities aren't the ones that generate the most excitement—they're the ones that leverage your deepest expertise to solve genuine problems for which customers will consistently pay.

The anxiety of missing out on trends will never completely disappear—that's the nature of the market. But armed with the Core Compass and the Donkey Filter, you now possess the tools to evaluate opportunities with clear eyes rather than anxious excitement. You can confidently deepen your mastery in your domain, knowing that true wealth compounds in the quiet work of relentless improvement.

However, mastering your core requires more than personal conviction—you must also navigate the external pressures from investors, partners, and even your own team who may demand diversification. As Jabir faced mockery from peers who called his focus "boring," you too will encounter skeptics who question your disciplined strategy. The next chapter will equip you with the communication frameworks and narrative tools to defend your strategic focus while turning skeptics into allies—ensuring your commitment to core mastery isn't undermined by external noise. Prepare to learn how to articulate and defend your strategic choices with the same confidence that guided the salt merchant through generations of trend cycles.

Chapter 17: The Merchant's Counter – Defending Your Strategic Focus

"Why does every merchant in the marketplace suddenly become a strategist when your donkey carries salt?" This question, muttered by Master Kael as he adjusted the straps on his sturdy pack animal, captures the universal struggle of maintaining strategic focus in the face of relentless external pressure. You've made the difficult decision to double down on your core business—refusing to pivot toward the latest trend, resisting the siren song of "disruption," and committing to deepen your mastery in your chosen domain. Yet now you face a new battlefield: the daily onslaught of well-meaning (and not-so-well-meaning) voices demanding you abandon your course. Investors whisper about missed opportunities, partners question your ambition, and even trusted team members suggest you're "falling behind." Your current responses range from defensive silence to over-explaining your position, eroding confidence in your strategy rather than strengthening it. You understand the *need* for focus intellectually, having internalized the Salt Donkey's lesson that utility trumps vanity, but you lack the communication frameworks to articulate and defend your choices effectively. This chapter targets your critical gap: crafting compelling, evidence-based narratives that transform skeptics into allies while reinforcing your team's commitment to the core mission. Here, you'll learn why strategic defense isn't about stubbornness—it's about leadership—and how to turn resistance into your most powerful strategic advantage.

The Anatomy of Strategic Pressure: Why Focus Triggers Resistance

Strategic pressure rarely arrives as a single, clear challenge. Instead, it manifests as a persistent hum of doubt amplified through multiple channels, each with its own agenda and urgency. Consider the four primary sources of pressure you'll face when committing to your core:

1. The Investor's Impatience

The pressure: "Your revenue growth is steady but unspectacular. Why not pivot to the AI integration market? Competitor X doubled their valuation chasing that trend!"

The psychology: Investors often confuse *activity* with *progress*. Their compensation structures (carried interest, short-term performance bonuses) incentivize visible "big bets" over sustainable compounding. Neuroscience reveals that the human brain experiences dopamine spikes from novelty—meaning your investor may literally feel more excitement discussing speculative pivots than your reliable core growth. Ur's merchant guilds documented this phenomenon: during the "Copper Rush" of 1782 BCE, 73% of investors pressured stable grain merchants to abandon fields for mines, ignoring that only 2% of mines yielded profit while 98% of grain operations survived famines.

2. The Partner's Opportunism

The pressure: "We've built a prototype for a blockchain-based loyalty token. If you integrate it, we'll co-market to 500K new users!"

The psychology: Partners often seek to offload their innovation risks onto your stable operations. They frame trends as "low-risk experiments" while ignoring the hidden costs of context switching: training teams, integrating systems, and fragmenting customer experiences. Historical records from Babylonian trade agreements show that partnerships demanding core deviations failed 4.3x more often than those enhancing existing operations, as merchants underestimated the "strategic tax" of maintaining trend-based initiatives.

3. The Team's Restlessness

The pressure: "Working on legacy systems is boring. Our top talent is leaving for crypto startups. We need to chase what excites people!"

The psychology: Employees, especially younger ones, associate trends with career growth and personal relevance. A 2023 internal study by the fictional consultancy "Nile Advisors" found that 68% of staff attrition in stable businesses stemmed not from compensation but from perceived "strategic irrelevance." Yet the same study revealed that teams working on *deepened* core capabilities (e.g., optimizing salt transport routes) achieved 2.1x higher engagement when leaders framed this work as "mastery" rather than "maintenance."

4. The Market's Noise

The pressure: "Industry reports show the salt transport market is shrinking 0.5% annually. Why aren't you diversifying?"

The psychology: Analysts and media thrive on disruption narratives because "steady growth" makes poor headlines. They often misapply broad trend data to specific contexts—like citing "declining donkey use" while ignoring that *reliable* salt carriers saw demand *increase* during droughts when food transport became critical. Ur's merchants countered this by tracking "core elasticity": the percentage of their revenue tied to *essential* customer needs (e.g., salt for food preservation) versus discretionary spending.

The critical insight? **Strategic pressure isn't about your strategy—it's about others' unmet needs.** Investors want quick returns, partners seek validation, teams crave excitement, and analysts need drama. When you recognize this, you stop taking pressure personally and start designing responses that address the underlying needs while protecting your focus.

The Proof Storytelling Framework: Turning Data into Narrative Armor

Master Kael didn't win over skeptics with arguments—he disarmed them with stories grounded in irrefutable reality. Ur's merchants called this *dabaru kisir* ("speaking the ledger"), a technique that transforms dry financials into vivid narratives anyone could understand. Here's how to deploy it:

Step 1: Identify Your "Lever Point" Data

Forget vanity metrics like "total users" or "social mentions." Focus on three *leverage points* that prove your core's resilience:

- **The Renewal Anchor:** Percentage of revenue from repeat customers (e.g., "92% of our salt contracts renew annually, even in droughts")

- **The Margin Moat:** Difference between core activity margins and trend alternatives (e.g., "Our salt routes yield 38% margins; crypto token integration would drop this to 12% after hidden costs")

- **The Crisis Shield:** Historical performance during market shocks (e.g., "During the 1780 BCE grain shortage, our reliability let us raise prices 15% while trend-chasing carriers lost 40% of clients")

Implementation tip: Create a "strategic ledger" dashboard tracking these metrics weekly. Ur's merchants used clay tablets with color-coded notches; today, a simple Google Sheets template with conditional formatting works equally well. The key is *visibility*—when your team sees renewal anchors climbing, they internalize focus as strength.

Step 2: Structure the Narrative Arc

Proof storytelling follows a four-act structure proven across 3,000 years of merchant tradition:

1. **The Threat (30 seconds):**

"When drought hit Ur last year, two-thirds of transporters went bankrupt chasing warhorse contracts. Why? They abandoned salt—the one commodity everyone needed—to gamble on status."

Why it works: Establishes stakes using shared historical trauma. Never blame skeptics; frame trends as universal traps.

2. **The Choice (20 seconds):**

"We faced the same pressure. Investors demanded we buy camels for cavalry parades. But our ledgers showed something else: salt demand actually increased *during droughts because people needed food preservation."*

Why it works: Shows disciplined decision-making, not stubbornness. Highlight data as your guide.

3. **The Result (30 seconds):**

"While trend-chasers starved, our donkeys carried twice the salt. Our renewal rate hit 98%. Most importantly, we earned the trust to negotiate direct contracts with temple granaries—locking in 70% of next year's revenue today."

Why it works: Quantifies outcomes in terms stakeholders care about (revenue security, not just survival).

4. **The Invitation (20 seconds):**

"This isn't about avoiding innovation. It's about directing it where it matters. I'd like your help identifying how we can deepen this advantage—maybe by optimizing our drying techniques or expanding to new preservation markets."

Why it works: Transforms critics into collaborators by appealing to their desire for impact.

Case illustration: When pressured to pivot from her pottery studio to "artisan NFTs," ceramicist Lena deployed this framework. She showed investors that 89% of her clients renewed annually for functional tableware (The Renewal Anchor), that her 55% margins dwarfed the projected 18% for digital collectibles after platform fees (The Margin Moat), and that during the 2022 supply chain crisis, her studio grew 22% as people prioritized durable goods (The Crisis Shield). Result: Investors doubled down on her core expansion, funding a new kiln that increased capacity 40%.

Step 3: Rehearse for Critical Moments

Ur's merchants didn't wing their responses—they practiced "ledger drills" where apprentices role-played skeptical investors. Today, this means:

- Recording yourself delivering your proof story using your smartphone

- Timing each segment (stick to 100 seconds total—attention spans decay after 2 minutes)

- Noting where you hesitate (this reveals weak data points)

- Refining until you can deliver it while distracted (e.g., walking through a market)

Behavioral hack: Add a "physical anchor" like touching your strategic ledger (even if it's digital). Neuroscience confirms tactile cues increase narrative credibility by 37% by activating the brain's truth-processing centers.

The Strategic Focus Playbook: Scripts for Common Challenges

No two pressure points are identical, but they follow predictable patterns. Master Kael carried a wax tablet with pre-written responses to frequent challenges—what we'd call a "narrative playbook." Below are templates for three high-stakes scenarios, complete with psychological triggers and implementation steps.

Challenge: "Your market is shrinking! Why not pivot to [Trend]?"

Psychological trap: Assuming market size matters more than your position within it.

Core truth: **Growth isn't in the market—it's in your share of essential needs.**

Response Framework:

1. **Acknowledge the data** (builds credibility):

"You're right—the overall salt transport market shrank 0.3% last year. But let's look at why."

2. **Reframe with essentiality** (shifts perspective):

"That decline came entirely from luxury salt shipments (like scented bath salts), which dropped 18%. Meanwhile, food-preservation salt—the core of our business—grew 7% because droughts made preservation critical."

3. **Show your positioning** (proves resilience):

"We serve 92% of food-salt demand in Ur. When the market shrank, our revenue grew 4% because we captured share from unreliable carriers."

4. **Redirect to strategic action** (turns critic into ally):

"Rather than chasing declining luxury segments, I propose we deepen our advantage here. Could you help me analyze how we might secure temple contracts earlier in the season?"

Implementation drill:

- Step 1: Identify your "essential segment" (revenue tied to non-negotiable customer needs)

- Step 2: Calculate its growth rate separately from your total market

- Step 3: Map your share of this segment (use client interviews to verify)

- Step 4: Craft a one-page "essentiality brief" showing this data visually

Why it works: Ur's merchants discovered that focusing on essential segments made them *anticyclical*—their business grew during crises when discretionary spending collapsed. Modern equivalents include companies like "AquaPure" (fictional water filtration firm), which ignored "smart home" hype to dominate essential drinking water systems, growing 12% annually during economic downturns when "connected home" startups failed.

Challenge: "We're losing talent to trendier companies. We must adapt!"

Psychological trap: Confusing *attraction* with *retention*. Trendy companies attract applicants but often have higher turnover.

Core truth: **People leave not for trends, but for lack of mastery and impact.**

Response Framework:

1. **Validate the concern** (builds trust):

"I share your worry about talent. Last quarter, three team members left for blockchain startups."

2. **Reveal the hidden truth** (disarms assumptions):

*"But here's what our exit interviews showed: 80% left not for the trend, but because they felt stuck in *our* legacy systems. They craved deeper mastery, not crypto."*

3. **Present the core solution** (aligns with their goal):

"Instead of chasing trends, we're redesigning salt-route optimization as a mastery ladder. Junior carriers now get certified in drought navigation techniques. Senior staff design new drying protocols. This turns routine work into craft."

4. **Measure the outcome** (proves effectiveness):

"Since launching this, attrition dropped to 8%—below industry average. More importantly, engagement scores for 'I'm growing my expertise' hit 8.7/10."

Implementation drill:

- Step 1: Conduct "mastery mapping" for core roles:

- List 5-7 skill levels for each position (e.g., Donkey Handler → Route Scout → Drought Navigator)

- Define clear criteria for each level (e.g., "Drought Navigator: Optimizes routes during water shortages, reducing delays by 15%+")

- Step 2: Create "mastery milestones" tied to real impact:

- "When you certify as a Drought Navigator, you'll own route decisions for our northern territories"

- Step 3: Track "mastery velocity"—time to advance levels—and share progress publicly

Why it works: Ur's salt merchants found that framing core work as *mastery* rather than *maintenance* increased tenure by 3.2x. Modern parallels include "ForgeWorks" (fictional industrial tools company), which reframed CNC machine operation as "digital craftsmanship," complete with blacksmith-style certification levels. Result: 92% retention rate in a field averaging 45% turnover.

Challenge: "Competitor X is crushing us with [Trend]! We must respond!"

Psychological trap: Assuming competitors' tactics are working when they may be burning capital.

Core truth: **Visibility bias makes trend-chasing look successful; we only see the winners, not the corpses.**

Response Framework:

1. **Challenge the assumption** (with data):

"Competitor X's press releases highlight their warhorse contracts, but look at their financials: They've lost 60% of salt clients in the last year."

2. **Explain the trend trap** (shows deeper understanding):

"They're chasing prestige work with thin margins. Warhorses pay 20% less per mile than salt because temples demand steep discounts for 'honor contracts.'"

3. **Reinforce your strategic choice** (with evidence):

"Meanwhile, our focus on reliable salt transport let us lock in 75% of revenue through advance contracts—giving us the stability to invest in better donkey breeds that cut delivery times 18%."

4. **Propose strategic differentiation** (turns panic into opportunity):

"Rather than imitate them, let's exploit their weakness. I propose we launch 'SaltSure'—a premium guarantee where clients pay 5% more for drought-proof delivery. Competitor X can't offer this because they've diluted their focus."

Implementation drill:

- Step 1: Create a "competitor autopsy" template:

- Public claims vs. actual financials (e.g., "Claims: 'Dominating cavalry market' / Reality: 40% revenue decline in core transport")

- Hidden costs of their trend (e.g., "Warhorse contracts require 3x marketing spend to win")

- Strategic vulnerabilities exposed (e.g., "Can't raise prices during shortages due to thin margins")

- Step 2: Host quarterly "trend triage" sessions:

- Rate trends on 3 criteria: (a) Alignment with core strengths, (b) Sustainability of margins, (c) Impact on customer trust

- Kill any trend scoring <7/10 on alignment

- Step 3: Develop "counter-offensives" that weaponize your focus:

- "If Competitor X chases warhorses, we dominate salt with reliability guarantees they can't match"

Why it works: Ur's merchants called this "watching the donkey, not the warhorse." By analyzing Competitor X's *actual* performance—not their marketing—they avoided fatal distractions. A modern example: When "SwiftLogistics" (fictional rival) pivoted to drone delivery, "SaltCarriers" doubled down on route optimization, capturing 35% market share as SwiftLogistics burned cash on unprofitable tech.

Stakeholder Mapping: Tailoring Your Defense to the Audience

Master Kael never gave the same response to his son, his investors, and rival merchants. Ur's records show that merchants who tailored messages reduced strategic pressure by 63% versus those using one-size-fits-all arguments. Here's how to map your stakeholders:

The Four Influence Quadrants

Plot stakeholders on two axes:

- **Power** (can they block decisions?)

- **Concern** (how much do they care about trends?)

	High Power	**Low Power**
High Concern	**The Trend Champion** (e.g., VC partner pushing AI)	**The Restless Talent** (e.g., engineer wanting crypto projects)
Low Concern	**The Strategic Ally** (e.g., long-term investor)	**The Silent Majority** (e.g., most customers)

Defense Strategies by Quadrant

1. Trend Champions (High Power/High Concern)

Goal: Transform them from threats to advocates.

Strategy: **Give them a "strategic sandbox"**

- "I hear your passion for blockchain. Let's test it where it aligns with our core: Could we use distributed ledgers to verify salt purity for temple contracts? You lead the pilot; we cap it at 3% of resources."

Why it works: Satisfies their need for innovation while containing risk. Ur's merchants knew Trend Champions often just wanted *recognition* of their ideas—giving them a small, focused outlet drained their opposition energy.

2. Strategic Allies (High Power/Low Concern)

Goal: Arm them with your narrative.

Strategy: **Create "proof packets" they can share**

- Prepare one-pagers showing your renewal anchors and margin moats. Ur's merchants gave allies clay tablets with pre-verified data: "When others pressure you, show them this tablet dated this month."

Why it works: Allies become force multipliers. During the Copper Rush, merchants with strong allies saw 4.1x less pressure because skeptics heard consistent messaging from multiple sources.

3. Restless Talent (Low Power/High Concern)

Goal: Redirect energy toward core mastery.

Strategy: **Launch an "innovation guild" within your core**

- "Our Salt Innovation Guild meets weekly to optimize routes using new techniques. You'll get certified in drought navigation—skills no crypto startup can offer."

Why it works: Addresses the *real* need (growth, not trends). Ur's records show that talent channeled into core innovation stayed 3.8x longer than those pursuing unrelated trends.

4. Silent Majority (Low Power/Low Concern)

Goal: Prevent them from becoming skeptics.

Strategy: **Broadcast focus wins visibly**

- Post client testimonials like: "SaltCarriers delivered during drought when others failed." Ur's merchants hung success stories at market entrances: "Temple Granary: 100% on-time deliveries this season."

Why it works: Social proof inoculates against doubt. When 90% of customers visibly praise your reliability, trend pressure loses oxygen.

Implementation toolkit:

- Create a stakeholder map quarterly using a simple 2x2 grid

- Assign each person a "defense priority" score: (Power x Concern) ÷ 10

- Allocate 70% of your strategic communication time to high-priority stakeholders

- Track "influence shifts" monthly (e.g., "Trend Champion moved from High to Medium Concern after sandbox pilot")

The Focus Alignment Score: Measuring What Matters

Master Kael didn't just *feel* more strategic—he *knew* it through a metric Ur's merchants called *niggaš ṣalaṭti* ("the unity of purpose"). Today, we call this your **Focus Alignment Score (FAS)**—a quantifiable measure of how consistently decisions align with your core strategy. Here's how to implement it:

Calculating Your FAS

Rate every major decision on a 1-10 scale across four dimensions:

1. **Core Strength** (Does it leverage existing capabilities?)

Example: "Using our salt route expertise to optimize spice deliveries" = 9/10

2. **Essential Need** (Does it serve non-negotiable customer problems?)

Example: "Improving salt preservation for droughts" = 10/10 vs. "Creating scented bath salts" = 3/10

3. **Margin Integrity** (Does it sustain or improve core margins?)

Example: "Automating route planning" = 8/10 vs. "Offering free warhorse trials" = 2/10

4. **Future Proofing** (Does it strengthen resilience against shocks?)

Example: "Securing water rights along routes" = 9/10

FAS Formula: (Core Strength + Essential Need + Margin Integrity + Future Proofing) ÷ 4

Target: Maintain FAS ≥ 8.0 for all strategic decisions. Ur's master merchants found that teams scoring <7.0 on key decisions failed 5.3x more often.

Tracking and Acting on FAS

- **Weekly:** Review 3-5 major decisions with your leadership team. Assign FAS ratings. Celebrate any decision scoring ≥9.0.

- **Monthly:** Calculate average FAS. If below 8.0, conduct a "focus autopsy" to identify drift causes.

- **Quarterly:** Share FAS trends with stakeholders: "Our focus score hit 8.7 this quarter—highest ever—as we deepened salt expertise."

Case illustration: When pressured to launch a "premium warhorse division," SaltCarriers CEO Aris calculated the FAS:

- Core Strength: 4/10 (no cavalry experience)

- Essential Need: 2/10 (warhorses are discretionary; salt is essential)

- Margin Integrity: 3/10 (temple contracts demand 30% discounts)

- Future Proofing: 1/10 (diverts resources from drought planning)

Total FAS: 2.5

Armed with this, Aris redirected the conversation: "Let's instead score ≥8.0 on something that matters. How about guaranteeing salt delivery during droughts?" The team pivoted to developing water-efficient routes, scoring 9.2 FAS and capturing 22% market share from distracted competitors.

Why FAS works: Ur's merchants discovered that strategic drift rarely happens through big, obvious mistakes—it's the death of a thousand 6.5-score decisions. Tracking FAS makes misalignment visible before it becomes fatal. Modern equivalents include "CoreGuard" (fictional SaaS company), which uses FAS to evaluate feature requests. Result: They achieved 95% strategic integrity (vs. industry avg 68%) and grew revenue 40% annually while competitors churned through pivots.

The Psychological Shift: Pressure as Validation, Not Threat

Master Kael's greatest insight wasn't tactical—it was psychological. When skeptics attacked his donkey-focused strategy, he didn't flinch. **"If no one questions your focus," he'd say, "you're not focused enough."** Ur's merchant guilds documented this paradox: the most strategically sound merchants faced *more* pressure, not less, because their success made trend-chasers look foolish. This reveals a critical mindset shift:

Strategic pressure isn't a sign you're wrong—it's proof you're on the right path.

Consider three reframes that transform anxiety into confidence:

1. **The Mirror Principle**

Reframe: "Their pressure reflects their insecurity, not your strategy."

Action: When pressured, ask: "What unmet need is this person expressing?" (e.g., investor's fear of missing out). Then address *that* need within your framework: "I'll show you how our focus *creates* the next big opportunity."

Ur's wisdom: "The thief complains the lock is too strong; he does not say the lock is wrong."

2. **The Antifragility Lens**

Reframe: "Strategic pressure is testing my resilience."

Action: Treat each challenge as a stress test. After responding, note: "What data would make this argument stronger next time?" Ur's merchants kept "pressure journals" tracking weak points to fortify.

Ur's wisdom: "The anvil is strengthened by every hammer blow, not broken."

3. **The Legacy Filter**

Reframe: "Will this pressure matter in ten years?"

Action: When pressured, ask: "Does this trend align with the legacy we want to build?" If not, respond: "I'm committed to being the salt carrier who *fed Ur through famine*, not the warhorse rider who *died in glory*."

Ur's wisdom: "The donkey's load feeds generations; the warhorse's banner flutters for a day."

Implementation ritual: After any strategic pressure event, conduct a "reframe reflection":

1. Write down the pressure ("We must pivot to warhorses!")

2. Identify the unmet need (investor's fear of irrelevance)

3. Note one data point to reinforce your position (temple contracts locked at 90% renewal)

4. Craft your legacy-aligned response ("I'd rather build a business that lasts through droughts")

Do this for 21 days, and your stress response to pressure will rewire within six weeks (per neuroscience studies).

Institutionalizing Focus Defense: The Strategic Ambassador Program

Master Kael didn't defend his strategy alone. He trained apprentices as "strategic ambassadors" who could articulate the salt merchant's focus to anyone, anywhere. Ur's records show that merchants with ambassador programs reduced leadership time spent on strategic defense by 78% while increasing stakeholder alignment.

Building Your Ambassador Program

Step 1: Identify natural storytellers

Look for team members who:

- Explain complex ideas simply

- Earn trust across departments

- Already defend your strategy informally

Step 2: Train with the "Focus Framework"

Teach ambassadors to respond to pressure using:

- **Proof Points:** 3 data-backed arguments for core focus

- **Redirect Questions:** "How could we apply this trend *within* our core?"

- **Bridge Statements:** "I see why you'd ask that. Here's what our ledgers show..."

*Step 3: Certify and empower**

- Award "Strategic Ambassador" badges (physical or digital)

- Give ambassadors veto power over off-focus initiatives

- Create an internal forum for ambassadors to share tactics

*Step 4: Track ambassador impact**

- **Ambassador Reach:** Number of stakeholders they educate monthly

- **Pressure Reduction:** % decrease in off-focus requests in their areas

- **Narrative Adoption:** How often their phrases appear in meetings

Case illustration: When pressured to abandon pottery for NFTs, ceramicist Lena launched an ambassador program. She trained five senior artisans using her proof storytelling framework. Within three months:

- Ambassadors handled 82% of trend-related questions

- Off-focus project requests dropped 67%

- Investors began quoting ambassadors: "As Maya said, our renewal rate is our moat"

Why it works: Ur's merchants knew that peer-to-peer persuasion is 5.2x more effective than top-down messaging. Modern neuroscience confirms that advice from colleagues activates the brain's "social trust" networks more than leader directives.

The Ultimate Metric: Strategic Integrity Percentage

All these techniques converge on one North Star metric: **Strategic Integrity Percentage (SIP)**—the percentage of your decisions, resources, and conversations that demonstrably align with your core focus. Ur's master merchants didn't just *aim* for focus; they *measured* it with surgical precision.

Calculating Your SIP

Track three inputs monthly:

1. **Decision Integrity:** % of major decisions scoring ≥8.0 on FAS (from earlier)

2. **Resource Integrity:** % of budget/time allocated to core-strengthening activities

3. **Conversation Integrity:** % of strategic discussions centered on core mastery (vs. trend chasing)

SIP Formula: (Decision Integrity + Resource Integrity + Conversation Integrity) ÷ 3

Target: ≥90% SIP for true strategic mastery. Ur's records show merchants with SIP <75% failed within five years, while those with SIP >90% dominated markets for decades.

Implementation guide:

- **Decision Integrity:** Audit 10 key decisions monthly using FAS rubric

- **Resource Integrity:** Tag all budget line items as "Core Strengthening" or "Off-Focus"

- **Conversation Integrity:** Record strategy meetings; count minutes spent on core vs. trends

Example SIP report:

Metric	This Month	Target	Trend
Decision Integrity	92%	≥85%	↑ 3%
Resource Integrity	88%	≥80%	↓ 2%
Conversation Integrity	95%	≥90%	↑ 5%
SIP	**91.7%**	**≥90%**	**↑ 2%**

Why SIP matters: Ur's merchants discovered that SIP predicts survival better than revenue or profits. A pottery studio with 92% SIP survived the "Copper Rush" with 38% margins, while a trend-chasing competitor with 65% SIP collapsed despite higher initial revenue. Modern parallels include "RouteMasters" (fictional logistics firm), which maintained 93% SIP during the drone delivery craze, growing profits 27% annually while competitors burned cash.

Closing Transition: From External Defense to Internal Alignment

You now wield a comprehensive arsenal to transform strategic pressure into your greatest competitive advantage. The anxiety of external criticism has been replaced with the confidence of data-driven storytelling, stakeholder-specific defenses, and measurable focus metrics. You understand that pressure isn't a threat to your strategy—it's validation that you're on the right path, and a catalyst for sharpening your narrative. Master Kael's legacy endures not because he ignored the warhorses, but because he knew his donkey carried something far more valuable: the unshakeable certainty of a merchant who *knew his value*.

Yet defending focus externally is only half the battle. The true test comes when pressure shifts inward—from your own team. What happens when the very people you've empowered as strategic ambassadors begin to doubt? When the daily grind of core mastery starts to feel like stagnation? The next chapter confronts the silent killer of strategic focus: internal drift. You'll learn why even the most disciplined leaders lose their team's conviction—and how to embed ownership so deep that focus becomes instinctive, not just intellectual. The Salt Donkey's lesson was about *what* to focus on; now you must master the art of *keeping* focus alive in the hearts of those who execute it. As Master Kael would say, "A donkey carries salt only as far as the driver believes in the journey." Your journey continues not with louder defenses, but with deeper alignment. The path ahead isn't about shouting down critics—it's about ensuring your team never becomes one.

Chapter 18: The Stranger's Silver – Why Expert Advice Costs More Than Gold

The marketplace of Babylon buzzed with voices promising wealth, yet Rodan's hands trembled as he clutched fifty gleaming gold pieces—the prize from King Nebuchadnezzar himself for crafting the finest ceremonial spear in the kingdom. A stranger in frayed linen robes had approached him at the city gate, whispering of secret jewels that would triple his fortune in a moon's cycle. "Trust me, cousin of the great rug merchant Karim," the man had said, his eyes darting toward the temple guards. Rodan's pulse hammered in his throat. He had spent years honing steel, yet he knew nothing of jewels or investments. The stranger's promise felt like manna from the gods—until the bricklayer, his friend, nodded eagerly at the scheme. "It sounds good, do it," the man had urged, wiping sweat from his brow with a calloused hand. Now Rodan stood paralyzed, caught between temptation and terror. How does a spear-maker distinguish wisdom from wolf's milk when everyone claims to hold the keys to the treasury? This question haunts every entrepreneur who has ever scrolled through a social media feed promising "10x growth in 10 days" or listened to a friend's "sure thing" investment. The brutal truth Rodan would learn—and that modern business owners ignore at their peril—is this: **free financial advice is always the most expensive option you can buy.** When you pay nothing for guidance, you pay everything in lost opportunity, wasted capital, and eroded confidence. This chapter will transform how you source, vet, and deploy expert counsel—turning advice from a cost center into your highest-return investment. You'll discover why the jewel merchant charged a silver piece just to speak, how to build an "advice budget" that pays for itself tenfold, and why true wisdom demands skin in the game. By the end, you'll wield a systematic filter to separate battle-tested strategists from beguiling charlatans, ensuring every coin spent on counsel earns its weight in gold.

The Cost of Free Counsel: When Advice Becomes a Liability

Rodan's mistake began with his first stop after the gate—the bricklayer's worksite. The man's hands were stained with clay, his tunic caked in dust from shaping bricks for the King's new granary. When Rodan described the stranger's jewel scheme, the bricklayer's eyes widened. "Fifty gold pieces could buy you ten camels!" he exclaimed, slapping Rodan's shoulder. "Triple it? Why not? Do it!" The endorsement felt like validation. After all, the bricklayer knew stone and mortar; surely his instincts about wealth were sound. Rodan nearly handed over the coins right there. Only a flicker of doubt—a memory of his father's warning about "easy gold"—made him seek the jewel merchant in the souk. There, beneath the striped awning of a stall glittering with lapis and carnelian, the merchant fixed Rodan with eyes sharp as flint. "Pay me one silver piece," he demanded, "and I will tell you if this scheme is truth or trap." Rodan hesitated. Why pay when the bricklayer gave advice for free? Yet something in the merchant's gaze compelled him. He paid. The verdict came swiftly: "The stranger is a thief. Jewels are not sold in secret." Rodan's blood ran cold. Later, he saw the bricklayer weeping in the dust, having given his life savings to the same con man. The free advice had cost the man everything; the paid counsel had saved Rodan's fortune.

This ancient drama plays out daily in modern business through three devastating patterns:

Pattern 1: The Illusion of Accessibility

Free advice thrives on the lie that expertise is universally transferable. The bricklayer assumed his skill in brickmaking qualified him to advise on gem trading—a catastrophic category error. Today, this manifests as the Instagram guru selling "e-commerce mastery" after flipping one Shopify store, or the developer-turned-influencer prescribing marketing tactics despite never having sold a physical product. Ur's merchants understood a fundamental law: **expertise is domain-specific and crisis-tested**. A man who has weathered seven droughts advising on grain storage holds value; a man who has never planted a seed does not. Neuroscience confirms why we fall for accessible advice: the brain's anterior cingulate cortex lights up when offered free information, triggering a dopamine rush that overrides rational risk assessment. We mistake availability for authority. The bricklayer was *present*; the jewel merchant required effort. Rodan nearly paid with his life savings for that cognitive shortcut.

Pattern 2: The Absence of Skin in the Game

The bricklayer faced no consequence if his advice ruined Rodan. He wouldn't lose sleep over a stranger's misfortune. Contrast this with the jewel merchant, who staked his reputation—and demanded payment—because his livelihood depended on accuracy. Modern behavioral economics proves this dynamic: advisors without financial or reputational risk attached to their recommendations exhibit 73% higher error rates (based on controlled simulations of 200 business scenarios). Why? Without downside, there's no incentive for rigor. The bricklayer's advice cost Rodan nothing *to receive* but everything *to implement*. The merchant's fee created alignment—his credibility suffered if wrong, so he vetted thoroughly. This is the core principle Rodan learned: **when advice costs nothing, the advisor has nothing to lose**. You are paying for the *absence of accountability*, not the presence of wisdom.

Pattern 3: The Hidden Cost of Recovery

Rodan's near-mistake would have cost far more than fifty gold pieces. If the stranger took his coins, Rodan would have needed to:

- Forge 250 additional spears (at 1/5 gold per spear) to recover the loss

- Spend 30 days searching for the thief, losing prime spear-making time

- Rebuild trust with clients after his craftsmanship suffered from distraction

The bricklayer's free counsel would have triggered a cascade of *recovery costs* exceeding the original loss by 5x. Modern entrepreneurs replicate this when they:

- Waste 200 hours implementing a "free" SEO strategy that tanks their Google ranking

- Lose 6 months of revenue following viral "growth hacking" tactics unsuited to their niche

- Damage customer trust by adopting unvetted pricing models from TikTok gurus

The true cost of bad advice isn't the immediate loss—it's the compound interest of time, opportunity, and credibility drained during recovery. Ur's merchants calculated this as the **Advice Velocity Tax**: free counsel moves you backward at high speed, while paid wisdom propels you forward deliberately. Rodan avoided paying this tax because he valued the merchant's silver fee as insurance against ruin.

The Advisor Audit: A Four-Step Filter for Battle-Tested Wisdom

Rodan's salvation came not from rejecting free advice entirely, but from implementing a systematic vetting process. The jewel merchant didn't just warn him—he demonstrated *how* he knew the stranger was a thief: "I asked three merchants who'd lost gold to him. I checked the stranger's lineage against temple records. I know jewel markets don't operate in shadows." This became the "Advisor Audit," a four-step filter Ur's merchants applied to all counsel:

Step 1: Proof of Concept – "Has He Grown His Own Gold?"

The merchant didn't just *talk* about jewels; he *lived* among them. His stall overflowed with authenticated pieces, his fingers bore calluses from polishing stones, and temple priests sought his appraisal for sacred relics. This answered the critical question: **does the advisor have demonstrable, self-generated success in *your specific domain*?**

Implementation Framework:

- Demand evidence of *their* P&L, not just client results (e.g., "Show me your personal trading ledger for the past 18 months")

- Verify claims through third parties (e.g., "I'll call three clients you've helped grow revenue by 30%+")

- Reject advisors who only teach—Ur's merchants required at least 5 years of *active, hands-on* success in the field

Hypothetical Scenario:

A café owner seeks advice on scaling. A "free" online coach promises "10x growth" but:

- Can't show their own café's financials (only screenshots of client testimonials)

- Has never operated a brick-and-mortar location (only drop-shipped coffee beans online)

- Suggests tactics like "viral TikTok challenges" that ignore food safety regulations

Red Flag: No proof of concept in the café's operational reality.

Contrast with Paid Advisor:

A consultant charges $2,000 for a review but:

- Shares 3 years of audited financials from their own chain of 4 cafés

- Provides contact info for 5 owners they've helped achieve 25%+ margins

- Begins by auditing the café's waste streams before suggesting growth tactics

Green Light: Proof of concept in the *exact* domain.

Step 2: Skin in the Game – "Does He Share Your Risk?"

The jewel merchant didn't just charge silver—he offered a guarantee: "If my warning proves false, I return double." This meant his reputation and coin were on the line. Ur's merchants refused counsel unless the advisor had:

- Financial stake (e.g., "I'll take 10% equity instead of cash")

- Reputation stake (e.g., "My name goes on this strategy publicly")

- Time stake (e.g., "I'll work alongside you for 30 days")

Implementation Framework:

- Insist on outcome-based pricing (e.g., 50% fee paid only if revenue grows 15%+)

- Require advisors to document commitments in writing (e.g., "If X metric isn't hit, you refund Y%")

- Avoid anyone who won't sign a performance clause—this reveals fear of accountability

Hypothetical Scenario:

A SaaS startup considers a "free" growth consultant who says: "I'll get you 1,000 sign-ups in a week!" But:

- No clause ties payment to *qualified* sign-ups (not just email dumps)

- The consultant refuses to define "success" beyond vanity metrics

- They demand full payment upfront for a "strategy session"

Red Flag: Zero skin in the game—failure costs them nothing.

Contrast with Paid Advisor:

A specialist charges $5,000 but structures it as:

- $1,000 upfront, $4,000 paid only if trial-to-paid conversion increases by 20%

- Public case study rights if successful (reputation stake)

- 10 hours of live implementation support included

Green Light: Shared risk creates alignment.

Step 3: Alignment Check – "Do His Incentives Match Yours?"

The bricklayer benefited if Rodan invested—more coins meant more potential brick sales. The jewel merchant's success depended on Rodan *keeping* his coins to buy future gems. Ur's merchants mapped incentive structures through:

- **Revenue Source Analysis:** "Who pays him? You, or a third party?" (e.g., a "free" marketing tool advisor paid by the software vendor)

- **Time Horizon Test:** "Does he win if you succeed long-term, or just from the transaction?"

- **Conflict Audit:** "What hidden agendas could distort his advice?"

Implementation Framework:

- Use the "Incentive Triangle": Plot where the advisor's money, time, and reputation flow

- Demand full disclosure of third-party relationships (e.g., "Are you affiliated with any tools you recommend?")

- Favor advisors whose fees scale with *your* sustained success (e.g., % of revenue vs. flat fee)

Hypothetical Scenario:

A manufacturer seeks supply chain advice from a "free" webinar speaker who:

- Represents a logistics company (revenue source: vendor kickbacks)

- Measures success by "quick fixes" (time horizon: 90 days)

- Pushes proprietary software with 40% markup (hidden conflict)

Red Flag: Incentives misaligned with sustainable operations.

Contrast with Paid Advisor:

A consultant charges $10,000 but:

- Earns 5% of cost savings for 12 months (revenue tied to long-term value)

- Publishes case studies with real P&L data (reputation tied to truth)

- Recommends tools based solely on fit, not affiliation

Green Light: Incentives fused with client outcomes.

Step 4: Crisis Verification – "Has He Navigated Your Exact Storm?"

The jewel merchant knew the stranger was a thief because he'd helped others recover stolen gems during past market crashes. Ur's merchants only valued advice tested in *comparable adversity*. Rodan needed counsel on *jewel scams during grain shortages*—not general wealth tips.

Implementation Framework:

- Ask: "Describe a client who faced *this exact challenge*—what broke, how did you fix it?"

- Demand war stories, not theory (e.g., "Tell me about the time your strategy failed in a drought")

- Reject advisors who only discuss "best-case scenarios"—true experts obsess over failure modes

Hypothetical Scenario:

A restaurant owner seeks turnaround advice during a recession. A "free" advisor says: "Just add delivery!" But:

- Their only experience is pre-pandemic fine dining (no recession navigation)

- They cite "viral success" without mentioning cost overruns

- They avoid questions about labor shortages or supply chain collapse

Red Flag: Untested in real crisis conditions.

Contrast with Paid Advisor:

A specialist charges $7,500 but:

- Shares financials from a client who grew 18% during the 2020 lockdowns

- Details how they pivoted to "meal kits" *after* delivery failed due to driver shortages

- Shows contingency plans for ingredient scarcity (e.g., substituting lamb for beef)

Green Light: Battle-tested in analogous chaos.

Building Your Advice Budget: Turning Counsel into Compound Growth

Rodan's wisdom wasn't just in paying the merchant—it was in treating advice as *seed capital*, not an expense. Ur's merchants allocated 5% of all new revenue to "wisdom acquisition," knowing this investment would:

- Prevent 83% of costly mistakes (based on clay tablet records)

- Accelerate decision speed by 6.2x (reducing opportunity cost)

- Compound through network effects (advisors introduced better opportunities)

This became the **Strategic Advice Budget**, a system modern entrepreneurs must institutionalize:

Step 1: Calculate Your Baseline

- *Formula:* (Annual Revenue × 0.05) ÷ 12 = Monthly Advice Budget

- *Example:* A $240,000/year business allocates $1,000 monthly ($240,000 × 0.05 = $12,000/year)

- *Critical Adjustment:* Increase to 7-10% during pivots, crises, or hyper-growth phases

Step 2: Categorize Advice Tiers

Ur's merchants segmented spending based on risk/reward:

Tier	Purpose	% of Budget	Example Use Case
Foundation	Core system validation	50%	Hiring a fractional CFO to audit cash flow architecture
Opportunity	High-impact growth bets	30%	Paying a niche specialist to vet a $50K marketing channel
Crisis	Threat mitigation	20%	Consulting a legal expert during a supply chain collapse

Hypothetical Implementation:

A $60,000/month e-commerce brand allocates $250 weekly ($1,000 monthly):

- **Foundation ($125):** Quarterly review with operations specialist to stress-test fulfillment

- **Opportunity ($75):** Paying $500 for a 5-session sprint with a conversion rate expert

- **Crisis ($50):** Retainer for PR advisor to manage potential product recalls

Step 3: Track Advice ROI Relentlessly

Ur's merchants carved "advice ledgers" into clay, tracking:

- *Cost per counsel point* (e.g., $50/silver for jewel verification)

- *Revenue impact* (e.g., $500 saved by avoiding theft)

- *ROI multiplier* (e.g., $500 ÷ $50 = 10x)

Modern Implementation:

Create an "Advice Dashboard" with:

- **Counsel Cost:** Total fees paid

- **Verified Impact:** Revenue saved/gained (e.g., "Avoided $20K mistake")

- **ROI Multiplier:** (Impact ÷ Cost)

- **Velocity:** Time from payment to impact realization

Real-World Hypothetical:

A service business paid $3,000 for a pricing strategy review:

- Counsel Cost: $3,000

- Verified Impact: $42,000 (from optimized tiered pricing)

- ROI Multiplier: 14x

- Velocity: 45 days

Result: The business now allocates 8% of revenue to advice, targeting 10x+ ROI.

Step 4: Institutionalize Wisdom Sourcing

Rodan didn't just pay once—he joined the jewel merchant's "council," a paid advisory group where members:

- Shared anonymized failure data ("Three lost gold to salt merchants posing as jewelers")

- Vouched for vetted specialists ("Seek Zabdiel for emerald authentication")

- Paid annual dues to access the network

Modern Implementation:

Build your "Wisdom Council" through:

- **Paid Masterminds:** Join groups where members contribute verified case studies (e.g., $500/month for a niche operator collective)

- **Advisory Retainers:** Lock in priority access with top experts (e.g., $300/month for 2 hours with a supply chain specialist)

- **Failure Libraries:** Document and share mistakes internally (e.g., "The $8,000 Facebook Ads Blunder")

Hypothetical Case Study:

A manufacturing firm created a "Crisis Council" after nearly collapsing during a raw material shortage:

- Paid $15,000/year for access to 3 vetted advisors (logistics, procurement, finance)

- Required each advisor to share 2 failure stories quarterly

- Tracked ROI: $187,000 saved in 12 months through preemptive interventions

Result: Advice ROI hit 12.5x, funding further wisdom acquisition.

The Psychological Architecture of Paid Wisdom

Rodan's deepest lesson wasn't financial—it was psychological. Paying the merchant transformed his relationship to the advice. Free counsel feels disposable; paid wisdom demands integration. Ur's merchants engineered this through three cognitive levers:

Lever 1: The Sunk Cost Catalyst

When Rodan handed over silver, his brain registered an investment—not a transaction. Neuroscience shows paid advice activates the *endowment effect*: we value what we pay for 2.3x more than free alternatives. The bricklayer's words evaporated; the merchant's warning echoed for months. Modern application: **always pay something for advice, even if symbolic**. A $1 consultation fee creates psychological ownership where free PDFs gather digital dust. Ur's merchants paid one date for financial counsel, knowing this tiny cost would make the advice *stick*.

Lever 2: The Credibility Filter

The merchant's fee acted as a quality screen. Rodan subconsciously reasoned: "If he risks shame by charging and being wrong, his advice must hold weight." This leverages *signaling theory*—payment proves confidence in value. Free advice carries zero credibility signal; paid counsel broadcasts competence. Modern entrepreneurs misuse this by:

- Taking "free" advice from influencers (zero credibility signal)

- Ignoring paid specialists because "it's just their job" (misreading the signal)

The fix: **interpret fees as truth indicators**. When the merchant charged silver, he wasn't being greedy—he was saying, "My reputation is worth more than your doubt."

Lever 3: The Accountability Mirror

Paying forced Rodan to confront his own readiness. Would he implement the advice? Could he justify the cost? The fee created a mirror reflecting his commitment level. Ur's merchants called this "the price of conviction"—if you won't pay for advice, you won't act on it. Modern data proves this: entrepreneurs who pay for counsel implement 89% of recommendations versus 37% for free advice. The silver piece wasn't the merchant's fee—it was Rodan's *commitment tax*.

Implementing Your Wisdom System: From Theory to Daily Practice

Transforming these principles requires operationalizing them into daily habits. Here's how to build your unshakeable advice framework:

Daily Practice: The 10-Minute Credibility Scan

When offered unsolicited advice:

1. *Identify the advisor's revenue source* (e.g., "Is he selling a course?")

2. *Ask: "What have you lost using this method?"* (tests crisis verification)

3. *Calculate potential recovery cost* (e.g., "If this fails, how much time/ money is lost?")

4. *Decide: "Would I pay 1% of that recovery cost for verification?"*

Example: A "free" SEO tip promises "1,000 organic visitors/month." Recovery cost if wrong: 40 hours × $50/hour = $2,000. 1% = $20. If you won't pay $20 to verify, ignore the advice.

Weekly Practice: Advice Budget Reconciliation

Every Friday:

1. Review all counsel received that week (free or paid)

2. Score each on the Advisor Audit (1-5 per step)

3. Calculate ROI for paid advice (Impact ÷ Cost)

4. Adjust next week's budget allocation based on ROI

Template:

Advice Source	Cost	Audit Score (1-20)	Impact	ROI	Action
LinkedIn guru	$0	4	Lost $300 on bad tactic	N/A	Block
Procurement specialist	$450	18	Saved $8,200 on materials	18.2x	Increase engagement

Monthly Practice: Wisdom Council Meeting

Gather your top 3 paid advisors (or idealized versions if starting):

1. Share one *failure* you prevented using their advice

2. Present one *current challenge* for pre-mortem analysis ("How could this go wrong?")

3. Agree on one *micro-experiment* to test new counsel (e.g., "Try pricing tactic with 5% of clients")

Critical Rule: No one speaks without having implemented the prior month's advice.

Pitfalls to Avoid

- **The Guru Trap:** Paying one "oracle" for all advice. Ur's merchants consulted specialists per domain (jewels ≠ grain). *Fix:* Diversify your wisdom sources like a caravan.

- **Analysis Paralysis:** Over-vetting to avoid paying. *Fix:* Set a 48-hour decision window for advice under $500.

- **ROI Myopia:** Only tracking direct revenue impact. *Fix:* Measure soft ROI (e.g., "Reduced stress hours by 10/week").

The Ultimate Metric: Counsel as Compounding Capital

Rodan's final transformation came when he stopped seeing the merchant's fee as cost and started viewing it as *seed capital*. That one silver piece:

- Saved 50 gold pieces (100x return)

- Funded his first bricklayer contract (learning construction)

- Enabled future advice purchases (creating a wisdom flywheel)

This reveals the **Counsel Compounding Curve**:

- Year 1: Pay $1,000 advice → Save $15,000 mistakes (15x ROI)

- Year 2: Reinvest $15,000 → Pay $3,000 advice → Save $60,000 (20x ROI)

- Year 3: Reinvest $60,000 → Pay $12,000 advice → Save $300,000 (25x ROI)

The multiplier grows because:

1. You attract higher-caliber advisors as your budget grows

2. Your implementation speed increases with practice

3. Wisdom networks refer better opportunities

Ur's records show merchants who institutionalized advice budgets achieved 3.8x higher net worth growth over 10 years versus peers. The math is irrefutable: when advice ROI exceeds your cost of capital (e.g., 15x ROI vs. 8% loan interest), *not* buying counsel is financial malpractice. Rodan learned this when he became a merchant himself—he charged silver for advice because he knew it was worth more than gold.

As dusk settled over Babylon, Rodan stood at the jewel merchant's stall, not as a desperate spear-maker, but as a student of wisdom. "Why do you charge silver?" he asked, placing a coin on the counter. The merchant smiled, weighing the silver in his palm. "Because if I gave it free, you'd forget it by dawn. But this?" He tapped Rodan's chest. "This will live in your bones. Now—tell me what you *really* need to know." Rodan leaned in, ready to pay for the questions that would shape his legacy. The marketplace still buzzed with free promises, but he had learned the first law of mastery: **true wisdom isn't found—it's forged in the fire of paid attention, and its value is measured not in the coins you spend, but in the ruin you avoid.** As you navigate your own marketplace of noise, remember Rodan's silver. The cost of ignorance is always higher than the price of insight. Next, you'll confront the most dangerous gap between wisdom and results—the art of adapting advice to your unique reality without losing your strategic compass. For even the purest counsel becomes poison when swallowed whole. The path forward demands not just finding wisdom, but making it your own.

Chapter 19: The Oath Before the Tablets – Integrating Wisdom with Conviction

The Stranger's Silver and the Weight of Decision

How many gold pieces would you sacrifice for a single piece of advice that could save your business? The answer seems obvious—any amount, surely. Yet throughout the markets of ancient Ur, Babylon, and Memphis, merchants routinely paid dearly for the wrong counsel, while spurning wisdom that could have secured their fortunes. Consider this: in the bustling clay tablet archives of Nineveh, records show that 68% of merchant failures stemmed not from lack of opportunity, but from implementing someone else's strategy without testing it against their own reality. The tragedy isn't that Rodan nearly lost fifty gold pieces to the stranger at the gate—that was merely the symptom. The true crisis was his inability to distinguish between the bricklayer's free but worthless advice and the jewel merchant's costly but invaluable warning. You've likely faced this dilemma yourself: inundated with free business advice from podcasts, social media gurus, and well-meaning colleagues, yet paralyzed when it comes time to implement. You understand intellectually that not all advice is created equal, but in the heat of decision-making, you still find yourself oscillating between two dangerous extremes—blindly following the latest guru's framework or stubbornly dismissing all external counsel as irrelevant to your situation. This chapter will transform that tension into synergy, providing you with an actionable methodology to integrate external wisdom with your internal conviction, ensuring every piece of advice you act upon has been stress-tested against your unique business ecosystem.

Rodan's near-disaster with the stranger's jewel scam illustrates a fundamental business truth that remains as relevant today as it was in ancient Mesopotamia: advice without verification is merely opinion wrapped in confidence. When the stranger appeared at Rodan's gate, promising to triple his fifty gold pieces in a month through secret jewel investments, Rodan's instinct for caution should have been his first defense. Instead, he sought validation from those around him—a fatal error in judgment. The bricklayer, who gave free advice based on no expertise whatsoever, nearly cost Rodan everything he had earned from the King. It wasn't until Rodan paid a silver piece to the jewel merchant—a man with actual experience handling precious stones—that he uncovered the truth. This sequence reveals a critical pattern: valuable advice demands investment, both in terms of money and in the effort required to verify it. Modern entrepreneurs often fall into the same trap, chasing free content while undervaluing expert guidance that could prevent costly mistakes. The psychological phenomenon known as "zero-price bias" explains this tendency—our brains irrationally favor free options, even when they deliver minimal value. In business, this manifests as entrepreneurs spending hours consuming free YouTube videos while hesitating to invest in a $500 consultation that could save them $50,000 in misguided strategy.

The deeper issue isn't merely paying for advice—it's understanding how to integrate it without surrendering your strategic autonomy. Rodan could have avoided his crisis entirely if he had possessed a framework for evaluating counsel before acting on it. This represents your critical knowledge gap: the absence of a systematic process to transform external wisdom into context-specific action that aligns with your unique business reality. Without such a framework, you're condemned to either become a slave to every new business trend or an island unto yourself, missing opportunities for growth through valuable outside perspectives. The solution lies not in rejecting external counsel but in developing what the Ur merchants called "the discerning ear"—the ability to hear advice for what it truly is: raw material to be shaped by your own experience and context, not a blueprint to be followed blindly.

The Four Pillars of Wisdom Integration

Ancient merchants developed sophisticated frameworks for transforming advice into action, frameworks that modern business has only recently begun to rediscover through behavioral economics and organizational psychology. At the heart of this methodology lies the "Oath Protocol," a four-step process that Ur merchants performed before inscribing any significant decision onto clay tablets. This ritual wasn't superstition—it was a cognitive forcing function designed to prevent impulsive implementation of untested counsel. When Rodan finally understood this protocol, his approach to business decisions transformed from reactive to strategic. Let's examine each pillar in depth, revealing how you can apply these ancient principles to your modern business challenges.

The first pillar is **Source Verification**—the systematic evaluation of an advisor's credibility before giving their counsel serious consideration. Ur merchants never accepted advice at face value; they investigated the advisor's track record through three critical lenses: proof of concept, skin in the game, and alignment of incentives. Proof of concept required evidence that the advisor had successfully implemented their own advice in relevant scenarios. When the jewel merchant charged Rodan a silver piece for his consultation, he wasn't merely profiting—he was demonstrating that his advice had sufficient value to warrant payment, separating theoretical knowledge from practical wisdom. Skin in the game demanded that the advisor had personally risked something valuable on their recommendations. The jewel merchant's reputation—and potentially his license to operate—hung in the balance with every consultation he provided. Alignment of incentives ensured that the advisor's success was directly tied to the client's success; if Rodan had lost his gold, the merchant would have faced public disgrace and likely lost future business. Modern equivalents require you to ask three specific questions before implementing any significant advice: (1) Can the advisor show concrete results from applying this themselves? (2) Do they stand to lose something meaningful if their advice fails? (3) Will they benefit primarily from your success, not just from giving the advice? A simple verification checklist you can implement immediately includes: requesting three references from clients who faced similar challenges, verifying the advisor's own business metrics (not just testimonials), and structuring engagements so the advisor's compensation is partially tied to your outcomes.

The second pillar is **Contextual Mapping**—the process of translating generic advice into your specific business environment. This represents where most entrepreneurs fail, implementing strategies designed for entirely different contexts and wondering why they don't work. When the jewel merchant warned Rodan about the stranger's scam, the advice wasn't simply "don't trust the stranger." It was "verify the stranger's lineage through the temple records and cross-reference with three independent merchants." This specificity transformed generic caution into actionable intelligence. Modern businesses often miss this nuance, adopting frameworks like "growth hacking" or "agile development" without adapting them to their unique market position, team capabilities, or customer base. Contextual mapping requires you to identify the core principle behind any advice and then rebuild it for your specific circumstances. For example, if an advisor suggests "raise your prices by 20%," the universal principle might be "capture more value from your established customer base." But the implementation must consider your specific context: Are your customers price-sensitive? Does your brand promise value or luxury? What's the competitive landscape? A practical contextual mapping exercise involves creating a "context scorecard" rating how closely your situation matches the advisor's original context across five dimensions: market maturity, customer sophistication, team experience, competitive intensity, and regulatory environment. Only when the cumulative score exceeds 70% should you consider direct implementation; below that threshold requires significant adaptation.

The third pillar is **Micro-Experimentation**—the practice of testing advice at minimal scale before full implementation. This represents Rodan's most crucial insight: wisdom must be verified through personal experience, not merely accepted on authority. Ur merchants never implemented major strategic shifts based on advice alone; they first conducted "clay shard tests"—small-scale experiments designed to validate principles without risking significant resources. When Rodan suspected the stranger might be a thief, he didn't immediately confront him or withdraw his gold; he discreetly checked the stranger's claims through multiple independent channels. Modern equivalents include A/B testing pricing changes with 5% of your customer base, running pilot programs with a single product line before company-wide rollout, or implementing new processes in one department before scaling organization-wide. The key is designing experiments that provide meaningful data while minimizing risk and resource commitment. A robust micro-experimentation framework includes four elements: a clearly defined hypothesis ("If we implement X, then Y will happen"), a specific metric to track ("customer retention rate"), a defined success threshold ("increase of at least 5%"), and a predetermined timeline ("two weeks"). Crucially, Ur merchants recorded these experiments on temporary clay shards, not permanent tablets, symbolizing their provisional nature—advice remained unproven until validated through action. When implementing this today, designate specific projects as "advice tests" with capped budgets (never more than 5% of the potential full implementation cost) and strict kill criteria (if metric X doesn't improve by Y% in Z time, terminate the experiment).

The fourth and final pillar is **Integration Rituals**—the systematic process of weaving validated wisdom into your ongoing operations. This transforms isolated insights into organizational capability. Ur merchants didn't treat wisdom as one-off fixes; they created "wisdom journals" where verified advice was recorded alongside the context of its validation and specific implementation protocols. Each successful experiment became a new standard operating procedure, but only after being tested across three different scenarios to ensure robustness. Modern equivalents include creating "playbooks" for validated strategies, embedding key metrics into regular operational reviews, and establishing feedback loops that continuously assess effectiveness. The most sophisticated organizations develop what we might call "wisdom circuits"—closed-loop systems where advice is tested, validated, implemented, monitored, and refined in an ongoing cycle. For example, a manufacturing company might establish a monthly "advice sprint" where one promising external insight is tested across a single production line, with results reviewed by cross-functional teams before potential scaling. These rituals transform advice from episodic events into continuous improvement processes, ensuring your organization becomes increasingly adept at integrating external wisdom without losing strategic autonomy.

Building Your Wisdom Integration System

Implementing the Oath Protocol requires more than theoretical understanding—it demands concrete systems that operationalize these principles in your daily decision-making. Let's explore how to construct your own wisdom integration system through a practical, step-by-step framework you can implement immediately. Think of this as creating your personal "clay tablet" for business decisions—a structured process that transforms advice into action while preserving your strategic sovereignty.

Start by establishing your **Advice Triage System**, a method for categorizing counsel based on its universality and your context. Ur merchants instinctively understood that not all advice requires equal scrutiny—some principles are nearly universal, while others are highly contextual. Create a three-tiered system for evaluating incoming counsel: Universal, Contextual, and Speculative. Universal advice applies to virtually all business situations (e.g., "track your cash flow," "understand your customer," "honor your commitments"). These require minimal verification—implement them immediately with minor adaptation to your systems. Contextual advice has proven value but requires significant adaptation to your specific situation (e.g., "raise prices by 20%," "pivot to digital marketing"). These demand rigorous contextual mapping and micro-experimentation before implementation. Speculative advice represents unproven theories or highly specialized tactics with limited applicability (e.g., "invest in cryptocurrency," "adopt blockchain for supply chain"). These should be treated as hypotheses requiring extensive validation before consideration. To operationalize this, create an Advice Triage Matrix with two axes: applicability across contexts (low to high) and evidence strength (weak to strong). Plot all incoming advice on this matrix to determine the appropriate level of scrutiny. Universal advice falls in the high applicability/strong evidence quadrant; Speculative advice occupies the low applicability/weak evidence space. Contextual advice spans the middle ground. When Rodan received the bricklayer's suggestion to invest with the stranger, placing it on this matrix would have immediately revealed its speculative nature—zero evidence from a non-expert in a highly specific situation.

Next, design your **Micro-Experimentation Framework**, the engine that transforms advice from theory into validated practice. This requires moving beyond vague intentions to create specific protocols for testing wisdom at minimal risk. Begin by establishing your "experiment budget"—the maximum resources you'll allocate to test any single piece of advice. Ur merchants typically limited experiments to 5% of the resources required for full implementation, ensuring failure wouldn't threaten their business. For a modern business, this might mean allocating no more than 5% of your marketing budget to test a new channel, or dedicating just one team member to pilot a new process. Crucially, define your experiment parameters before beginning: What specific outcome will validate the advice? How will you measure it? What constitutes failure? How long will the test run? When Rodan investigated the stranger's claims, he didn't wander aimlessly—he specifically checked three verifiable facts (the stranger's lineage, his connection to the rug merchant, and recent jewel transactions) through predetermined channels (temple records and merchant associations). Create an Experiment Design Template with these essential elements: hypothesis statement ("If we implement X, then Y metric will improve by Z%"), measurement protocol (exactly how you'll track results), success criteria (minimum improvement required to continue), kill criteria (conditions requiring immediate termination), and resource allocation (people, time, and money committed). For example, if testing a pricing increase recommendation, your template might specify: "If we raise prices by 15% for customers with 12+ months tenure, then retention rate will remain above 85% with a 20% increase in revenue per customer. We'll measure this through our CRM system over six weeks. Success requires retention above 85% and revenue per customer increase of at least 10%. Kill criteria include retention dropping below 80% or customer complaints increasing by 25%. Resources: one marketing specialist for 10 hours/week, $500 for targeted communications."

Now, establish your **Wisdom Journal**, the institutional memory system that transforms isolated experiments into organizational capability. Ur merchants maintained meticulous records of tested advice on special clay tablets, noting not just what worked but why and under what conditions.

Your Wisdom Journal should capture four critical elements for each tested piece of advice: the original counsel, the contextual adaptation you applied, the experiment design and results, and the integration protocol for successful strategies. Structure your journal digitally or physically with consistent fields: Advice Source (who provided it and their credentials), Core Principle (the universal insight behind the specific recommendation), Context Score (how well it matched your situation on a 1-10 scale), Experiment Design (your test parameters), Results (quantitative and qualitative outcomes), and Integration Path (how you'll implement if successful). When Rodan documented his experience with the jewel merchant's advice, he didn't merely note "stranger was a thief." He recorded the verification process, the specific evidence that confirmed the scam, and the broader principle about verifying high-stakes opportunities through multiple independent channels. Modern equivalents might include using a shared document system where team members contribute tested wisdom, with successful strategies automatically feeding into standard operating procedures. Crucially, schedule regular Wisdom Review Sessions—weekly for tactical advice, monthly for strategic guidance—where your team examines new journal entries, discusses insights, and updates implementation protocols. These sessions transform individual learning into collective wisdom, ensuring your organization compounds knowledge rather than constantly reinventing the wheel.

Finally, create your **Adaptation Feedback Loop**, the mechanism that ensures wisdom integration remains dynamic rather than dogmatic. Many businesses fail by treating validated advice as permanent truth, ignoring changing market conditions that may render yesterday's wisdom obsolete. Ur merchants understood that even proven strategies required periodic revalidation—they called this "checking the tablet's edges" to ensure the clay hadn't cracked with time. Your feedback loop should include three elements: regular revalidation schedules (e.g., review pricing strategies quarterly, marketing approaches semi-annually), trigger events that prompt immediate reassessment (e.g., 10% drop in key metrics, major market shift), and a formal process for sunsetting outdated strategies. Implement a "Wisdom Expiration Date" for each integrated strategy, requiring review before the date to confirm continued relevance. When Rodan began using the jewel merchant's verification process for all high-value opportunities, he didn't apply it rigidly—he adjusted the number of verification channels based on opportunity size and risk. A $5 transaction might require only one verification step, while a $500 opportunity demanded three independent confirmations. Your adaptation protocol should specify how strategies evolve with changing conditions: perhaps your pricing strategy includes automatic adjustments based on competitor moves, or your marketing approach scales verification rigor with customer lifetime value. Track two critical metrics: Adaptation Speed (time from advice receipt to validated implementation) and Wisdom Yield (revenue impact per advice point), aiming for adaptation under 14 days and yield exceeding 15x.

Navigating the Common Traps

Even with a robust wisdom integration system in place, you'll encounter predictable challenges that can derail your efforts. Understanding these traps—and how to navigate them—is essential for transforming advice into sustainable advantage. The Ur merchants documented these pitfalls on special "warning tablets" kept near their decision-making spaces, recognizing that awareness alone could prevent costly errors. Let's examine the most common traps and their antidotes, equipping you to maintain clarity when implementing external wisdom.

The first trap is **Context Blindness**—the failure to recognize how your specific business environment alters the applicability of general advice. This manifests when entrepreneurs implement strategies that worked for industry giants without considering their own scale, resources, or market position. Imagine a small pottery workshop owner reading about Amazon's "two-pizza teams" and immediately restructuring her 12-person operation into autonomous squads—ignoring that Amazon's approach depends on sophisticated technology infrastructure, vast resources, and a completely different business model. Context blindness often stems from what psychologists call the "curse of knowledge"—once we understand a concept, we forget what it's like not to know it, making us overestimate its universal applicability. Ur merchants avoided this by developing what they called "context scoring," a systematic method for evaluating how closely their situation matched the conditions under which advice was developed. Create your own context scoring protocol by identifying five to seven critical dimensions where business contexts differ (e.g., team size, market maturity, customer sophistication, competitive intensity, regulatory environment, technological infrastructure, cash reserves). Rate each dimension on a 1-10 scale for both the advisor's context and your own, then calculate a context match percentage. Only when this exceeds 70% should you consider direct implementation; below 50% requires significant adaptation or rejection. When Rodan considered the stranger's jewel investment opportunity, a context score would have immediately revealed the mismatch—he was a spear-maker with limited trade experience, while the opportunity required specialized knowledge of gem valuation and international markets. A practical exercise: take a piece of advice you're considering implementing and conduct a formal context assessment. You'll likely discover dimensions you hadn't considered that significantly alter the advice's applicability.

The second trap is **Verification Bias**—the tendency to seek evidence confirming our preexisting beliefs while ignoring contradictory information. This explains why Rodan initially trusted the bricklayer's free advice: it confirmed his hope for a quick, easy return on his gold. Modern entrepreneurs fall prey to this when they selectively remember the successes of business strategies while ignoring failures, creating an illusion of effectiveness. Verification bias operates through three mechanisms: cherry-picking data that supports our preferred outcome, misinterpreting ambiguous information as confirmation, and dismissing contradictory evidence as "special cases." Ur merchants countered this with their "three witnesses" rule: no significant decision could be made based on a single verification channel. Rodan's breakthrough came when he sought multiple independent confirmations of the stranger's claims rather than relying on the bricklayer's single endorsement. Implement your own verification protocol requiring multiple independent validation channels for any significant advice: for market-related counsel, consult at least three customers, two competitors (discreetly), and industry data; for operational advice, test with two different teams or processes; for financial strategies, model outcomes under three different scenarios. Crucially, build in "disconfirmation requirements"—specific evidence that would prove the advice wrong—and actively seek this information. When testing pricing changes, for instance, deliberately look for customer segments where the change reduces revenue, not just those where it increases. Track your verification completeness score (percentage of required validation channels completed) and never implement advice scoring below 80%.

The third trap is **Implementation Rigidity**—the failure to adapt validated wisdom as circumstances change. Many businesses successfully test and implement advice only to cling to it long after it has ceased delivering value. This occurs because we confuse the principle behind the advice with its specific expression, treating tactics as permanent truth. Ur merchants called this "worshipping the tablet instead of the wisdom," recognizing that even proven strategies require periodic revalidation. The antidote lies in building adaptability into your implementation from the start. When Rodan adopted the jewel merchant's verification process, he didn't create a rigid checklist but established flexible principles: verify high-value opportunities through multiple independent channels, with verification rigor scaling with opportunity size. Create "strategic flexibility points" in every implemented strategy—specific conditions triggering automatic review or adjustment. For pricing strategies, this might include automatic reassessment when competitor pricing shifts by more than 10%, or when customer acquisition costs increase by 15%. Implement "wisdom expiration dates" for all implemented advice, requiring formal revalidation at predetermined intervals. Track two critical metrics: Adaptation Speed (time from advice receipt to validated implementation) and Context Drift (how much your business environment has changed since implementation), aiming for revalidation whenever context drift exceeds 30%. A practical exercise: review your current business strategies and identify their built-in flexibility points. If you can't find them, redesign those strategies to include specific triggers for reassessment.

The fourth and most insidious trap is **Wisdom Debt**—the accumulation of unverified or outdated advice that continues to influence decisions despite lacking validation. This resembles technical debt in software development: shortcuts taken today that create mounting costs tomorrow. Wisdom debt often enters organizations through three channels: inherited practices ("we've always done it this way"), uncritically adopted trends ("everyone's doing agile"), and partially implemented strategies ("we tried content marketing but it didn't work"). Ur merchants maintained meticulous "debt tablets" tracking unverified assumptions and outdated practices, reviewing them quarterly to prevent compounding errors. Modern businesses can implement Wisdom Debt Audits by creating an inventory of current practices, classifying each as: Verified (tested and proven), Assumed (operating without verification), or Outdated (once-verified but potentially obsolete). For each Assumed or Outdated practice, calculate its Wisdom Debt Score based on impact (how much it affects results) and uncertainty (how confident you are in its effectiveness). Prioritize addressing high-impact, high-uncertainty items first. When Rodan examined his business practices after the stranger incident, he discovered several Wisdom Debts: assuming all gate visitors were legitimate opportunities, trusting free advice over paid expertise, and neglecting verification for small transactions. Each had contributed to his near-disaster. Implement a quarterly Wisdom Debt Review where you: catalog current practices, score each for impact and uncertainty, select top three to address, and design validation protocols. Crucially, track your Wisdom Debt Ratio (unverified practices divided by total practices), aiming to keep it below 20%. This metric serves as an early warning system for accumulating strategic risk.

The Transformation of Rodan: From Victim to Visionary

To truly understand wisdom integration in action, let's follow Rodan's journey as he transforms from a near-victim of bad advice into a master of contextual wisdom. After his encounter with the jewel merchant, Rodan didn't merely avoid future scams—he developed a systematic approach to advice that propelled him from successful spear-maker to respected merchant-advisor in his own right. His transformation illustrates the practical application of the principles we've explored, providing a roadmap for your own journey from advice consumer to wisdom integrator.

Rodan's first step was establishing his **Personal Oath Protocol**, a ritual he performed before making any significant business decision. Each morning, he would inscribe his intended decisions for the day on a temporary clay shard, then subject each to the four verification questions: (1) Whose advice influenced this, and have I verified their credibility? (2) How well does this align with my specific business context? (3) Have I tested this through a small-scale experiment? (4) How will I know if this is working, and when to adjust? Only decisions passing all four checks would be transferred to permanent tablets. This ritual transformed Rodan's decision-making from reactive to deliberate. When a cloth merchant later approached him with an opportunity to invest in a new loom technology, Rodan didn't immediately dismiss it (as he might have before) or jump in (as he did with the stranger). Instead, he followed his protocol: he verified the merchant's track record by speaking with three other weavers who had used the loom; he mapped the technology to his context, realizing it would only benefit him if he doubled production capacity; he arranged to test the loom for one week at minimal cost; and he defined clear success metrics before implementation. The result? He avoided a costly investment that would have sat idle (the loom required specialized materials unavailable in his region), while identifying a modified version that proved highly profitable when adapted to his specific needs.

Rodan next developed his **Community Wisdom Network**, recognizing that individual verification has limits. He formed a council of five trusted merchants from different trades, each committing to share tested wisdom and provide independent verification for high-stakes decisions. Crucially, they structured this as a paid network—each member contributed one silver piece per verified insight shared, creating skin in the game that ensured quality contributions. When Rodan considered expanding into shield-making (a natural extension of his spear business), he didn't rely on a single advisor. He presented his plan to the council, paying each member a silver piece for their verified assessment. Their collective wisdom revealed critical gaps: the shield market was dominated by established artisans with temple connections, and Rodan's spear-making techniques didn't directly transfer to shield construction. Instead of abandoning the idea, Rodan used this feedback to pivot—focusing on spear-and-shield matching sets, a niche none of the council members had considered. This adaptation, born from integrated wisdom, became his most profitable line. Your modern equivalent might be creating a mastermind group where members pay to participate, ensuring commitment to quality contributions, or establishing formal advisory relationships with clear verification protocols. The key is designing structures that incentivize truth over politeness and verification over opinion.

Most significantly, Rodan institutionalized wisdom through his **Apprentice Integration System**. As his business grew, he faced the challenge of ensuring new team members could independently evaluate and implement advice. Rather than simply teaching them his current practices, he trained them in the wisdom integration process itself. Each apprentice began with a "Wisdom Journal" where they documented every piece of advice they encountered, including their verification process and adaptation decisions. Rodan structured their learning through progressive responsibility: first observing his verification process, then conducting verifications under supervision, then implementing micro-experiments, and finally making independent decisions with post-implementation reviews. Crucially, he celebrated "intelligent failures"—instances where apprentices followed the process correctly but still encountered negative outcomes—as learning opportunities rather than mistakes. When a promising apprentice nearly lost a shipment by trusting a new carrier's claims, Rodan didn't punish him. Instead, they reviewed where the verification process broke down (the apprentice had relied on only one reference check instead of the required three) and strengthened the protocol accordingly. This created a culture where the process mattered more than any single outcome, ensuring Rodan's business could continue thriving even in his absence. Your equivalent might involve onboarding new team members with explicit training in your advice evaluation framework, creating "wisdom pathways" that map skill development in contextual integration, or implementing regular team exercises where hypothetical advice is collectively evaluated and tested.

Rodan's ultimate transformation came when he stopped viewing advice as something received and began generating wisdom through structured experimentation. He established his **Wisdom Incubation Program**, dedicating 10% of his business resources to systematically testing promising but unproven ideas. Each quarter, he and his team would select three potential innovations, design micro-experiments to validate core principles, and document results in their collective Wisdom Journal. When a traveler described "water-powered looms" used in distant lands, Rodan didn't dismiss it as irrelevant or immediately invest in recreating the technology. Instead, he designed a series of escalating experiments: first verifying the basic principle with a small waterwheel demonstration, then testing adaptation to local river conditions, and finally piloting a modified version with one weaver. Though the full water-powered loom proved impractical for his scale, the experiments revealed valuable insights about tension control that improved all his looms' output. This systematic approach to wisdom generation transformed Rodan from a passive advice consumer into an active knowledge creator, positioning him as the go-to advisor for other merchants. Your modern equivalent might involve creating a dedicated innovation budget, establishing regular "advice sprint" cycles, or implementing a formal process for capturing and testing customer suggestions.

Becoming a Wisdom Integrator: Your Path Forward

As Rodan discovered through his near-disastrous encounter with the stranger at the gate, the masterful integration of external wisdom with internal conviction isn't merely a business skill—it's the foundation of enduring entrepreneurial success. You now possess the frameworks to transform from advice victim to wisdom integrator: the Oath Protocol for systematic verification, the Advice Triage System for intelligent categorization, the Micro-Experimentation Framework for low-risk validation, and the Wisdom Journal for institutional memory. These aren't theoretical constructs but practical tools forged in the crucible of real business challenges, proven across millennia of merchant experience. The true measure of your progress won't be how many concepts you've absorbed, but how consistently you apply them when faced with the next piece of advice that promises to transform your business.

Your immediate next step is to conduct a Wisdom Audit of your current decision-making processes. Identify three significant business decisions you've made in the past six months and subject each to the Oath Protocol: (1) How thoroughly did you verify the advice sources? (2) How rigorously did you map recommendations to your specific context? (3) What micro-experiments did you conduct before full implementation? (4) How have you institutionalized lessons from the outcomes? This audit will reveal your specific Wisdom Integration gaps, allowing you to prioritize which element of the system to strengthen first. Most entrepreneurs discover they're surprisingly strong in one or two areas while dangerously weak in others—perhaps you excel at source verification but neglect micro-experimentation, or you're great at contextual mapping but fail to institutionalize lessons. Focus your initial efforts on your weakest link, as it represents your greatest vulnerability to costly advice missteps.

To operationalize your learning immediately, implement the "Single Advice Sprint" challenge: select one piece of business advice you've been considering (whether from a podcast, article, or colleague) and subject it to the full Wisdom Integration process within the next 14 days. Begin by verifying the source's credibility through at least three independent channels, then map the advice to your specific context using the context scoring protocol. Design a micro-experiment with clear success metrics that consumes no more than 5% of the resources required for full implementation, and document everything in your new Wisdom Journal. At the end of the sprint, make a conscious decision: scale the advice, adapt it further, or discard it based on evidence rather than emotion. This single sprint will teach you more about wisdom integration than months of theoretical study, while potentially uncovering a valuable new strategy for your business. Record your results and share them with a trusted colleague to create accountability—this transforms the exercise from individual learning to collective wisdom building.

The true transformation occurs when wisdom integration becomes instinctive—when you no longer need to consciously apply the Oath Protocol because it has become your natural decision-making rhythm. This represents the highest level of business mastery, where external counsel flows through your verification filters automatically, emerging as context-specific action without conscious effort. Rodan achieved this state when, years after his encounter with the stranger, he found himself instinctively verifying high-stakes opportunities through multiple channels, adapting proven strategies to his evolving business, and teaching his apprentices the wisdom integration process as naturally as breathing. You'll know you've reached this level when team members begin asking the Oath Protocol questions unprompted, when micro-experiments become standard operating procedure rather than special projects, and when your Wisdom Journal becomes the living document that guides your strategic evolution. This isn't a destination but a continuous journey—one where each piece of advice becomes an opportunity to refine your integration process, strengthening your business's immune system against bad counsel while accelerating adoption of transformative wisdom.

As you seal your own wisdom tablets with verified insights, remember Rodan's ultimate lesson: advice has no inherent value—it gains worth only through intelligent integration. The bricklayer's free counsel nearly cost him everything, while the jewel merchant's silver-charged warning preserved his fortune, not because of their relative cost but because of how Rodan processed and applied them. Your business's resilience and growth depend not on how much advice you consume, but on how skillfully you transform it into context-specific action. In the next chapter, we'll explore how to take this integrated wisdom and drive organizational change—how to align your entire team around tested insights, especially when they challenge sacred cows and established practices. You're now equipped to discern and implement wisdom individually; the next challenge is scaling this capability across your organization, ensuring your entire team operates with the same discerning ear that saved Rodan from ruin. As the Ur merchants knew, true mastery isn't found in any single piece of advice, but in the flow connecting wisdom to action—a flow you now command with confidence.

Chapter 20: The Master Merchant's Seal – Synthesizing Wisdom into Unstoppable Flow

When Fragments Become Symphony: The Final Revelation

Why do so many entrepreneurs master individual business principles—cash flow management, risk mitigation, reputation building—yet still fail to achieve sustainable growth? Why do some merchants accumulate vast knowledge yet remain perpetually reactive, never quite reaching the level of true mastery where opportunity flows to them rather than being chased? The answer lies not in the absence of knowledge, but in the failure to integrate knowledge into a cohesive system. For every Arad who successfully filled his fifth jar during famine, there were ten weavers who understood the Five Jars principle yet missed the famine opportunity because they hadn't connected it to their reputation with wool farmers or their ownership stake in dye production. This chapter reveals the final, transformative insight: business mastery isn't about executing isolated tactics perfectly, but about orchestrating all principles into a self-reinforcing cycle where each element amplifies the others, creating unstoppable momentum.

You've journeyed through the essential components of business wisdom—the Five Jars for cash flow discipline, the Caravan Strategy for risk management, the Engraver's Mark for reputation engineering, the Clay Pit Dividend for ownership thinking. You've learned to identify hidden assets, monetize waste streams, align incentives, forecast strategically, and defend your core focus. Yet, if these principles remain siloed in your consciousness—treated as separate chapters in a manual rather than movements in a symphony—you'll never access the exponential power that comes from their integration. Your current state reflects this fragmentation: you apply cash flow principles rigorously during budgeting season but abandon them when opportunity knocks; you understand reputation's value yet sacrifice it for short-term gains during cash crunches; you recognize byproduct potential but lack the capital to monetize it because your risk management strategy is disconnected from your ownership thinking. This chapter targets your critical gap: the absence of a unified operating system that transforms isolated insights into perpetual motion, turning you from a practitioner of business into a true master merchant who moves with the current rather than against it.

The Capital Symphony Framework: Orchestrating Four Movements

Ur's master merchants didn't view business as a collection of tactics but as a living symphony with four essential movements that must play in harmony. Just as a single instrument produces sound but not music, isolated business principles generate activity but not sustainable growth. The Capital Symphony Framework—perfected over generations by merchants who weathered famines, wars, and market collapses—reveals how cash flow, risk management, reputation, and ownership must interweave to create unstoppable momentum. This isn't theoretical; Babylonian merchant records show that traders who implemented integrated systems grew wealth 7.3x faster than those using isolated tactics during the 20-year drought of 1792 BCE. Let's examine each movement in the symphony and how they must interact.

Movement I: The Cash Flow Rhythm (The Five Jars Revisited)

The foundation of the symphony is cash flow management—specifically, the Five Jars methodology transformed from a static allocation system into a dynamic rhythm that responds to market conditions. Most entrepreneurs treat the Five Jars as fixed percentages: 10% tithes, 35% household, 20% debt, 15% tools, 20% opportunity. But master merchants adjust these ratios like a musician adjusting tempo—faster during growth phases, slower during contraction. During the Bronze Age trade boom, successful merchants reduced household allocation to 25% to accelerate opportunity capital growth to 30%, while during the famine, they temporarily increased tools allocation to 25% to acquire undervalued resources.

The critical evolution is viewing cash flow not as revenue allocation but as energy distribution. Every shekel earned carries potential energy that must be directed intentionally through the jars. The tithes jar isn't just community contribution—it's your connection to the economic ecosystem, ensuring stability when markets fluctuate. When Arad reduced his tithes during lean times, he unknowingly severed this connection, making farmers reluctant to sell him wool during famine. The household jar isn't just personal expenses—it's your psychological anchor; merchants who allocated less than 25% here suffered decision fatigue that eroded all other allocations. The debt jar isn't just repayment—it's your leverage multiplier; Babylonian records show merchants who maintained debt below 30% of assets could secure emergency loans at half the interest rate of over-leveraged peers.

Master merchants implemented "cash flow cadence checks" three times daily: at market opening (verifying today's revenue allocation), at midday (adjusting for unexpected opportunities), and at closing (auditing deviations). They used physical tokens—bronze for opportunity capital, silver for household, copper for debt—to make allocations visible and tangible. Most crucially, they recognized that cash flow management's ultimate purpose isn't survival but creating the liquidity that enables the other symphony movements. Without sufficient opportunity capital, risk management becomes theoretical; without stable household allocation, reputation suffers from owner burnout; without debt discipline, ownership opportunities remain out of reach.

Movement II: The Risk Management Counterpoint (The Caravan Strategy Evolved)

Risk management isn't merely diversification—it's creating a counterpoint melody that harmonizes with cash flow while providing resilience. The Caravan Strategy's evolution recognizes that true diversification requires uncorrelated revenue streams that respond differently to market shocks. Most merchants diversify into related activities (e.g., a weaver adding rug dyeing), creating false security—when demand for textiles drops, both streams collapse simultaneously. Master merchants instead created "negative correlation portfolios" where one stream thrives when another struggles.

Consider the caravan merchant who allocated resources across four uncorrelated streams: grain caravans (prosper during droughts), wool shipments (prosper during cold snaps), temple lending (prosper during famines), and date farming (prosper during trade embargoes). Babylonian records show that when drought hit, grain revenue increased 40% while wool dropped 30%, date farming remained stable, and temple lending surged as temples sought emergency funds—resulting in net revenue growth of 18% despite the crisis. Crucially, this merchant funded these streams through his opportunity capital jar, creating a self-reinforcing cycle where cash flow enabled diversification which stabilized future cash flow.

Modern entrepreneurs replicate this through "strategic correlation mapping." For instance, a textile merchant might allocate opportunity capital across: core weaving (vulnerable to fashion shifts), textile recycling (thrives when core demand drops), weaving workshops (thrives when unemployment rises), and fabric design licensing (thrives during innovation booms). Each stream requires different resource inputs yet shares operational infrastructure, creating efficiency. The master merchant's innovation was stress-testing correlation assumptions through "what-if" scenarios: "If a plague reduces weavers by 50%, which streams compensate?" Babylonian merchants used clay tablet simulations tracking 12 market variables, while modern equivalents use tools like Monte Carlo simulators projecting thousands of market scenarios.

Most importantly, risk management must interact with cash flow through dynamic allocation. During stable periods, opportunity capital might fund 30% growth in new streams; during volatility, it shifts to strengthening uncorrelated core streams. The merchant who survived the 1792 BCE drought didn't just have diversified streams—he temporarily reallocated 50% of his opportunity capital from new ventures to securing grain supply contracts, recognizing that existing uncorrelated streams needed reinforcement more than expansion.

Movement III: The Reputation Melody (The Engraver's Mark Transformed)

Reputation isn't a separate concern—it's the melody that gives emotional resonance to the entire symphony, determining how customers, suppliers, and partners respond to your business during both calm and crisis. Master merchants understood that reputation compounds like interest but erodes like sandcastles, requiring constant nurturing through visible quality commitments. The Engraver's Mark evolved from a simple quality indicator to a dynamic reputation system with three critical components.

First, "reputation anchoring"—publicly committing to standards that become synonymous with your brand. Drios didn't just engrave his mark; he swore oaths before temple elders that every shield would withstand forty hammer strikes, creating social accountability. Modern equivalents include public service level agreements where merchants promise specific outcomes (e.g., "All rugs delivered within seven days or double compensation") visible to all customers. Babylonian records show merchants with public commitments charged 22% premiums yet maintained 30% higher customer retention because their reputation became a self-fulfilling prophecy—customers expected excellence and merchants delivered to protect their public oath.

Second, "reputation resonance"—ensuring quality signals reach the right audiences at the right time. Drios engraved his mark prominently where battle damage would reveal it first (the shield's edge), ensuring warriors saw his craftsmanship during combat. Today, this means placing quality indicators where they impact decision points: a weaver might showcase thread density at the rug's fringes (where customers first touch it) rather than hidden centers. Master merchants mapped "reputation touchpoints" across the customer journey, allocating resources to maximize visibility where it mattered most—like placing quality certifications on transaction receipts where customers review purchases.

Third, and most crucially, reputation must harmonize with cash flow and risk management through "reputation elasticity"—the ability to maintain quality during crises when others cut corners. When famine hit Ur, many weavers diluted wool with goat hair to survive, destroying their reputation. Arad maintained pure wool because his opportunity capital jar funded premium materials during shortages, while his diversified streams provided alternative income. Babylonian merchant guilds tracked "reputation elasticity scores" measuring how merchants maintained quality during stress; those scoring above 8/10 (on metrics like material consistency and delivery reliability during crises) grew wealth 4.7x faster than peers.

The master merchant's insight was recognizing reputation as liquid capital—during the 1792 BCE famine, Arad's reputation allowed him to negotiate 30-day payment terms with desperate wool farmers when competitors demanded immediate payment, giving him flexibility to leverage his opportunity capital strategically. Reputation wasn't just about customer loyalty; it was operational leverage that amplified all other symphony movements.

Movement IV: The Ownership Crescendo (The Clay Pit Dividend Amplified)

Ownership thinking transforms from passive income pursuit to the crescendo that elevates the entire symphony, converting linear growth into exponential expansion. Master merchants didn't just acquire assets—they created "ownership ecosystems" where each asset generated not just income but new opportunities to acquire additional assets, creating compounding momentum.

The Clay Pit Dividend evolved through three critical innovations. First, "asset chaining"—using income from one asset to acquire the next, creating a daisy chain of compounding ownership. Hapu didn't just buy clay pit shares; he used clay pit dividends to acquire a kiln, then kiln income to fund a pottery stall, then stall profits to buy a brick factory. Babylonian records show merchants who implemented asset chains grew passive income 8.3x faster than those acquiring isolated assets, as each new asset amplified the others (clay pit supplied kiln, kiln increased clay demand).

Second, "byproduct ownership"—monetizing operational waste streams as independent revenue sources that required minimal additional investment. While Sharru sold excess stone for housing, master merchants took it further, using stone sales to acquire ownership stakes in complementary businesses (e.g., a wood supplier for housing frames). The true innovation was recognizing that every operational output contains hidden ownership opportunities if viewed through the right lens—a weaver's discarded threads might become stuffing for cushions sold to potters, with cushion profits funding loom upgrades.

Third, and most transformative, ownership must interact with risk management through "optionality"—structuring asset acquisitions to create future choices rather than fixed commitments. Rather than buying full ownership of the clay pit, master merchants often secured first refusal rights or profit-sharing agreements that required minimal upfront capital but offered disproportionate future upside. During the famine, these flexible arrangements let Arad acquire distressed wool farms at 30% of market value because he wasn't locked into rigid ownership structures.

Modern entrepreneurs replicate this through "phased ownership": acquiring micro-stakes (1-5%) in related businesses with clear paths to increased ownership as value grows. A textile merchant might start by taking 2% ownership in a dye supplier for preferential pricing, then increase stake as volume grows, eventually gaining control without massive upfront capital. Crucially, ownership income must flow back into the opportunity capital jar, creating a self-fueling cycle where passive income accelerates active growth.

Implementing the Capital Symphony: Rhythms, Metrics, and Rituals

Mastering the symphony requires more than understanding its components—it demands implementation systems that make integration automatic. Babylonian merchant records reveal four critical implementation frameworks that transformed theory into daily practice.

The Orchestration Rhythm System

Rather than treating business principles as occasional considerations, master merchants embedded them into daily, weekly, monthly, and quarterly rhythms that reinforced integration. These weren't abstract plans but physical rituals performed with tangible objects:

- **Daily (Cash Flow Cadence)**: At market opening, merchants placed physical tokens (bronze, silver, copper) into jar replicas representing today's expected revenue, allocating immediately rather than waiting for month-end. At midday, they adjusted allocations based on morning activity, moving tokens between jars as opportunities arose. At closing, they audited actual revenue against allocations, using clay tablets to track deviations. This made cash flow allocation visceral and immediate rather than theoretical.

- **Weekly (Reputation Resonance)**: Every seventh day, merchants conducted "reputation walks" through their operations, physically inspecting quality touchpoints with engraved marking tools ready to apply their mark where quality met standards. They collected customer feedback through tablet interviews, categorizing comments by impact on the four symphony movements (e.g., "slow delivery" affected cash flow and reputation).

- **Monthly (Risk Rebalancing)**: On the new moon, merchants reviewed caravan performance across all streams, recalculating correlation coefficients using bead counters on abacuses. They stress-tested portfolios against three hypothetical crises, reallocating opportunity capital based on emerging threats. Most crucially, they verified that no single stream exceeded 25% of total revenue, maintaining true diversification.

- **Quarterly (Ownership Audits)**: Every three months, merchants conducted "asset chain reviews," mapping how income from one asset flowed into acquiring the next. They calculated ownership velocity (time for asset income to cover acquisition cost) and identified new byproduct opportunities through waste stream walks inspecting operational outputs.

These rhythms transformed integration from an abstract concept into embodied practice. Babylonian records show merchants who implemented full rhythm systems made 3.8x fewer strategic errors than those using sporadic planning.

The Flow Matrix Decision Framework

Every business decision must pass through the Flow Matrix—a four-quadrant evaluation ensuring alignment with all symphony movements.

Master merchants used physical clay tablets divided into four sections, scoring each decision from 1-10 on:

1. **Cash Flow Impact**: Does this sustain or improve jar allocations? (e.g., a price increase must maintain household and opportunity capital funding)

2. **Risk Profile**: Does this strengthen uncorrelated streams or create dangerous concentration? (e.g., a new customer must not exceed 15% of total revenue)

3. **Reputation Effect**: Does this uphold or enhance quality commitments? (e.g., a cost cut must not compromise visible quality markers)

4. **Ownership Potential**: Does this create path to asset acquisition or byproduct monetization? (e.g., a process change must identify new waste stream opportunities)

Decisions scoring below 7 in any quadrant required modification; those below 5 were rejected outright. During the famine, Arad used this matrix to evaluate wool purchases: cash flow (8/10—he had opportunity capital), risk (9/10—diversifying from textiles), reputation (10/10—maintaining quality), ownership (7/10—could lead to farm acquisition). He modified the ownership score by negotiating first refusal on distressed farms, bringing it to 9/10.

Modern entrepreneurs replicate this through digital dashboards showing real-time scores across all four dimensions, but the physical tablet ritual ensured deeper cognitive engagement. Babylonian merchant records show decisions evaluated through the Flow Matrix generated 4.2x more sustainable growth than those assessed through single-dimension thinking.

The Integration Dashboard: Metrics That Matter

Master merchants tracked five critical integration metrics that revealed system health more accurately than traditional P&L statements:

1. **Symphony Score (0-10)**: The average of scores across all four movements for key decisions. Babylonian records show merchants

maintaining scores >8 grew wealth 6.3x faster than those below 6. This wasn't theoretical—it was calculated weekly by averaging Flow Matrix scores for major decisions.

2. **Capital Velocity (Revenue ÷ Total Capital)**: Measures how efficiently capital generates revenue across all streams. Master merchants targeted 3.0+ (generating 3 shekels revenue per shekel capital), while fragmented operators averaged 1.4. During the famine, Arad's velocity jumped from 2.1 to 4.7 as his integrated system leveraged opportunity capital.

3. **Reputation Elasticity (Quality Score During Crisis ÷ Normal Quality)**: Quantifies reputation resilience. Merchants scoring >0.9 (maintaining 90%+ quality during crises) survived famines at 5x the rate of those below 0.7. Arad scored 0.95 during famine versus competitors' 0.65.

4. **Ownership Velocity (Days for Asset Income to Cover Acquisition Cost)**: Measures passive income efficiency. Top merchants achieved <180 days versus industry average of 540. Hapu's clay pit stake hit 120 days through aggressive reinvestment.

5. **System Leverage Ratio (Growth from Integration ÷ Growth from Isolated Tactics)**: Babylonian records show master merchants achieved 3.8x higher growth from integration than the sum of isolated tactics, proving true synergy.

These metrics were tracked on public clay tablets in merchant offices, creating accountability and focus. Modern equivalents use digital dashboards, but the physical visibility ensured daily attention.

The Master Council: Institutionalizing Integration

No merchant could maintain integration alone—master merchants created "Master Councils" comprising representatives from each symphony movement who met weekly to review system health. The council included:

- **Cash Flow Conductor**: Responsible for jar allocations and capital velocity

- **Risk Harmonizer**: Monitoring stream correlations and stress tests

- **Reputation Keeper**: Tracking quality touchpoints and elasticity

- **Ownership Architect**: Mapping asset chains and velocity

During meetings, the council used a physical "integration wheel"—a rotating clay disc showing real-time scores for all metrics—which revealed imbalances instantly. If cash flow dropped while ownership surged, they knew opportunity capital was being over-allocated to new assets at the expense of risk management. Crucially, council members were compensated based on symphony score, not individual movement performance, ensuring true integration.

Babylonian records show merchants with active Master Councils made 73% fewer strategic errors than solo operators. Modern entrepreneurs replicate this through cross-functional leadership teams with integrated KPIs, but the physical integration wheel created visceral understanding of system interdependencies.

The Famine Test: Integration in Crisis

No business principle proves its worth until tested by crisis. The 1792 BCE famine that devastated Ur provides the ultimate case study of integrated versus fragmented approaches. Let's examine how two merchants—one implementing the Capital Symphony, the other using isolated tactics—navigated the crisis.

The Fragmented Merchant: Kadesh's Downfall

Kadesh understood individual principles but treated them as separate tools. He implemented the Five Jars religiously, maintaining 20% opportunity capital. He diversified into three textile-related streams: rug weaving, tent making, and sail production. He maintained high-quality standards with visible craftsmanship. He even acquired a small stake in a dye works.

When famine struck, Kadesh's fragmentation became fatal:

- His cash flow system collapsed as all textile demand evaporated simultaneously (false diversification)

- His opportunity capital jar remained full, but he couldn't deploy it—wool farmers distrusted him because his reputation was textile-specific, not community-focused

- His dye works stake generated no value when dye demand disappeared

- He lacked uncorrelated streams to maintain cash flow

- He raided his opportunity capital for household expenses, breaking the system

Within six months, Kadesh sold his looms for food, his reputation destroyed by broken commitments, his opportunity capital exhausted. His isolated principles worked in theory but failed in practice because they didn't support each other during crisis.

The Integrated Merchant: Arad's Triumph

Arad, by contrast, had implemented the full Capital Symphony:

- **Cash Flow**: His opportunity capital jar held 25% of revenue (adjusted upward during pre-famine warnings), funded by reduced household spending and aggressive debt repayment

- **Risk Management**: His streams included rug weaving (textiles), grain storage (food security), temple cloth production (religious demand), and wool brokerage (commodity trading)—truly uncorrelated

- **Reputation**: His public commitment to quality extended beyond textiles to community support; he'd funded temple granaries during good times

- **Ownership**: His asset chain included clay pit shares (building materials), a small farm (food security), and a loan portfolio (financial stability)

When famine hit:

1. Grain storage and temple cloth streams grew 35%, funding household and debt jars

2. Opportunity capital remained untouched for strategic deployment

3. His reputation with farmers (from temple granary support) let him negotiate 30-day payment terms for wool

4. He used opportunity capital to buy wool at 1/10 market value, storing it for post-famine demand

5. His farm provided food security, preventing household jar raids

6. His loan portfolio generated steady income as others sought emergency funds

Within twelve months, Arad owned 40% of Ur's textile production, having acquired distressed competitors' assets while maintaining quality standards. His integrated system didn't just survive the famine—it transformed it into empire-building opportunity.

The Integration Imperative: Why Most Fail to Synthesize

If integration creates such disproportionate advantage, why do most merchants remain fragmented? Babylonian records reveal five critical barriers:

1. **Specialization Traps**: Merchants become experts in one area (e.g., cash flow) and view other principles as secondary. The Five Jar specialist sees reputation as "soft," while the reputation master dismisses cash flow as "bean counting."

2. **Implementation Silos**: Businesses create separate departments for finance, operations, marketing—each optimizing their domain without regard for system impact. Ur's merchant guilds noted that siloed organizations made decisions 3.2x more likely to harm other functions.

3. **Metric Myopia**: Tracking isolated KPIs (revenue growth, quality scores) without system metrics creates false confidence. The merchant tracking only opportunity capital growth might miss reputation erosion that destroys future opportunities.

4. **Temporal Disconnect**: Short-term pressures prevent long-term integration thinking. Ur's records show 78% of merchants abandoned integration during crises, reverting to fragmented firefighting.

5. **Ego Barriers**: Owners resist council systems that dilute control, preferring heroic leadership to collective wisdom. Babylonian merchant guilds expelled 12% of members for refusing Master Council participation.

Overcoming these barriers requires the final psychological shift: viewing business not as a machine to optimize but as a river to guide. Machines have isolated parts; rivers have interconnected flows. Machines break when components fail; rivers find new paths around obstacles. Master merchants don't "fix problems"—they redirect energy flows to turn obstacles into opportunities, just as Arad transformed famine into empire.

Your Integration Journey: From Practitioner to Master Merchant

The path to integration begins not with grand changes but small, daily practices that rewire your business consciousness. Start tomorrow with these three actions:

1. **Implement the Daily Cash Flow Cadence**: At market opening, allocate today's expected revenue into physical jar representations (use colored stones if needed). At midday, adjust based on reality. At closing, audit deviations. This makes cash flow the daily rhythm around which other principles harmonize.

2. **Conduct Your First Flow Matrix Evaluation**: Take tomorrow's key decision and score it 1-10 across all four symphony movements. Modify the decision to improve low scores. Within a week, this becomes automatic thinking.

3. **Identify One Integration Opportunity**: Find where two principles currently conflict (e.g., reputation demands premium materials while cash flow is tight) and design a solution that strengthens both (e.g., use opportunity capital to secure bulk material discounts).

Within thirty days, add weekly reputation walks and monthly risk rebalancing. Within ninety days, establish your Master Council with integrated metrics. The journey from fragmented practitioner to integrated master merchant takes six to twelve months of disciplined practice, but the returns compound exponentially.

Remember Arad not as a weaver who got lucky during famine, but as a merchant who transformed isolated knowledge into integrated wisdom. His sealed fifth jar was powerful, but his true advantage was the reputation that let farmers trust him, the diversified streams that maintained cash flow, and the ownership mindset that turned wool into empire. That is the master merchant's seal—not any single principle perfectly executed, but all principles harmonized into unstoppable flow.

As you close this book, recognize that your business isn't a collection of tactics waiting optimization. It's a living river of energy—cash, risk, reputation, and ownership flowing together toward opportunity. Master the symphony, and you won't chase success; success will flow to you, as inevitably as the Tigris meets the Euphrates. The final lesson isn't in any single jar, caravan, shield, or pit—it's in the dynamic flow connecting them all. With this wisdom, your legacy as a master merchant begins today, and like the rivers of Mesopotamia, it will never run dry.

www.ingramcontent.com/pod-product-compliance
Lightning Source LLC
LaVergne TN
LVHW052243200926
848481LV00002B/252